Selling the Serengeti

Selling the Serengeti

THE CULTURAL POLITICS OF
SAFARI TOURISM

BENJAMIN GARDNER

THE UNIVERSITY OF GEORGIA PRESS
Athens & London

Set in 10/13 Minion Pro by Graphic Composition, Inc., Bogart, Georgia
Printed and bound by Thomson-Shore
The paper in this book meets the guidelines for
permanence and durability of the Committee on
Production Guidelines for Book Longevity of the
Council on Library Resources.

Most University of Georgia Press titles are
available from popular e-book vendors.

Printed in the United States of America
20 19 18 17 16 P 5 4 3 2 1

Library of Congress Cataloging-in-Publication Data

Names: Gardner, Ben (Benjamin Richard), author.
Title: Selling the Serengeti : the cultural politics of safari tourism /
    Benjamin Gardner.
Other titles: Geographies of justice and social transformation ; 23.
Description: Athens : The University of Georgia Press, 2016. | Series:
    Geographies of justice and social transformation ; 23 | Includes
    bibliographical references and index.
Identifiers: LCCN 2015015512 | ISBN 9780820345079 (hardcover : alk. paper) |
    ISBN 9780820345086 (paperback : alk. paper) | ISBN 9780820348186 (ebook)
Subjects: LCSH: Maasai (African people)—Tanzania—Economic conditions. |
    Maasai (African people)—Tanzania—Social conditions. | Identity
    politics—Tanzania. | Neoliberalism—Social aspects—Tanzania. | Land
    use—Tanzania—Serengeti Plain. | Land tenure—Tanzania—Serengeti Plain.
    | Culture and tourism—Tanzania—Serengeti Plain. | Safaris—Social
    aspects—Tanzania—Serengeti Plain. | Ecotourism—Social
    aspects—Tanzania—Serengeti Plain. | Community-based
    conservation—Tanzania—Serengeti Plain.
Classification: LCC DT443.3.M37 G37 2016 | DDC 305.896/5—dc23 LC record available
at http://lccn.loc.gov/2015015512

For Jennifer, Stella, and Maylie

CONTENTS

PREFACE

Is the Serengeti a place or an idea? The stakes of this seemingly simple question lie at the heart of this book, as I have tried to understand how safari tourism has changed the very meanings and geographies of places and people living in the greater Serengeti region of northern Tanzania. I now realize that I was initially drawn to the idea of the Serengeti when I first went to Tanzania in 1992 as an undergraduate anthropology student. As much as I wanted to see Serengeti National Park and its surrounding areas with my own eyes, I know that I wanted to experience what I had already determined to be one of the most important and valuable places in the world. I didn't question why I believed the Serengeti was so important and valuable a place. I just knew it was. I didn't see the historical and geographical discourses that shaped my understanding of this place from the position of a white male student from the United States or how it was that I might be involved in preserving or protecting a particular image or representation of this place. After years of living and working in Tanzania and then researching the political economy and cultural politics of tourism in the Serengeti region, I have come to understand how the production of the Serengeti as both a place and an idea influences current debates and practices concerning economic development, conservation, and tourism in Tanzania.

As geographer Doreen Massey explains, places "are always constructed out of articulations of social relations (trading connections, the unequal links of colonialism, thoughts of home) which are not only internal to that locale but which link them to elsewhere. Their 'local uniqueness' is always already a product of wider contacts; the local is always already a product in part of 'global' forces" (1995, 183). This idea of places and their pasts enables us to see the Serengeti not simply as the crown jewel of national parks in Africa but also as a landscape that has been produced in the image of an idea of African nature and what it should be.[1] Scholars like Massey point out how "global" social relationships, including the ideas, values, and interests of Westerners longing to see and experience the Serengeti actually help construct the meanings and geographies of the place. Cultural studies scholar Stuart Hall makes a similar argument as he explains, "'the West' is as much an idea as a fact of geography" (1992, 57).[2] Hall uses the metaphor of "the West and the Rest" to describe how understandings and beliefs about the history and meaning of a specific geography and the actual lived experience of a place like the Serengeti are inseparable. He shows that the idea of the West came into being through a biased system of representation during a period of European exploration, expansion, and conquest that not only described the West as a place but also provided a set of criteria to evaluate its relative value, which provided a new logic to explain difference. "A discourse is a way of talking about or representing something. It produces knowledge that shapes perceptions and practices" (Hall 1992, 317).

Tourism in the Serengeti is more than the enjoyment or appreciation of African nature. It is a critical site where cultural, political, and economic ideas and practices shape the activities and encounters among tourists, tour companies, state agencies, local communities, as well as the flora and fauna. It is a particular form of consumption in which the commodity is the landscape itself. The idea of the Serengeti is a powerful one. Geographer Rod Neumann's groundbreaking book, *Imposing Wilderness*, describes the production of the dominant idea of nature in Africa. Neumann starts by quoting a traveling companion: "This is the way that Africa *should* look" (1998, 1). He draws on archival sources, as well as interviews with residents, to show how the production of nature in Africa transformed the identities and rights of African subjects. His research is a significant intervention in how understandings of African parks were forged through historical struggles over who should have rights and access to African natural resources. Neumann's book is essential reading for anyone interested in the relationship between protected areas and livelihoods around the world.

The contributions of scholars like Hall, Massey, and Neumann go well beyond learning important histories. They enable us to recognize how contemporary understandings, ideas, and practices draw their authority and even their legitimacy from the very discourses that shape what people value in a place like the Serengeti. How discourse shapes landscape became an important lens as I researched and observed different forms of tourism in the Serengeti region. Tourism is commonly framed as a way to add value to place, where visitors will pay simply to passively enjoy the environment. Such narratives pay scant attention to how that environment is framed and preserved or to how prioritizing a certain kind of experience actually shapes the landscape in question. In one of the examples I discuss in this book, a U.S.–based tourism company purchased a former barley farm in the middle of three Maasai villages to establish a nature refuge and promote ecotourism. As I describe in detail, the company met considerable resistance from Maasai residents, who claimed that it had received the land illegally and the refuge would dispossess them of essential grazing land that they had used for well over a century. In a promotional video made by the company in 2012, the owners of Thomson Safaris describe their project to prospective clients and supporters. Missing completely from the video is the fact that the company gained access to the land by purchasing a lease agreement for $1.2 million.[3] The project justification and rationale as laid out in the video tell a very different story about how land rights are allocated to investors. The video's narrative relies on a universal claim that ownership of African nature is granted to those who can best take care of the land. Implicit in this narrative is the commonsense idea that the primary value of this land, in the general vicinity of the Serengeti, is for conservation. The American general manager of the company, John Bearcroft, describes the company's relationship to the place. "We borrowed this land from our children, our children's children; we don't own it. It's for the future of all that come after us. You know we are guardians of this land, it's not ours so we do the best we can within our resources . . . and what we do is tourism" (Thomson Safaris 2012). For many of the people I have shown this video to, including a number of my undergraduate and graduate students in the United States, this statement appears to make a lot of sense. The video's framing of a philanthropic-oriented company from the United States that wants to use its economic power to promote conservation, tourism, and community empowerment in Africa was seen to deliver the promise of development that many of my students wanted to help foster themselves. But the more we examined the origin stories and histories on which these claims were being made, the clearer it became that the company was drawing on a discourse of African conservation that relies on the implicit idea that foreign whites are in a better position to care for African nature than are the African residents of that place, in this case the Maasai.

Such a framing is precisely what Hall means when he says that discourse is not innocent. In describing the creation of the discourse of "the West and the Rest," Hall explains that in the encounter between Europeans and the New World, "Europe brought its own cultural categories, languages, images, and ideas to . . . describe and represent it. It fit the New World into existing conceptual frameworks, classifying it according to its own norms, and absorbing it into Western traditions of representation" (Hall 1992, 294). Europe, he asserts, also "had certain definite purposes, aims, objectives, motives, interests, and strategies in setting out to discover what lay across the 'Green Sea of Darkness.'" Similarly, tourism companies have their own cultural categories for understanding and explaining places like the Serengeti, as well as their own purposes, motives, and objectives to make a good living while also promoting their deeply held values of conservation.

Such narratives are not created anew but rather draw directly on persistent historical ideas that often go unquestioned as representing truth. The narrative framing of the Thomson Safari promotional video is reminiscent of another landmark film that argued to a largely Western audience for the Serengeti to be preserved. The 1959 German film *Serengeti Shall Not Die* chronicled the famous veterinary professor and Frankfurt Zoo director Bernhard Grzimek and his son Michael as they fought to protect and preserve the Serengeti from a variety of what they saw as local threats, including African poachers and a poorly equipped park service. The film, released in 1959 two years before Tanganyika gained its independence from the British, marks an important moment coalescing the ideas and interests of a relatively small group of people and presenting them as the commonsense understanding of African nature and why it should be preserved for all of "mankind."[4] Grzimek draws on a nostalgic image of African nature as a countervailing representation for the decline of urban civilization. He uses this binary to help justify Western intervention in Africa in the name of conservation.

> Today the human population of our earth is multiplying at a staggering rate. Our numbers are increasing by 180,000 per day or 700 million every ten years, more than the total population of China. As we become more crowded in our concrete cities, our grandchildren will be able to see less and less of the wonders of nature. These last remaining herds of African game are a cultural heritage of the whole of mankind. . . . If today, any government of whatever political shade dared to pull down the Acropolis in Athens in order to build workers' flats, the whole civilized world would cry out furiously against such outrage. Similarly, no man, black or white, should ever be allowed to endanger the future of these last living cultural treasures of Africa. God made the earth subject to the will of man, but surely not that he might completely destroy his creation.

Part of the power of this film, as well as of the Thomson Safari promotional video, is that each appears to be speaking on behalf of humankind rather from their own historically situated position, with all its specific ideas, values, and interests.

Thinking about the production of places in this way helps us ask questions such as who benefits from the creation of a nature refuge for tourism? In the Thomson video, Bearcroft continues to explain the company's intentions in setting up the nature refuge. "We're trying to preserve a piece of heaven that we can share with our guests, that will touch them, that will make them think, and that will change them. They will go back home, and they will go inspired, and maybe they can use that in their future life when they are thinking about the world in general and educating their kids." Although the video is clearly targeted toward a Western audience, foreign clients who can take a piece of Africa back home with them are not its only constituents. Bearcroft also describes what he sees as benefits for the local community. "This was an opportunity . . . to give some value to the community for what conservation can be as a resource to them." Throughout the film, Bearcroft and the co-owners of Thomson Safaris describe the real long-term benefits of the project when the community and the company come together to use tourism to their mutual advantage. I am in no position to judge the intentions of the company, but in analyzing this promotional video along with many other communications and actions, I began to realize that their very right to represent this area and its value is derived from the dominant discourses of Western conservation and the unquestioned role of well-meaning foreigners in preserving, protecting, and creating new value out of African nature. Such relational understandings lie at the heart of questions about the political ecology and geography of northern Tanzania, its world-famous national parks, and the communities that still live in the shadow of both the place and the idea of the Serengeti.

I first visited Tanzania in 1992 as an undergraduate from the United States. I studied wildlife management and learned Swahili, the country's national language. I spent my final month at Loliondo, an area just east of Serengeti National Park, studying the influence of tourism on the Maasai people who lived there. Tourism has played an increasingly prominent role in the economic development of Tanzania. In the late 1980s, Tanzania, along with many nations in Africa, Asia, Latin America, and the Caribbean, had little choice but to accept structural adjustment programs (SAPs) and other neoliberal reforms. With their economies in crisis and their debt burdens expanding because of rising interest rates, mismanagement, and bad investments, countries like Tanzania surrendered their policy decisions to the mandates of the Bretton Woods institutions, including the World Bank (WB) and the International Monetary Fund (IMF). A group of influential economists and politicians known collectively as the Washington consensus gained influence at the time as the global debt crisis signaled the failure of past development policies.[5] Although those failures were multidimensional, the confluence of a Reagan administration in the United States, a Thatcher-led government in England, and the popularity of economic theories promoting austerity led to a new orthodoxy in international development known as neoliberalism. As a theory and set of policy prescriptions, neoliberalism is based on the principle that too much state intervention in the economy creates bad investments and excessive bureaucracy, distorts monetary policy, and encourages corruption. Policy makers used this new consensus to implement reforms to reduce the role of the public sector, prioritize balancing national budgets, promote foreign trade, privatize state-owned companies, and rationalize social service provision. For a relatively large cohort of economists and politicians from all sides of the political spectrum, a global assault on state power was seen as a positive move toward political and economic freedom around the world.

Along with profound economic changes that drastically reduced public payrolls and contributed to rising costs of living, the liberalization of Tanzania's economic and political system in the 1980s set in motion reforms that altered the relationship among state institutions, economic markets, and civil society. "The balance sheet of structural adjustment in Africa . . . includes capital flight, collapse of manufactures, marginal or negative increase in export incomes, drastic cutbacks in urban public services, soaring prices, and a steep decline in wages . . . [and] a virtual demolition of the local state," writes Mike Davis (2006, 155) in his book *Planet of Slums*, describing the effects of SAPs. There is now considerable agreement that SAPs demanded changes too quickly and placed significant burdens on the very citizens they were supposed to help.[6] The rapid adoption of neoliberal policies in the late 1980s led to what is commonly described as "the lost decade" in Africa. Geographers, anthropologists, and other scholars have spent much of the 1990s and the twenty-first century thus far documenting and analyzing the consequences of neoliberalization in countries such as Tanzania. Much of this research has emphasized the increased burden placed on the rural farmers who cannot easily access markets or must leverage their most vital assets, including their land, to secure loans to compete with private companies. Other scholars have focused on the growing numbers of urban unemployed who rely on the informal sector to make a living, and shifting the risk of economic production and reproduction from the state to individuals.[7]

Neoliberalization, however, is more than an economic program. Its effects are as much cultural as they are economic. Like previous systems of economic and political rule, neoliberal governance shapes how different groups understand the value of people and places and sets the frameworks for economic and political activity. Situating questions of value and values within a political and economic framework enables us to see the relationships between symbolic and material practices under a capitalist mode of production. As Don Mitchell notes, "Values—meanings, knowledge about good and bad and about truth and falsehood, about moral ways of life—are inexorably, if not completely, imbricated in the production of capitalist value" (2000, 72). This connection does not mean, however, that capitalism determines the shape of these relationships. In part what is produced in this political economic space are meanings and possibilities. Commonsense discourse is a powerful force reproducing dominant ideas, values, and interests. Yet history is a dynamic process, and new forms of production and consumption lead to new possibilities for how spaces are shaped and reproduced.

For many Tanzanians reducing government programs meant that few if any social safety nets remained in place. For upper-middle-class Tanzanians, this new economy organized around ideas of freedom and competitiveness could provide new economic prospects. For the majority of Tanzanians, however, there were too few opportunities to go around. Groups like the Maasai, who never enjoyed the full benefits of Tanzanian citizenship and received little in the way of social services or infrastructure development, did not necessarily lament the weakening of the state. For a large number of Tanzanian Maasai, the emerging international consensus that states stood in the way of development created new possibilities to claim long-sought land rights. Many Maasai people whom I interviewed between 1991 and 2010 associated Maasai land dispossession as much with the nationalist state since independence in 1961 as with the German- and then British-led colonial state and considered the neoliberal assault on the state a potentially promising change.

Scholars such as Dorothy Hodgson and James Igoe who have studied Maasai politics and land struggles in Tanzania since the 1990s have focused their attention on the important role of civil society and the remarkable rise of Maasai nongovernmental organizations (NGOs), which are fundamental in advocating for pastoralist rights in the changing national and international context. Much of this scholarship documents the work of NGOs in building new transnational coalitions and giving political representation to marginalized groups, especially ethnic minorities and women. These scholars also describe the limitations of NGOs as agents of social change, including the often narrow interests pursued by identity-based groups, the overreliance on foreign donors and their agendas, and new opportunities for corruption.[8] Much of this literature is divided on the potential of NGOs to foster a new era of democratic and participatory development.

The role of foreign investment and the actions of specific investors have received much less attention by ethnographers seeking to understand how neoliberal development is experienced by its subjects and how it is remaking places and creating new possibilities.[9] As important as NGOs have been to the politics of the Maasai people in Loliondo, foreign investors have played a crucial although largely concealed role in reshaping the Tanzanian landscape. In Tanzania state actors often view NGOs with suspicion as being excessively influenced by external agendas. Investors, however, are typically given a pass in this regard for they are represented largely as nonpolitical actors, simply interested in creating business opportunities and producing profit in the country. Because of the near-desperate need for foreign financing, national leaders, as well as large numbers of people looking for betting paying jobs and economic opportunities, commonly embrace investors as partners, if not saviors, in underdeveloped and highly indebted nation-states like Tanzania.

Arriving in Loliondo

Foreign investors are attracted to Loliondo primarily for safari tourism, including the area's two main activities, big-game trophy hunting and adventure-oriented ecotourism. National park restrictions against hunting and walking (visitors are not permitted to get out of their vehicle, except at their campground, picnic site, or hotel) have made Maasai village lands adjacent to Serengeti National Park valuable sites for a range of safari tourism practices, including hunting and ecotourism. The deregulation of the tourism sector in the late 1980s helped transform village lands into tourist landscapes, radically changing their meanings and values.

When I first arrived in Loliondo, I spent two days in the headquarters of the newly registered Maasai NGO KIPOC (Korongoro Integrated People Oriented to Conservation). Despite being the central government seat for Ngorongoro District, Loliondo is quite isolated from the rest of Tanzania. Located only 400 kilometers (approximately 250 miles) north of the nearest city, Arusha, it is one of the most difficult places to reach in the country with no all-season road connecting it to the rest of Tanzania.[10] It is easier for Maasai in Loliondo to cross the border north into Kenya to sell livestock and buy basic goods such as tea and sugar than it is for them to travel to Arusha or the de facto capital city of Dar es Salaam.

The final project for my study-abroad semester was to investigate how Maasai villages in Loliondo might benefit from new forms of tourism. In May 1992, I set out to start my study, and I was thrilled to have simply arrived in Loliondo. There was no public transportation, but I had been lucky to arrange a ride with Lazaro Parkipuny, who had served as a member of parliament (MP) for the Ngorongoro District (which included the Ngorongoro, Sale, and Loliondo political divisions) from 1980 to 1990 and had left national politics to start KIPOC in 1991. The trip to Loliondo felt like an accomplishment in itself. But despite the distance I had come, I was still uncertain how I would reach my ultimate destination, the Maasai villages that were only twenty to thirty kilometers outside Loliondo town. In my mind a Maasai village in this faraway place represented the authentic Africa I had traveled all this way to see.

With only a month to conduct my research, I was eager to arrive at my final destination and meet with real Maasai people living in their homesteads together with their livestock, just as I had read in my undergraduate anthropology classes. John ole Monte, one of the KIPOC staff members, told me to be patient.[11] Ole Monte and other KIPOC staff would figure out some way to get me out to "the villages." I spent my first day walking around Loliondo town. The place was a curious mix of Tanzanians who had moved to the district headquarters and established homes and small farms in the high-altitude plains. By May the maize fields were tall and green, awaiting the end of the rains in June for harvesting in July or August. Maize fields were a common sight across Tanzania. But not, I knew, in real Maasai villages. Unlike most peasant farmers, who lived on beans, maize, and a variety of green leafy vegetables, tomatoes, and onions, the Maasai lived primarily on milk and occasionally meat. Loliondo town fascinated me, but I couldn't help but feel that I had yet to arrive in the real Africa. I did not have to wait much longer. In the middle of my second night, loud knocking and shouting awaked me. Maasai people throughout the district and the country knew Parkipuny as the go-to leader for pastoralists, especially when it came to handling trouble with state authorities. On this night, Maasai from the villages of Ololosokwan and Soitsambu came seeking his assistance. I heard the group of men speaking to Parkipuny in the room next to me. After several minutes of animated conversations, of which I understood not a word, Parkipuny knocked on my door. In Swahili he told me to grab my bag. There was a problem in one of the villages, he said, and he would be driving out to help resolve the matter. This, he told me in no uncertain terms, was my best chance to get a ride to a Maasai village.

I piled into the back of Parkipuny's personal vehicle, a short-chassis Land Rover affectionately named "baby KIPOC." For most of the ride, I sat quietly in the back taking in the scene. These six men had walked through the night over twenty-five kilometers to reach the KIPOC offices to find Parkipuny. They were clearly upset and spoke rapidly in the Maasai language, Maa. After about fifteen minutes of driving, Parkipuny explained to me what was going on. Serengeti National Park rangers had detained two young boys who were being held at Klein's Camp ranger station in Ololosokwan village. He was going to help the elders and village officers get the boys released. Traditional and elected leaders had been seeking Parkipuny's assistance for years to mediate and resolve disputes such as this. Not only did he speak Swahili and English fluently; having been the district's MP also gave Parkipuny a particular gravitas when it came to dealing with state officials. Parkipuny wasn't a lawyer, but he had pursued several lawsuits against the state during his tenure as MP. He was not afraid to confront state officials, especially if he believed they were treating the Maasai unfairly based on ignorance or discrimination. During his time in office, he had grown all too familiar with the accepted contempt and lack of respect for pastoralism as an acceptable way of life in Tanzania.

As I had learned on the way to Loliondo, Parkipuny's reputation for driving fast was well deserved. That it was pitch black only seemed to encourage his desire for speed. The Land Rover careened across the red dirt roads, frequently hitting bumps that would send the little vehicle into the air and then forcefully back down again. I was only partially reassured, as the other passengers did not seem particularly afraid. My fear of dying was mitigated by my excitement at getting a lift to a real Maasai village. Beyond this ride, I had not given a moment's thought to the logistics of my trip. During the forty-minute drive, Parkipuny broke off his conversations twice to speak to me. The first time was to inform me that we were passing through a part of Soitsambu village known as Sukenya. "This land," he told me, "is Maasailand. The government tried to take this from us and turn it into a barley farm in the 1980s, but they failed. We took them to court and we won. This land is ours now, and people are afraid of us here in Loliondo. They know they can't take our land. We started KIPOC to make sure they wouldn't ever take our land."

We drove another twenty minutes or so; then Parkipuny turned off the dirt road. Without reducing speed, he wove across the plains, avoiding trees, dry riverbeds, and occasionally zebra, gazelle, and wildebeest standing motionless in the open grasslands between scattered homesteads. We eventually stopped in front of a thorn fence enclosure. Parkipuny told me to get out here. "The boy next to you is Marcus Nalang'o. He speaks English and will be your host for the next four weeks. I will pick you up here at the end of the month." With that, I followed Marcus out the back door of the Land Rover. During the ride Marcus had not spoken a word to me. Although younger than the other men in the car, he resembled them wrapped in a red-hued blanket with a staid expression on his face. For no good reason, I had assumed that he spoke only the Maasai language, Maa. A young man of about my own age of twenty-two clearly hadn't come to Loliondo that evening to pick up a Mzungu (white person of European ancestry) visitor. He had walked the twenty kilometers from Soitsambu to Loliondo town with the other men to help get the young boys from his clan out of trouble. But in Maasai society it is quite difficult for younger Maasai, who can still be considered youth into their late twenties, to confront their elders. In many places having a foreign visitor foisted upon you for a month is less than ideal, if not utterly absurd, but Marcus never raised a question about taking me into his care. As it turned out, I could not have asked for a more gracious host; Marcus would become a close friend and research assistant for many years following our month together in May 1992.

After about twenty minutes, three young boys from Marcus's *enkang'* (Maasai homestead) managed to remove the thick thorn-strewn branches acting as a barrier for the small entrance in the otherwise tightly wrapped enclosure. The design of these elaborate living fences varied across pastoral communities in Tanzania. The exceedingly strong weave of this fence was a sign that threats from predators like lions, hyenas, and wild dogs were very real. Hundreds of cows, sheep, and goats slept in the paddock in the middle of the homestead, which Marcus's father shared with his three adult sons and their families. As a member of a polygamous society, Marcus's father had three wives, and each woman had her own *enkaji* (Maasai house) within the family compound.

After contorting our bodies to pass through the small opening, I followed Marcus along a muddy pathway that ran outside the central animal enclosure and then into his house. Marcus cleared his throat with a deep guttural sound. He helped me maneuver around the wooden posts that held the roof up, avoiding the goat kids and lambs that slept inside to keep warm in the cold high-plateau climate. I sat next to Marcus on the "men's bed." The bed, which doubled as a sitting and sleeping place, was made of dried and cured cattle skins stretched over an elaborate gathering of sticks. Marcus and his brothers, as well as any male visitors, slept here. If his father was staying in the house, the boys and the guests would all sleep elsewhere, in one of his "other mother's" homes. On the other side of the home, across from a fire pit, was his mom's bed. Upon our arrival, she awoke and quickly began to relight the fire, which provided both heat and light. Blowing on the end of a metal pipe, she slowly and deliberately restarted the flame on a dormant log. She added dry wood from her extensive collection meticulously stored in the walls of her house.

Only after the orange flames illuminated the room did Marcus's mother set her eyes on me. Although she never said so, Marcus assured me that I was the first Mzungu to stay in her home. She looked at me closely and then at Marcus. It was the middle of the night, and although I can't be certain, I think she assumed she was hallucinating. She boiled a pot of water to which she added tea leaves, sugar, and milk. After about fifteen minutes, she handed me the hottest metal cup I had ever held. My inability to hold the cup was comical compared to her lifting the aluminum pot from the three stones in her fire pit over and over as she added ingredients to the chai.

Only after all of these preparations did she ask Marcus who I was. He told her that I was a student from "America" and that I had come to stay with them for a month. Her only question was, "What will he eat?" Marcus turned to me and asked if I had brought my own food. I told him I had not but that I was happy to eat whatever they ate. This information eased everyone's mind. I told Marcus a bit more about myself while we drank our tea. Soon afterward, I unrolled my sleeping bag. Marcus covered himself in his blanket, and we both fell asleep for the night. While with Marcus and his family, I bought basic food supplies like tea, sugar, maize, and beans to help compensate for the burden of taking care of me. I quickly came to realize that my resilient stomach was a great asset for living and working among pastoralists.

Over the next month I traveled around Marcus's village of Soitsambu as well as the neighboring villages of Ololosokwan to the north and Oloipiri to the southeast. I helped herd cattle, visited Marcus's friends, went to the monthly market in Soitsambu, attended church, and crossed the invisible boundaries separating Tanzania and Kenya to the north and Maasai villages from Serengeti National Park to the east. I conducted interviews with people about the history of the area and their experience with tourism.

Since that first visit and initial research, I have closely followed the efforts of tour operators, conservation NGOs, state officials, and Maasai leaders and groups to create tourism opportunities and how these political and economic relationships have influenced pastoralist land rights and livelihoods. Over that time my research focus shifted from the policy prescriptions of designing tourism projects that would benefit communities to asking how tourism projects shape Maasai culture and influence Maasai political ideas and tactics.

Although I had read several critical accounts of colonial conservation, much of my understanding of conservation in the early 1990s was based on a commonsense Western belief that conservation was inherently good. As an eager student, I thought that informed and well-meaning experts, the kind I might one day become, could resolve environmental conflicts by educating the different groups with better knowledge about the problems. Achieving conservation seemed an obvious win-win scenario to me at the time. I learned many things that month in Loliondo in 1992. One of the biggest lessons was that the Maasai saw conservation up to that point in their history primarily as a national and international agenda designed to dispossess them of their land.[12] They had nothing against wild animals per se; in fact they are one of the few groups with strict taboos against hunting and eating wild animals.[13] But the common methods of achieving conservation in Tanzania, modeled after the national parks system in the United States, reproduce a strict separation of people and nature, denying the possibility of people sharing the land with wildlife as a viable practice. According to many Maasai I interviewed, the inevitable result of conservation policies has been the complete enclosure of Maasailand. Understanding and promoting tourism and conservation were clearly more complicated than I had first assumed.

I would later learn that my first visit to Loliondo coincided with several significant events. That same year, 1992, marked the arrival of the Ortello Business Corporation (OBC), a high-profile hunting company from Dubai in Loliondo. The company was granted a controversial lease to two hunting areas in Loliondo. This would initiate a series of conflicts between hunting, nonconsumptive tourism and pastoralism in the area. One of the effects of this initiative was the 2009 eviction of the Maasai from their village lands to clear the area for hunting and the subsequent government effort to enclose fifteen hundred out of a total of four thousand square kilometers as a hunting game corridor (see chapter 4).

I also learned about legal efforts to permanently restore a farm formerly run by the state-owned Tanzania Breweries Limited (TBL) to collective grazing land. In 1987 Soitsambu village resident Isata ole Ndekerei and fourteen other villagers filed a lawsuit against TBL, claiming that the community had never agreed to allocate ten thousand acres of its land to the state.[14] Despite the ongoing legal action at the time, Parkipuny and other leaders were assured that TBL had not obtained a title to the property in question. It came as a surprise then when in 2006 TBL sold the land to a U.S.-owned safari company (see chapter 5).

Before arriving in Loliondo, I spent two weeks on a field course run by Dorobo Tours and Safaris (Dorobo Safaris), a travel company owned by U.S. expatriates. It was during that trip that I first learned of Dorobo Safaris's approach to community conservation and about its recent efforts, in 1991, to sign joint-venture contracts with village governments in Loliondo. The village contracts were presented as an alternative way to promote tourism without enclosing Maasai lands (see chapter 6).

As an enthusiastic twenty-two year old, I was thrilled to spend time with the Maasai in what appeared to me at the time as their "authentic landscape." The Maasai in Loliondo lived in dispersed homesteads spread out across several registered villages. Despite their relatively permanent attachment to a specific location within a village area, the Maasai continued to rely heavily on seasonal movement of their livestock. Young men would take their families' herds far from their homesteads and establish *ronjos* (temporary cattle camps) to take advantage of unpredictable rain patterns and availability of necessary grasses and minerals.

It took me many years and several return visits working with civil-society groups and as a researcher to appreciate that Maasai villages were not a feature of some timeless Maasai society. Rather, villages were created quite recently, formed in the mid-1970s as part of Tanzania's rural socialist strategy. Yet, I argue in this book that starting in the early 1990s and coinciding with the founding of KIPOC, the emergence of an institutionalized pastoral civil society, the rapid privatization of state functions, and the promotion of tourism on village lands, Maasai in Loliondo began to use villages to organize their collective interests and to engage with foreign investors and state actors.

Situating the Research and Researcher

I went to Tanzania as an undergraduate student seeking to get my feet wet in fieldwork that real anthropologists and geographers were meant to do. I still believe that ethnographic research in which an outsider immerses himself or herself in another culture, builds relationships, observes and participates in daily life, interviews a broad mixture of people, follows current events, and debates with others in order to ask and answer meaningful questions is an important research strategy. I am, however, much less naive about the problematic politics of this research and the inevitable inequalities that it reproduces. There could not be a more stereotypically problematic representation of this type of research than a white man from the United States, studying perhaps the most iconic African ethnic group, the Maasai. Although I did not specifically seek out this historically awkward position, I can now see that it was a product of my own training. My undergraduate mentor taught anthropology at a small liberal arts college in New England. He studied pastoralists in the Sudan and had his students read the classics in structural anthropology. Not only did we read the E. Evans-Pritchard ethnography *The Nuer* (1940), we also read the lesser-known books in the trilogy, *Kinship and Marriage among the Nuer* (1951) and *Nuer Religion* (1956).

I knew I wanted to study in Africa, and my professor recommended the St. Lawrence University semester in Kenya. The program was based in Nairobi and introduced students to the history, culture, and politics of Kenya. It was during that semester that I first visited Tanzania and met the directors of Dorobo Safaris. I spent the next semester based in Arusha, Tanzania, on another semester-abroad program run by the Vermont-based School for International Training. That program was similar to the first but was organized specifically around conservation and wildlife management. By spending the entire year in East Africa, I was able to improve my Swahili language skills and instill my instructors with enough confidence to allow me to travel to the otherwise off-limits Loliondo for the final month of the program. I am very grateful for the opportunities and experiences I gained while studying abroad from August 1991 to June 1992 in East Africa. Despite their mission to promote cross-cultural learning and communication, however, such programs also reproduce the historically unequal relationships between wealthy industrial nations like the United States and relatively poor countries like Tanzania. Such programs empower their students to explore countries like Tanzania with the hope that students will use their knowledge to "change the world for the better."

Had I been aware of the broader implications of my opportunities, I may never have left on that Pan American flight from John F. Kennedy International Airport in New York to Nairobi. But I have come to understand my ongoing work in Tanzania through a different lens. I returned to Tanzania throughout the 1990s, first leading trips for U.S. high school students to volunteer and travel over the summer. I parlayed these experiences into longer stays in the country working with a number of NGOs. I stayed in close touch with Tanzanian friends and colleagues, following their lives and struggles in Loliondo. Interested in pursuing development work, I returned to school to study natural resource management at the Yale School of Forestry and Environmental Studies. While there I took classes about the postcolonial state and global political ecology, as well as forest management and soil science. I returned to Tanzania in 1997 to study the evolution of village tourism partnerships begun by Dorobo Safaris five years after they began. At that time the owners of Dorobo Safaris founded a nonprofit foundation, the Dorobo Fund for Tanzania (Dorobo Fund). I introduced the company directors, the Petersons, to Marcus Nalang'o and his cousin Lucy Asioka. The Dorobo Fund hired these dynamic young Maasai to conduct research with me in July and August 1997. Together the three of us spent the summer interviewing Maasai throughout Loliondo and Simanjiro, another Maasai area south of Arusha. We met with district officials, village leaders, and a range of civil-society groups.

We researched how Maasai used their land and the role of village governments in regulating land management. We also sought to understand whether the tourism joint ventures between villages and Dorobo Safaris were widely known outside the core village leadership, and if so, what, if any, impact they had on people's understanding of their land and of conservation. In many ways we were testing the thesis of investors like Dorobo Safaris, which believed that paying villagers directly to use their land for tourism was not only more ethical than imposing external conservation agendas but also more effective. We did find that local meanings of tourism and conservation were changing as villagers directly benefited from tourism. Valuing tourism, however, is not the same thing as sharing an understanding of its meaning with tourists. To the dismay of many tour operators, not one Maasai person we interviewed shared their sense of awe or joy at "hearing a lion roar in the distance" or the knowledge that "elephants and hippos shared their land." Maasai had their own relations with nature, neither hostile nor nostalgic. Invariably Maasai appreciated wildlife as a part of what they understood as their landscape—a landscape created for and by pastoralists and their livestock, though not entirely of their own making.[15]

This book explores the contradictory discourses of market-led conservation, tourism, and land rights. I demonstrate that despite numerous challenges, the Maasai in Loliondo use their relationship with foreign investors together with community-based organizations (CBOS) and NGOS to try to remake their relationship with Tanzanian state institutions, with nature, and with their land. One consequence of neoliberal reforms was the liberalization of tourism on village land. This transformed villages throughout Loliondo into new forms of transnational commodities. The shift posed new threats of dispossession from foreign investors who were invited to Tanzania to transform "underutilized" spaces into valuable places. But these same policies and ideas opened new ways to understand and imagine Maasai villages as sites of belonging, rights, and international investment and reconfigured Maasai social relations with the local, national, and international institutions. If neoliberalism was going to transform the village into a new kind of commodity, Maasai residents and leaders were not going to sit idly by and see what happened. Instead they actively participated in the process of commodifying their villages and their landscapes. This book traces how the Maasai people are remaking the meaning of their landscapes and identities through their different arrangements with safari tourism. Much of this political room for maneuver relies on a new way to imagine, represent, and translate the meaning of Maasai villages as sites of belonging and rights. Much like the Serengeti, the Maasai village is both a place and an idea. Who gets to imagine, represent, and translate the contingent meanings of the village and of the greater Serengeti landscape will go a long way in determining the future possibilities for conservation and pastoralist livelihoods in northern Tanzania.

ACKNOWLEDGMENTS

This book owes a great deal to many individuals and groups. The inspiration to study and write about conservation, tourism investment, and Maasai livelihoods started during my junior year in college. It was then, in 1992, that I first met Maanda Ngoitiko, Daniel Ngoitiko, Dismas Metaiya and Makko Sinandei. These four people welcomed me to Loliondo and have embraced my curiosity and questions ever since. I am grateful for their candor, their humor, their friendship, as well as their tireless work on behalf of their communities. This book would not exist without their insights, encouragement, and convictions. I also want to thank Lazaro Parkipuny for giving me my first ride to Loliondo and putting up with me ever since. His passion for and commitment to Maasai rights and respect reshaped livelihoods and landscapes throughout northern Tanzania. Sadly, he passed away in 2013. Thanks to Alais Morindat and Francis Shomett for putting up with my questions and for encouraging me to ask more.

It is difficult to convey my gratitude to the residents of Loliondo and their willingness to talk with me about their lives, their history, and their aspirations. I also want to express my appreciation and thanks to numerous Tanzanians who assisted this research in various ways. The use of pseudonyms to protect people's privacy precludes many formal acknowledgments. I want to thank the staff of so many organizations that allowed me to use their archives, conduct interviews, and observe their activities and meetings. I especially want to acknowledge the Ujamma Community Resource Trust, Pastoral Women's Council, Pastoral Indigenous Non-Governmental Organizations Forum, Lawyers Environmental Action Team, Journalists Environmental Association of Tanzania, Legal and Human Rights Centre, and African Wildlife Foundation.

I offer profound thanks to my "family" in Arusha. Munka and Selina Killerai and their sons, Kip, Ntimama, and Killerai, have provided my family and me a home away from home and sincere friendship since I first came to Tanzania in the early 1990s. Thank you for always supporting me and for being *Babu* and *Bibi* to Stella and Maylie. Thanks also to Munka's mom, *kokoo* who provided me a home in Loliondo and is as formidable today at ninety years old as she was when I first met her over twenty years ago.

This research would never have happened if Dave, Thad, and Mike Peterson had not introduced me to the issues of community tourism, land use, and conservation in northern Tanzania. Although they do not always agree with my analysis, they have always encouraged and supported me to pursue my interests in understanding the complex relationships among development and conservation in Tanzania. Their genuine caring, enthusiasm, and wisdom are infectious. I also want to thank Trude, Lisa, and Robin Peterson, and all of their children for their support to my family and me over the years.

I received permission to conduct research in Tanzania from the Tanzania Commission for Science and Technology. A variety of institutions funded the various stages of this research. The National Science Foundation and the Fulbright-Hays Fellowship supported my dissertation research. The Walter Chapin Simpson Center for the Humanities at the University of Washington provided both financial and intellectual support through my participation in the 2011–2012 society of scholars. My sincerest thanks to members of that cohort, especially to Stephanie Camp, a wonderful historian who gave me exceptionally valuable suggestions on the manuscript. Sadly, Stephanie passed away in 2014. The Land Deals Politics Initiative funded a case study on land grabbing in Tanzania. And, finally, the University of Washington Bothell provided the financial means necessary to conduct follow-up research, to create the maps, and to index this book. I've presented portions of this project over the years at conferences of the Association of American Geographers, the African Studies Association, and the Cultural Studies Association and at invited lectures and seminars.

When I began this work I didn't know how I would contribute to the already rich research on the Maasai and conservation politics in Tanzania. I want to thank Dorothy Hodgson and Richard Schroeder for being so open to a junior scholar and for encouraging me to find my own voice in the field. They offered critical feedback and support from the earliest stages of this research until the end. I want to thank Rod Neumann for his advice and comments throughout this project. Both Rod and Rick read the entire manuscript with an incredibly detailed and supportive eye. James Igoe and Daniel Brockington also provided great feedback at different stages of this work.

In Tanzania I greatly benefited from my affiliation with the Department of Geography and the Institute of Resource Assessment at the University of Dar es Salaam. In particular I want to thank Hussein Sosovele, George Jambiya, N'gwanza Kamata, Festus Ndumbaro, Davis Mwamfupe, Idris Kikula, Tundu Lissu, Rugemeleza Nshala, and Issa Shivji. I also received invaluable insights from Elizabeth Garland, Mara Goldman, Fred Nelson, Andrew Williams, Elizabeth Singleton, Alan Rodgers, Katherine Homewood, and Peter Rogers.

At the University of California, Berkeley, my dissertation committee—

Louise Fortmann, Gillian Hart, Donald Moore, Nathan Sayre, and Michael Watts—guided me through my initial research and helped shape me into a cultural geographer. My advisor, Michael Watts pushed me to use geographic and political economic theory to see conservation politics in Tanzania from a different perspective. His own scholarship and teaching continue to inspire and motivate my work. Donald Moore opened my eyes to the importance of cultural studies and cultural politics, and I have never seen anything the same since. Gillian Hart helped me to understand the local as a historical and geographical production. Thanks are also due to a number of faculty mentors who not only were on my committee but also have shaped my interests and this project in profound ways: John Burton, Bill Burch, Kalyanakrishnan Sivaramakrishnan, Eric Worby, Michael Burawoy, Alan Pred, and Nancy Peluso.

Writing a book can be an isolating experience, and I am grateful for having wonderful colleagues. I especially want to thank Lynn Thomas, Johanna Crane, Nora Kenworthy, Danny Hoffman, and Ron Krabill, who commented on draft chapters and otherwise substantially supported this project and me. I have benefitted greatly from conversations and collaborations with Susan Harewood, Eric Stewart, Jackie Belanger, Lauren Berliner, Diane Gillespie, Martha Groom, Christian Anderson, Julie Shayne, Jin-Kyu Jung, Alyssa Deutschler, Bruce Burgett, Colin Danby, S. Charusheela, and Tony Lucero from the University of Washington. I particularly want to recognize Ron Krabill and Crispin Thurlow for the sincere interest they both took in my project and my overall development as a scholar and professor. I could not have wished for better colleagues or friends.

I had the privilege of studying together with some remarkable students at UC Berkeley, including Brinda Sarathy, Tracey Osborne, Sapana Doshi, Rebecca Lave, and Mark Hunter. Joe Bryan and I were classmates and itinerant travelers throughout graduate school. He has shaped my thinking and understanding of theory more than anyone. I also want to thank James McCarthy, Aaron Bobrow-Strain, Wendy Wolford, Geoff Mann, Scott Prudham, Julie Guthman, Amy Ross, Sharad Chari, and Jake Kosek, all of whom have offered insights and advice at various stages of this project.

I have had the pleasure of working with some remarkable students at UW Bothell whose intellectual curiosity and engagement have immensely strengthened this project. Thanks to Joyce Mwangi, Angela Macklin, Josh Heim, Debbie Brown, Trina Ballard, Julie Hurst, and Shana Hirsch. I especially want to thank Marcus Johnson for his work as a research assistant on this project and for his contagious passion for cultural studies and social justice. Ronnie Thibault has challenged me to do my best work and has been instrumental in putting together companion digital humanities resources for this book.

I want to thank Julie Van Pelt for her assistance editing early chapters of the manuscript and to Barbara Wojhoski for copyediting the final draft. xNR productions made the maps. John Joerschke guided me through the publishing process. Beatrice Burton produced the index. Derek Krissoff went to bat for this book from the beginning and introduced me to the world of publishing. This book was greatly improved by the comments and suggestions of two anonymous reviewers. Thank you also to Julie Felner and Amy Harrison, who gave me much needed late-night help to see more clearly the poignant stories that bring this research to life.

My parents and sister deserve many thanks for providing love, confidence, and plenty of constructive criticism. To my mom, Behna Gardner, you have always made me believe that anything is possible and that creativity matters. I am grateful for your unconditional love. To my sister, Abbey Gardner, thank you for reading my dissertation over and over and for reminding me to think of an audience outside of the social sciences. To my dad, Lanny Gardner, you have supported me at every step of this project. I could not have done this without you. As a father and an editor you are beyond compare.

My deepest gratitude is to the three people who influence and inspire me most. To my daughters Stella and Maylie, you have not always known what I was writing about, but my research, as much as my life have been shaped by your warm spirits, your infectious smiles, and your unbridled optimism. Your depth of caring about people all over the world is a constant source of delight. Finally, my heartfelt thanks go to my wife and partner in all things, Jennifer Meyer. Thank you for supporting me throughout this process. We met in East Africa in 1991, and this book represents one, albeit long, chapter of our mutual relationship with the people and places of Tanzania. You are and have always been my best friend and companion in the everyday things that make life worth living, which included many dusty, bumpy, daylong drives to and from Loliondo. Without your encouragement, reassurance, and love this book would never have been written. Simple thanks are not enough. This book is for you.

ABBREVIATIONS

AA	authorized association
ADDO	Arusha Catholic Diocese Development Organization
AWF	African Wildlife Foundation
CAMPFIRE	Communal Areas Management Program for Indigenous Resources
CBC	community-based conservation
CBNRM	community-based natural resource management
CBO	community-based organization
CCS	Community Conservation Service
CIDA	Canadian International Development Agency
FFU	Field Force Unit
FZS	Frankfurt Zoological Society
GCA	game controlled area
GTZ	Gesellschaft für Technische Zusammenarbeit
ILO	International Labor Organization
IMF	International Monetary Fund
IUCN	International Union for Conservation of Nature
IWGIA	International Working Group on Indigenous Affairs
KIPOC	Korongoro Integrated People Oriented to Conservation
LGCA	Loliondo Game Controlled Area
LHRC	Legal and Human Rights Center
LTOF	Loliondo Tour Operators Forum
MLDRMP	Maasai Livestock Development and Range Management Project
MNRT	Ministry of Natural Resources and Tourism
MP	member of parliament
MRG	Minority Rights Group International
NAFCO	National Farm and Agriculture Corporation
NCA	Ngorongoro Conservation Area
NCAA	Ngorongoro Conservation Area Authority
NGO	nongovernmental organization
OA	open area
OBC	Ortello Business Corporation

PINGOS	Pastoralists Indigenous Non-governmental Organizations Forum
PWC	Pastoral Women's Council
SAP	structural adjustment programs
SCF	Sand County Foundation
SRCS	Serengeti Regional Conservation Strategy
TAHOA	Tanzanian Hunting Operators Association
TANAPA	Tanzania National Parks Association
TANU	Tanganyika African National Union
TAWICO	Tanzania Wildlife Corporation
TBL	Tanzania Breweries Limited
TCL	Tanzania Conservation Limited
TNRF	Tanzania Natural Resources Forum
TWPF	Tanzania Wildlife Protection Fund
TYL	Tanganyika African National Union Youth League
USAID	United States Agency for International Development
WB	World Bank
WCA	Wildlife Conservation Act
WD	Wildlife Division
WMA	Wildlife Management Area
WSRTF	Wildlife Sector Review Task Force
WWF	World Wildlife Fund

Selling the Serengeti

CHAPTER 1

Introduction

Safari Tourism, Pastoralism, and Land Rights in Tanzania

On August 9, 2012, Avaaz.org, a self-described "global web movement" bringing "people-powered politics to decision-making everywhere," organized an online petition titled "Stop the Serengeti Sell-Off." The appeal highlighted the injustice of wealthy trophy hunters buying an area adjacent to Serengeti National Park for use as their own personal playground. The statement read: "At any moment, a big-game hunting corporation could sign a deal which would force up to 48,000 members of Africa's famous Maasai tribe from their land to make way for wealthy Middle Eastern kings and princes to hunt lions and leopards."[1] Avaaz was referring to the Ortello Business Corporation (OBC), a hunting company established by businessman and member of the Dubai royal family Mohammed Abdulrahim al-Ali, and the Tanzanian government's proposed plan to create a new protected area for trophy hunting, which would dispossess the Maasai people of over 37 percent of their land.[2]

Within twenty-four hours, over 400,000 people had signed the Avaaz petition, and after one week there were over 850,000 signatures. Together with local direct action including over 1,500 women turning in their CCM cards, the campaign seemed to work temporarily, putting pressure on the Tanzanian government to listen to the concerns of Maasai activists who claimed it was taking their land simply to appease the interests of powerful foreign investors. The reprieve was short-lived, as less than a year later, in April 2013, the government declared a new protected area that would split the Maasai people's land, creating a 1,500-square-kilometer protected area for hunting and leaving the Maasai pastoralists with the remaining 2,500 square kilometers. Local leaders and activists protested the action, calling on the president to intervene. The government eventually relented and called for a process to address conservation and tourism in Loliondo.

This remote part of Tanzania was quickly becoming a laboratory for how conservation and tourism were to be managed within a neoliberal context. Efforts to convert Maasai village land into a conservation area in Loliondo were not new. On the eastern edge of Serengeti National Park, conservationists had long wished to resettle the residents, move the villages and incorporate the area into the park. But Maasai leaders had repeatedly resisted efforts to do so, in the process organizing not only a regional social movement but also a new political understanding of the state, international conservation, and what it meant to be a Maasai living in Loliondo. The persistent political resistance shown by Loliondo residents is a direct effect of this legacy. Whether the increased global attention will mark a turn for Maasai activists fighting against this "land grab" is still uncertain. The fact that the remote Maasai area of Loliondo was now a critical site in a global struggle for the future meanings of conservation, pastoralism, and communal land rights was, however, coming clearly into view.

In 1992 the Tanzanian government had controversially granted the OBC exclusive hunting rights to Loliondo division, including the area made up of six villages that share a border with Serengeti National Park (map 1).[3] The OBC's continued presence in Loliondo over the past twenty years and its substantial influence with government officials have been a significant story line for critics of neoliberal globalization in Tanzania. Local journalists named the OBC's unparalleled influence over government officials "Loliondogate."[4] Examples were cited in the press that included the construction of a private international airstrip in the remote location, lax oversight of hunting quotas, state police working as private security whenever the OBC is hunting in the area, and allegations of illegal live animal capture and transport to Dubai.[5] Perhaps the most telling illustration of what journalists called "the privatization of Tanzania" was the OBC's supposed "hijacking" of the country's telecommunications system. When a cell phone is turned on near the OBC hunting camp, a message from the Abu Dhabi–based telecommunications corporation Etisalat greets you, "Welcome to the United Arab Emirates."[6]

National and international media exploited the ethnic and religious background of the OBC directors, commonly referring to them as "the Arabs."[7] Daily papers suggested that their extreme wealth and opulence distinguished their transnational political power and enabled a callous lack of ethics. As the sole leaseholder for both of Loliondo's designated hunting areas, the company garnered similar privileges granted to other foreign investors. The OBC was one of sixty registered companies, mostly foreign owned, that were granted a concession to one of the country's 140 designated hunting areas by Tanzania's Wildlife Division. While some of those hunting blocks, as they are called, are in game reserves with no permanent populations, the majority of hunting concessions in Tanzania overlap with established village land in either game-controlled areas or designated open areas (see chapter 3).

Between 1992 and 2009, local Maasai communities protested the OBC's rights to hunt on their lands (see chapter 4). But despite media representations that depicted the OBC as the worst of the worst, many Maasai in Loliondo had come

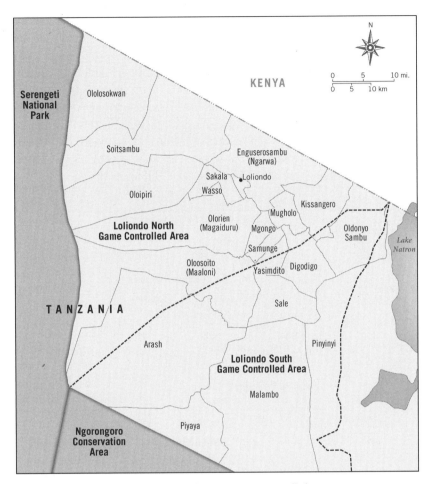

MAP 1. Loliondo Division villages and overlapping game controlled areas where safari trophy hunting is permitted. xnr Productions.

to see the obc as a marginally better option than other hunting investors with their own reputations as entitled foreigners and for harassing local communities. As long as the obc's activities did not interfere with the Maasai pastoralist land-use system that depended on the same designated hunting area for dry-season grazing, they were generally tolerated. However, the fear that the obc could wield extraordinary influence with the government if it chose to do so was substantiated on July 4, 2009. On that day Tanzanian police, using obc vehicles, evicted thousands of Maasai people and tens of thousands of live-stock from village land. The evictions were justified in the name of protecting the environment and maintaining the obc's state-sanctioned right to hunt in the area.[8]

The Avaaz campaign came two years after the evictions, on the heels of the government-proposed solution to the conflict. A new protected area put forward by state wildlife authorities and district officials would permanently create a new space for conservation and big-game trophy hunting, essentially expanding the boundaries of Serengeti National Park (map 2). If successful, the state plan would build on past efforts to separate important wildlife habitat from populated village areas.[9] According to officials, this was necessary to prevent future conflicts between "people and nature" in Loliondo. The rub was that the Maasai would lose 1,500 out of 4,000 square kilometers of communal grazing land that until then had been shared by wildlife and livestock. This was

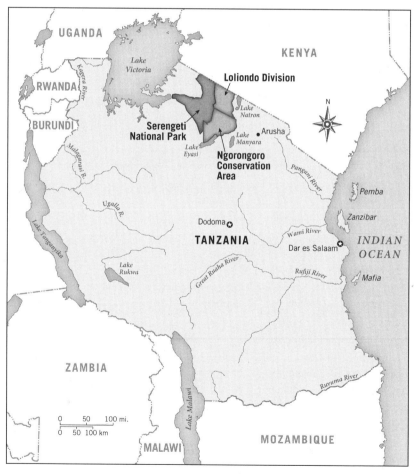

MAP 2. Ngorongoro Conservation Area and Loliondo Division in northeast Tanzania. XNR Productions.

the worst possible outcome for the Maasai living in Loliondo, who had already surrendered much land, first when colonial powers placed the international boundary dividing Kenya and Tanzania through the middle of Maasai land and communities and then with the creation of Serengeti National Park and the Ngorongoro Conservation Area in 1959.[10]

Tourism, Neoliberalism, and Conservation in Loliondo

I was drawn to Loliondo in the early 1990s to study the relationship between Maasai livelihoods, conservation, and tourism. I came to appreciate how the history of land dispossession in the name of conservation, first by colonial authorities and then by the newly independent national government of Tanzania, had led many Maasai leaders and residents to embrace the promises of neoliberal political and economic reforms as a way to gain recognition for long sought-after land and human rights. Neoliberalization is a term used by geographers and other scholars to describe the set of policies and discourses that promote economic liberalization as a solution to global poverty and underdevelopment. Neoliberalism generally entails promoting free trade, privatization, deregulation, and opening new markets. Invoking neoliberalization as a theory, as well as a set of policy reforms, its advocates call for increasing the role of the private sector and limiting the role of the state to create investment and economic growth.[11] Like most people and social groups in Africa, Asia, and Latin America, the Maasai were thrown into the new political economic context of neoliberalism that came to dominate the world capitalist system in the mid-1980s and early 1990s.

Throughout the colonial period (1891–1961) and under the socialist developmental state (1961–85), the Maasai had consistently struggled against the government to defend pastoralist livelihoods and protect their land rights. The pressure to take Maasai land for wildlife conservation and large-scale agriculture was supported by a developmental ideology that saw pastoralism as a premodern social and economic system. Ideas for efficient and market-oriented range management based on private-property rights, popularized by ecologist Garret Hardin's (1968) "Tragedy of the Commons" thesis, gave government officials and development experts the conviction they needed to justify massive interventions in pastoralist communities.

Market-oriented reforms arrived in Tanzania in the late 1980s at the same time that a crisis occurred in the "fortress conservation" model of wildlife protection, which called for the separation of people and wildlife (see chapter 3).[12] Despite Tanzania's extraordinary commitment to wildlife conservation, which entailed dedicating close to 35 percent of its land to protected status, the 1980s saw the rapid conversion of land bordering parks from rangelands to farmlands. The same period also saw an unprecedented rise in poaching activities within core-protected areas.[13] A lack of resources, as well as hostile relations with bordering communities, put pressure on the conservation community of donors, NGOs, scientists, and state agencies to reimagine conservation by including a role for rural communities. Range ecologists at this time began to push back against Hardin's thesis, arguing that pastoralism was in fact a highly productive system of land use that was more compatible with wildlife conservation than other rural production systems.[14] Presented with opportunities to commoditize their lands for tourism, the Maasai actively adopted market-based community conservation arrangements. The promise of devolved rights to land and natural resources led many Maasai, searching for a tactical advantage in their struggle for land rights, to embrace many of the neoliberal ideas and ideologies that underpinned these projects. Seeing possible benefits such as a path to securing long-term property rights, Maasai leaders in Loliondo often became vocal supporters of policies that enabled direct foreign investment for tourism on village lands. At the same time, they opposed the state's signature effort to manage tourism investment on village lands, the Wildlife Management Area (WMA) policy.

The recent evictions to create a lucrative hunting reserve and another controversial land deal in Loliondo to establish a private nature refuge expose the contingent practices through which the meanings of neoliberalism are produced. The Maasai in Loliondo have learned that trying to harness capitalism's power to make claims for collective rights is a politically fraught undertaking. Neoliberalism provided new opportunities for both Tanzanians and foreigners to exploit their land and labor. A market approach to development also meant fewer state resources devoted to public services and basic state functions. How Tanzanians view neoliberal reforms depends largely on their identities and where they are situated within the nation-state. The Maasai people in Loliondo had rarely enjoyed the benefits and protections of the Tanzanian state. Because of this marginalized position, they often viewed neoliberal reforms differently than did many other Tanzanians. Informed by this history of state-society relationships, Maasai leaders have attempted to use their ability to negotiate directly with foreign investors, participating in commoditizing their landscapes, to create openings that they believe will help them realize the level of autonomous development for which they have long strived. Such independence or freedom from the state is often seen as a key aspect of neoliberal reforms. For many Maasai people in Loliondo, pursuing economic and political freedom turned on their ability to advance their status within the nation-state. I argue in this book that the Maasai have attempted to achieve these new forms of recognition by reimaging the village as a legitimate site of community belonging and rights and representing this image of the village to different audiences including tourism investors, state officials, and their fellow Maasai citizens. As I describe in the following chapters, this process has opened up political spaces as well as presented challenges.

Safari Tourism as a Site of Meaning and Profit

This book is an ethnographic study that examines how tourism investment in the Loliondo area of northern Tanzania remakes the ideas and meanings of economic markets, land rights, and political struggle. I consider three tourism arrangements in Loliondo: village-based tourism joint ventures in which foreign-owned ecotourism companies lease access to land from Maasai villages; a "private nature refuge" established by Thomson Safaris, a U.S.-owned tourism company that purchased 12,617 acres of village land in 2006; and a government hunting concession on village land managed by the OBC.[15] I examine these projects to explain how state authority depends on articulating national agendas with the interests of private foreign investors (chapter 4); how the context of neoliberal development remakes social and spatial relationships, animating a new cultural politics of ethnic difference (chapter 5); and why Maasai activists have embraced some forms of investment as a way to assert their rights and defend their lands (chapter 6).

I contend that the context of neoliberalism has reshaped the meanings and values of Maasai landscapes and communities. This reshaping has altered the political tactics available to marginalized social groups like the Maasai. I argue neither for nor against the fairness of markets. Instead, I attempt to show that communities like the Maasai in Loliondo have little choice but to work within the discursive context of neoliberalism and attempt to use the techniques afforded by markets, such as contracts with investors and village land-use plans, as tactics in defending their right to land and access to natural resources. These tools were part and parcel of a development policy based on private property and the rights of landowners. History would tell the Maasai that such cadastral practices have rarely if ever promoted the interests of farmers and herders who depend largely on customary and collective rights that were dismissed under colonial rule. However, the promise of securing communal land through the market rationale of proof of ownership has appealed to many Maasai who have spent decades trying other strategies to defend their land. In doing so they open themselves up to risks, including deepening capitalist social relationships, enabling state interests to claim resources in the name of maximizing value and efficiency, and increased ethnic conflict based on new meanings of land as private property. I am especially interested in the cultural dimensions of neoliberalism and how incorporating market logic and relationships to pressure the state for recognition simultaneously transform landscapes and subjects, and the social relationships that reproduce them. My main argument in the book is that in the context of these entanglements between nature, capitalism, state authority, and social movements, historically marginalized communities such as the Maasai actively participate in commodifying their land and identity with the desire to fulfill long-standing aspirations for what they see as economically and socially just opportunities to secure their pastoralist livelihoods. For these reasons what we see as resistance to the current framework of neoliberal development might include acts that embrace commodification with the goal of gaining long-sought and long-denied land and citizenship rights. This seemingly contradictory practice of challenging some market ideologies while embracing others is an increasingly common practice of marginalized social groups and movements around the world. This book examines what such contradictory resistance looks like in practice.

A Happy Place for Tourism?

The same week of the August 2012 Avaaz.org petition, a group of European and Tanzanian activists launched their own online campaign through the social media sites Weebly and Facebook to boycott a U.S. safari company for illegally purchasing land near the OBC concession and for taking critical grazing land from Maasai communities. Their campaign was titled "Boycott Thomson Safaris and Stop Them Land Grabbing from the Maasai People!" Unlike the OBC, Thomson Safaris was not a big-game hunting company. It was a niche tour operator from the United States that specialized in adventure camping and family safaris, ecotourism, and philanthropic travel tourism in Tanzania.[16] Unlike many larger companies, Thomson Safaris operated only in Tanzania, and working from its office in Watertown, Massachusetts, it marketed its tours largely to United States clients. The company has won several prestigious awards, including being honored by *Travel + Leisure* as "World's Best" in the category of top safari outfitter, and as one of the "best adventure travel companies on earth" by National Geographic Adventure magazine. The company markets itself as a leader in sustainable travel and provides a guide with eleven green and sustainable travel tips on its website.[17] In 2008 the company was a finalist for *Condé Nast Traveler*'s "World Savers Awards," which are given to socially responsible tour companies.[18] And in 2009 the company received the Tanzania Conservation Award for "their community-based conservation project at their private nature refuge" in Loliondo, the project that I describe in this book.

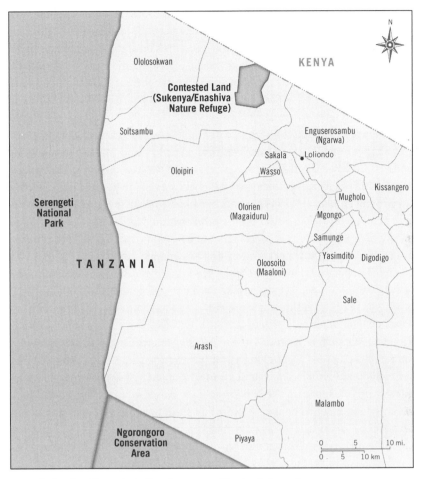

MAP 3. Loliondo villages, including the contested land at Sukenya/
Enashiva Nature Refuge. xnr Productions.

In 2006 the owners of Thomson Safaris had purchased a defunct farm, known locally as Sukenya, in the middle of Soitsambu village in Loliondo (map 3). The land had a brief history, from 1987 to 1989 as a national farm for the state-owned Tanzania Breweries Limited (TBL). The farm was one of several areas identified by government-employed consultants as prime properties to nationalize. The consultants saw the relatively large communal grazing land with few permanent settlements as a great opportunity to grow large amounts of barley for the rapidly expanding beer industry. However, the remote location far from major cities and towns coupled with the lack of all-season roads proved costly. The unreliable rainfall and a two-year drought signaled the project's demise.

After cultivating only seven hundred out of ten thousand acres over the first three years, the government abandoned the scheme in 1989. With few physical changes and no more government resources directed at the farm, the property reverted to communal grazing land used by Maasai pastoralists.[19] Questions remained about the property status of the land, but from 1989 through 2006, local Maasai residents exclusively used the area for grazing and watering their livestock.

In February 2006, to the surprise of Maasai leaders who had strongly challenged the initial TBL project and the government's claim that the land was not being effectively utilized, local newspapers advertised the land for sale. Mike Saningo, a Maasai man about thirty six-years old at the time, showed me a tattered copy of the announcement, posted in the *Arusha Times* on January 21, 2006.[20] It stated, "The farm comprises 10,000 acres" with "a labor camp and boreholes, for water supply." Potential developers and investors were told that "the farm is suitable for barley cultivation or eco-tourism undertakings."[21]

The Thomson Safaris owners, who lived part time in Tanzania and part time near Boston, Massachusetts, heard about the property and saw it as an opportunity to create a landmark community conservation project.[22] They created Tanzania Conservation Limited (TCL), a subsidiary of Thomson Safaris' parent company, Wineland-Thomson Adventures Inc., in order to purchase the farm.[23] Thomson Safaris/TCL was the highest bidder in an auction process, paying $1.2 million for a ninety-six-year lease for 12,617 acres. In one of their first acts, the new owners renamed the area Enashiva, a Maasai word for happiness. In its publicity material, the company states that it adopted the name from that of a creek running through the middle of the property.[24] Few people I interviewed knew the important seasonal watercourse by that name. Without any supporting documentation, the company explained that Enashiva was the name the Maasai had "long ago" called the creek. Thomson's rechristening of the property was seen by many local Maasai as an attempt to brand the area and to promote itself as a preservationist and restorer of the land.[25] For many Maasai this was just the latest episode in a history of conservation as dispossession.

When Maasai leaders learned of Thomson Safaris/TCL's imminent arrival, they wondered who had sold their land. Village leaders learned that the brewery, now a subsidiary company under the global corporation SABMiller was granted a title deed to the property in 2003, seventeen years after TBL first obtained the farm and fourteen years after abandoning the area.[26] The history of the transaction included forged minutes from a supposed village meeting where villagers willfully granted the land to TBL.[27] The title deed for 12,617 acres was significantly more land than the initial farm size of 10,000 acres. Nonetheless, and despite opposition to the sale by many village leaders Thomson Safaris/

TCL was granted a sublease from TBL for the remaining ninety-six years. Given the suspect nature of the lease, Maasai village leaders demanded that Thomson Safaris/TCL immediately return the land to the village. As the state-authorized titleholders of 12,617 acres of land, Thomson Safaris/TCL refused to bow to community pressure to return the land. The Thomson Safaris/TCL owners believed that a few "jealous individuals" and "corrupt" NGOs had organized opposition to the sale.[28] Mass protests of up to twelve hundred Maasai and several high-profile attempts to meet with national officials and political leaders, including the prime minister and the president of Tanzania, that led to an official government inquiry made clear that opposition to the project was far reaching.[29]

Soon after taking possession of the land, Thomson Safaris/TCL staff began restricting access to grazing land, encouraging local police to arrest trespassers, and confiscating or detaining livestock. Local residents also accused the company employees of burning permanent homesteads and shooting a Maasai herder.[30] The company directors vociferously denied these allegations, saying that they only burned vacated structures and that the shooting was entirely unrelated.[31]

The online petition against the Thomson Safaris/TCL land deal called for tourists to boycott Thomson Safaris and to spread the word about its abusive and self-serving practices. The activists highlighted the dire stakes of the deal: "The land ... provides vital grazing and access to water for the local Maasai people who have co-existed with, and safeguarded, the ecosystem for hundreds of years. Without access to this land, which they say they have never knowingly sold, they cannot survive."[32]

Hunting Reserves and Nature Refuges: Deadly Deals?

These two land deals represented what Maasai residents and civil-society organizations alleged were unjust appropriations of village land by private investors interested in capitalizing on Loliondo's spectacular landscape for safari hunting and tourism.[33] Local leaders worked hard to get the word out and used their connections with international organizations and national journalists to prevent these land deals from taking place outside public view, an all too common practice. The activist campaigns and numerous media reports on Loliondo represented these transactions between investors and government agencies as "deadly deals" for the Maasai people. Local activists were successful in getting their message out that Loliondo's market value as a hunting and ecotourism destination could create the conditions to justify government violence and efforts to remove the Maasai people from their land to further promote conservation. The Maasai activists were all too aware of the history of evictions and land dispossession associated with protected areas in Africa. Scholars like Rod Neumann (1998), Mark Dowie (2009), Dan Brockington (2002), and Brockington and James Igoe (2006), Paige West (2006), and Nancy Peluso (1993) have documented how the creation of parks and protected areas was commonly used to dispossess rural land users and enclose communal land for nature preservation and national development. Such scholarship has made the connection between demarcating lands for conservation and securing the foundations of modern nation-states around the globe. This is especially true in eastern and southern Africa.[34] In Tanzania almost 35 percent of the entire land base is under state protection and control as either a national park, a game reserve, a forest reserve, or a hunting concession.[35]

Maasai leaders and activists welcomed the international attention that the campaigns against the OBC and Thomson Safaris/TCL raised regarding the social costs of safari tourism and the threats posed to pastoral livelihoods and land rights in northern Tanzania. On August 31, 2012, a group of Tanzanian civil-society organizations circulated a press release supporting the Avaaz campaign. The organizations—Tanzania Land Alliance, Feminist Activist Coalition, Ngorongoro Non-Government Organization Network, and the Pastoralists Indigenous Non-Government Organization Forum—concluded their statement with several demands addressed to the government. The fifth and final request was "to immediately stop the use of excessive powers in handling conflicts between investors and villagers in Loliondo and elsewhere in the country."[36] Rather than asking the state to intervene and protect the rights of its citizens from the growing threat of foreign ownership and interests, the civil-society organizations bade the state to stop interfering in their lives. In many ways this response makes sense coming from Maasai organizations in Loliondo, where state projects and the interests of pastoralists have rarely been aligned. However, it is also a curious request given the tremendous stakes of the conflicts, the disproportionate power of foreign investors, and the ultimate role of the state as the enforcer of rights and arbiter of justice within the national boundaries of Tanzania.

In the past, states like Tanzania have justified evictions in the name of protecting African wildlife and wilderness as a world heritage and the basic duty of a modern nation-state. The public narrative surrounding the Tanzanian state's defense of the OBC hunting concession and the Thomson Safaris/TCL nature refuge were different and made no such scientific or nationalistic appeal. The new rationale was more pragmatic and more market-driven and held that Loliondo was too valuable a commodity to be left under the control of "backward," corrupt, or naive villagers. Tanzania's minister of tourism and natural resources, Shamsa Mwangunga, commented, "We cannot allow villagers to control such important activities [tourism and hunting] because some dishonest business-people will utilise that as a loophole to unlawfully exploit our resources."[37] The statement raised important questions: Was the state's role in wildlife management on village lands motivated by the need to protect its vulnerable citizens from unscrupulous business people? Or did state officials act to prevent the possibility that villagers would work directly with foreign investors, creating their own public-private partnerships at the local level? Regardless of motive, the political maneuvering over who has the right to represent African nature and to form partnerships with investors indicate the state's and the villagers' orientation to global capital. What becomes clear in such political struggles is that investors play a key role in shaping the discourse of conservation and helping to determine at which scale environmental governance is legitimated.

Village Joint Ventures: A Different Deal?

In 1997 I attended a meeting between the directors of another foreign-owned tour company, Dorobo Tours and Safaris (Dorobo Safaris), and the elected government representatives of Losoito/Maaloni village in Loliondo. Dorobo Safaris was the first company to sign tourism contracts with Maasai villages in Tanzania. In exchange for exclusive access to village land for walking and camping safaris, Dorobo Safaris paid the village government an annual rent, as well as usage fees for each visitor per day. Despite the obvious international value of gaining access to the greater Serengeti ecosystem for tourism outside Serengeti National Park, for the first time in Loliondo these contracts assigned a specific monetary value to tourism on village lands.

The meeting was to renegotiate a five-year contract between the tour company and the village. It was scheduled for noon but started about four hours later. Company representatives, including two of the three expatriate owners from the United States and their Maasai manager, waited outside the village office, a small room with a desk, chair, and bookcase with several black file folders arranged neatly on the shelves. After a quorum of village government representatives arrived, we entered one of the nearby primary-school classrooms and took our seats on the wood benches usually occupied by school students clad in their blue uniforms.

A Maasai man named Christopher Tipat stood in front of the room and welcomed everyone to the meeting, including the company directors and me, their "guest from America."[38] He said that the village had received many benefits from the arrangement with Dorobo Safaris, and he recommended moving forward by signing another contract. After Tipat finished, several other village government representatives rose, one by one, and took center stage in front of the classroom's cracked chalkboard. Each of the next five speakers gave lengthy preambles about the importance of their relationship with the company. They then all proceeded to say that they wanted higher payments in exchange for the company's exclusive access to their village land for tourism.

After several hours of deliberations, the Dorobo Safaris directors and manager agreed to increase the fees paid to the village. Between 1992 and 1997, three villages working directly with Dorobo Safaris—Olorien/Magaiduru, Losoito/Maaloni, and Oloipiri—had each earned approximately ten thousand dollars a year. Under the new contract they were likely to bring in about twice that amount. The money is either a lot or a little depending on your position in the global tourism commodity chain and what you think is a fair distribution of profits within the historically and geographically unequal system of transnational capitalism. Nevertheless, the village income represented a profound departure from the way that tourism revenue typically flowed in Tanzania. Rather than going directly to state-controlled parks and conservation areas, to private-property owners, or to the networks of organizations, consultants, researchers and state agencies responsible for promoting conservation interests and values, some portion of the money paid by tourists went directly to village governments and their members.

This was the first significant tourism revenue earned directly by villages in Loliondo. The money assisted Maasai residents to build school classrooms, rent lorries or tractors to transport maize and beans to market, excavate water sources, and pay student school fees, among other things. The annual income was important and gave Maasai villages some minimal level of autonomy from central government authorities. The profits earned from ecotourism on village lands was contrasted directly with the money paid by the OBC to the national Wildlife Division (WD) and other state agencies for trophy hunting. To the Maasai communities in Loliondo, state interest in controlling hunting and tourism on village lands was a way to earn significant revenue. The village joint ventures were their attempt to benefit from wildlife on their land.[39] Beyond profit, village joint-venture partnerships were also becoming an important aspect of demonstrating a visible challenge to the history of state-controlled tourism and conservation governance and oversight.

In the face of evictions from both the OBC hunting concession and the Thomson Safaris/TCL nature refuge, Maasai activists and leaders lobbied government representatives to intervene on their behalf. But while they have not abandoned the state as an important site for voicing their interests and securing their rights, they have increasingly understood the market, embodied in their direct relationships with tourism investors, as a local-state space in which to pursue their agendas and to influence national policy and culture. Throughout the struggles over the various land deals in Loliondo, Maasai communities have reasserted a long-held belief that they, and not the state, have the right to make

Loliondo's natural resources available for investors. In the process they hope to intervene in the ways that conservation discourse has historically worked to empower centralized authorities and transnational conservation networks.

As I discuss throughout this book, communities in Loliondo believed that based on their recent history of attracting and negotiating directly with foreign investors, they could handle these land deals "on their own" without "government intervention."[40] Their direct experiences with transnational tourism investors, who through their contracts recognized the villages as legitimate owners of land, created a new paradigm for Maasai land politics. Tourism presented Maasai communities in Loliondo with a way to commoditize their lands without, they believed, compromising their land-tenure rights. They saw ecotourism on village lands as a way to maximize the value of their territories without altering the material qualities of the land and to bolster their claims as owners. With the growing emphasis on foreign investment throughout the 1990s and into the twenty-first century, the Maasai in Loliondo trusted that contracts with tourism investors helped to make the value of their village lands for both livestock and wildlife legible in new and more meaningful ways.

A strong conviction about local land ownership is nothing new. These beliefs have been most frequently grounded in appeals to indigeneity or a special cultural status that entitles a social group to unique rights based on its relationship with the land and allows it to exclude other citizens and communities from access based on the idea that it is the best steward of the land.[41] Anthropologists Dorothy Hodgson and James Igoe have shown how the Maasai represent their history as pastoralists in an agrarian nation to align their claims over land and resources with other indigenous groups and first peoples across the globe.[42] The Maasai creatively used their status as members of a transnational indigenous community to contextualize their position within the Tanzanian nation and carve out a distinct relationship with foreign NGOs, government agencies, and investors to shift their status within the nation-state. Nonetheless, appeals to indigeneity have been markedly absent in the current struggles. In opposing the OBC and Thomson Safaris/TCL, the Maasai did not assert their rights as a unique ethnic group or as indigenous people. Rather, they expressed their claims as rights-bearing villages and villagers: as state-sanctioned local authorities with specific territorial jurisdiction. By relying on the village as the embodied community, the Maasai are reworking how identity articulates with space and place in their society.[43] The question remains, however, whether Maasai communities can exploit their own land and natural resources as village territories to preserve collective ownership and control over them. Can they use global markets to pressure the state to finally recognize their rights as Maasai, as pastoralists, and as Tanzanians?

As a historical and geographical process, neoliberalism is not a singular formation that can be entirely resisted. Rather it is a force that acts on the actions of others.[44] I agree with anthropologist James Ferguson (2010), who argues that a simple oppositional stance to neoliberalism is neither an effective political strategy to create social change and justice nor a compelling analytical approach to understand contemporary politics.[45] If we, as scholars, hope to contribute politically and analytically, "we have to come up with something more interesting to say about [neoliberal policies] than just that we're against them."[46] More than a set of economic policies and beliefs that promote privatization and free enterprise, rolling back the state, and deregulating currencies, neoliberalism should also be understood as a broad cultural force shaping how states and societies understand their roles and interact, as well as the ways in which subjects understand their lives and possible futures. For reasons I had not anticipated when I first arrived in Tanzania in 1992, contemporary Maasai land struggles offer scholars like myself a rich context to explore the everyday way that neoliberalism shapes people's beliefs, values, and interests, and in turn the meaning of places like the Serengeti.

Building a Modern African Nation

To understand the dimensions of neoliberalism in Tanzania, it is necessary to briefly consider the history of Tanzanian nationalism and the relationship between state-led agrarian reform and pastoralism. After independence in 1961, Tanzania adopted a socialist system of government. The first president of the new country, Julius Nyerere, was revered across Africa and around the world as a postcolonial visionary. For many radicals and left-leaning politicians, activists, and academics, Tanzania presented one of the best places to build a new socialist society based on principles of collective work and mutual self-reliance. Tanzania was a Mecca of sorts, attracting a pilgrimage of students, scholars, and donors hoping to build and document this grand new experiment: a truly progressive state that would counter the ingrained racial and class privilege of colonialism and replace it with a society based on a unified national identity, collective rural labor, and centralized national development.[47] Tanzanian nationalism meant strong solidarity with peasant and pan-African social movements and a deep suspicion of capitalism.

On the eve of independence, Nyerere gave a speech titled "National Property," in which he laid out the dangers of the so-called free market for a newly independent country like Tanganyika that had been systematically "underdeveloped" during colonial rule. "In a country such as this, where generally speaking, the Africans are poor and the foreigners are rich, it is quite possible that, within eighty or a hundred years, if the poor African were allowed to sell his land, all the land in Tanganyika would belong to wealthy immigrants, and the local people would be tenants."[48]

Despite his prescient words, the results of his alternative direction of state-led national development were mixed. Progressive reforms were commingled with authoritarian edicts.[49] Peasant empowerment rubbed up against the need for urban labor and industrial production. Political nonalignment met global tariffs and trade barriers. And the concerted effort to constitute a postcolonial national identity left some groups, specifically pastoralists and hunter-gatherers, well outside the normative image of a modern Tanzanian citizen.[50] Several prominent Maasai leaders were initially supportive of Tanzania's socialist path, believing it could best address the intense marginalization wrought by colonial policies.[51] But the techniques employed by the Tanzanian government to modernize the Maasai were seen as generally hostile to their pastoral mode of production and way of life.

Specifically, the independent government intensified colonial efforts to create national parks, dispossessing peasants and pastoralists in the name of wildlife preservation.[52] More than other cultural groups, pastoralists lost access to large territories integral to their system of migratory seasonal grazing, known as transhumance. Along with their assault on pastoral lands, government officials and development experts also attempted to change the Maasai and other pastoralists into ranchers with clear private-property rights. The early efforts to modernize and transform the Maasai in the 1960s and early 1970s focused on creating group ranches and pushing for the marketing and sale of livestock, over subsistence practices. Maasai critics pointed out that the project, funded by the United States Agency for International Development (USAID), was "not in the spirit of socialist development."[53] Although collective farms and ranches were at the core of socialist and Marxist policies across the globe, Maasai leaders identified an underlying tension in Tanzanian state socialism. They believed that African socialism should respond to historical and geographical circumstances and not universal models. Although group ranches were one way to address collective labor and marketing of livestock, they also undermined the flexible land-use system that enabled pastoralists to subsist in semiarid areas. The Maasai linked these early efforts to integrate them into a modern economy and society based on agriculture and other policies to the larger context of Tanzanian socialism, in which they felt culturally marginalized. In what many Maasai believed was a display of utter contempt for their culture, the state also created policies to regulate Maasai dress, essentially stating, "Maasai must wear pants."[54]

Within the first decade of independence (1961–71), many Maasai leaders considered the Nyerere government and its large state bureaucracy as directly hostile to their interests and values. Unlike the majority of Tanzanians, who could recite Nyerere's warnings on the evils of capitalism by heart, the Maasai did not share in the deep-seated belief that they were being oppressed by global capitalism.[55] For some Maasai, especially in Loliondo, it was instead clear that their oppressor was none other than their own government and its universal ideas about modernization and development. Lazaro Parkipuny was one of the most influential Maasai leaders in Tanzania and a prominent Maasai intellectual from Loliondo. In his article "Some Crucial Aspects of the Maasai Predicament," Parkipuny asserts, "the people should not be made to sit back and let the government do whatever it wants. Since the well-being of the people must be the purpose of development, they must take control of the situation by creating their own socialist institutions for local management of the process of production, without being overpowered by the centre's requirements of uniformity."[56]

Maasai leaders' unfailing focus on state power and interests as the driving force behind Maasai marginalization and dispossession suggests an ideological disposition toward alternative "rights talk" that displaces the state as the sovereign space of economic, political, and cultural citizenship.[57] To better understand the current politics in Loliondo and places like it around the world, it is useful to go beyond oppositional frameworks, and as Ferguson suggests look for "new and better ways of thinking about practices of government" and "how they might be linked in new ways to the aspirations and demands of the economically and socially marginalized people who constitute the majority of the population in much of the world."[58] This is not a view that sympathizes with the current direction of global politics and the trend toward the accumulation of property and wealth in fewer and fewer hands. Rather, it is an attempt to take seriously the lived experiences, ideas, and desires of people like the Maasai in Loliondo as they literally fight for their future. It is also to add complexity to our understanding of "rights." For here rights are not individual nor are they sought exclusively through the state. Instead rights accrue to collective groups like villagers and are pursued in a global marketplace that decenters the state as the only site of guaranteeing and adjudicating rights. Whether transnational relationships based on economic interests are capable of guaranteeing rights or putting pressure on the state to do so becomes one of the most fraught and contingent questions for the Maasai and other groups like them.

Economic Growth or Land Grab?

For many of the Maasai residents I interviewed, the OBC and the Thomson Safaris/TCL land deals were considered a "government effort to complete the 'land grab' started under colonial rule" in the late 1800s, and that continues through today.[59] It is not unreasonable to read the history of the Maasai in East Africa as one long land grab in the name of global conservation and national development. George Monbiot's popular book *No Man's Land: An Investigative Journey through Kenya and Tanzania* (1994), highlights the brutal history of pastoral land dispossession. The Maasai often compare their experiences to Native Americans and First Peoples in North and South America, whose land-use systems were misunderstood, disrupted, and in many cases destroyed in the name of progress.[60]

Whenever he had the chance, Parkipuny reminded his audience that the locations of the world-famous Serengeti National Park and the Ngorongoro Conservation Area are also home to tens of thousands of indigenous people.[61] The systematic erasure of these people and their histories from the landscape in the name of wildlife preservation has seeded "deep rooted feelings of antagonism towards conservation." For Parkipuny, a critical reading of protected-area maps in East Africa reveals a simple truth: "Most of the protected areas have been carved out of the once large commonlands, used jointly by wildlife and pastoralists. . . . It is not by mere accident of history that many of the most spectacular wildlife protection areas in East Africa were carved out in territories previously part of Maasailand." (map 4).[62]

The history of conservation and Maasai land dispossession is well known throughout Loliondo. The regional collective memory in Loliondo holds that the government—be it under German (1891–1914), British (1914–61), or Tanzanian (1961–present) rule—unjustly took land from the Maasai to promote both conservation and state interests. This history of national territorial ambition in the name of state building and modernization has been central to constituting the Maasai in Loliondo as a "collective subject." At a time in the 1990s when social movements throughout the world were concerned with the negative effects of neoliberal reforms that appeared to speed up the process of accumulation by dispossession, especially for marginal and indigenous people, Maasai leaders in Loliondo saw neoliberalism as offering new openings and prospects for political and social change. The Maasai sought to exploit the inherent contradictions of neoliberalization, trying to use the new playing field to challenge their position vis-à-vis the postcolonial state.

Despite the dangers posed by foreign investors like the OBC and Thomson Safaris/TCL, Maasai leaders and activist organizations saw private investment as a contingent practice that offered the possibility of benefiting them as well as hurting them. Rather than a one-way relation of domination, Maasai saw some investors as potential partners in their struggle for land rights and political freedoms.[63] According to many Maasai leaders and activists I have spoken with, it is not foreign investment itself that has dispossessed them of resources

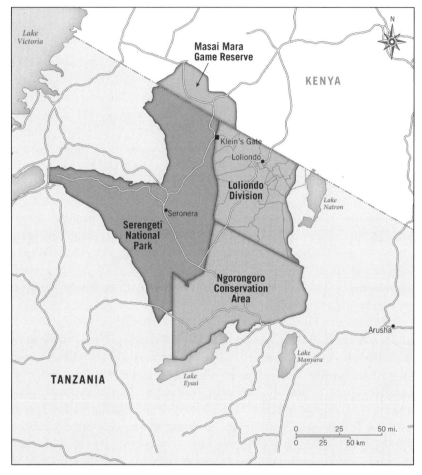

MAP 4. Northeast Tanzania, including Serengeti National Park, Ngorongoro Conservation Area, and Loliondo Division. XNR Productions.

and rights but rather what they see as the "skewed rules of capitalism" and the state's efforts to monopolize market opportunities and seek rents at the scale of the nation-state.[64] A string of political victories in support of their joint-venture partnerships with tourism investors in the 1990s and 2000s emboldened many Maasai in Loliondo to believe that they could rewrite those rules to promote their political aims for a future when pastoralism would be a viable cultural and economic system.

In a presentation to the Travelers Philanthropy Conference in Arusha in 2008 about the current conflicts in Loliondo, Maasai activist David Methau said, "What we need are real private sector partnerships that empower us."[65]

He contrasted these "real partnerships" that were based on "contracts between investors and villages" to investments in which the Tanzanian state "sold or leased" land rights directly to foreign investors.[66] For Methau and many other Loliondo leaders, remaking the social relations of investment presented one of the few possible paths for the Maasai to reshape their landscape, their relationship to the state, and ultimately control of their futures.

Are Methau's comments an example of false consciousness?[67] Do Maasai leaders have no other choice than to embrace market policies and opportunities, even as they may seed their demise? Or are activists such as Methau not naive but rather drawing on their historically and geographically situated experiences to analyze and act? Rather than dismissing Maasai people's interest in using market-based relationships as a way to challenge some of the features of global capitalism, I view them as emerging political tactics within a constrained neoliberal context. Again, I agree with Ferguson (2010) that if we are to understand contemporary social and political struggle in postcolonial countries today, we must "be willing at least to imagine the possibility of a truly progressive politics that would also draw on governmental mechanisms that we have become used to terming 'neoliberal.'"[68]

This book describes the history of recent Maasai efforts to engage shifting strategies to protect access to their resources and livelihoods within a complicated network of actors that include the state, hunting companies, ecotourism companies, and others. Understanding these efforts in a historical and geographical context provides valuable lessons and contributions for discussions and debates within political ecology, development studies, and neoliberal conservation.[69] Working alongside many Maasai activists and leaders over the past twenty years, I have been struck by how they artfully navigate the tricky political landscape of neoliberal development. On one hand, many leaders in Loliondo are wary of foreign investors who can use their money to influence state policies and officials to further dispossess and marginalize Maasai of their land and rights. On the other hand, many of the people I have interviewed and worked with express more faith in market relationships, with specific investors seen as allies against the bureaucratic state, as a way to force the state into making concessions to Maasai interests. From the trenches of political struggles, one can more clearly see the reasons for these seemingly contradictory positions.

Neoliberal Natures

Beyond telling an important story about tourism, conservation, and land struggles in Tanzania, this book engages three concepts important to contemporary understandings of development: neoliberalism and nature; the global land grab; and the social production of "the local" as the meaningful site of community interests. There is a robust literature challenging the market-led development paradigm and illustrating the costly social, political, and economic effects of neoliberalization.[70] Much of this literature critiques both the economics and the discursive power of neoliberalism or neoliberalization, showing how the new common sense toward market-oriented development and governance puts private profit over broader social benefits. One implicit assumption in much of this literature is that revealing the flaws in the hegemonic neoliberal consensus can help generate new discourses and mobilize new constituencies to advocate for alternatives. Such thinking often assumes that those groups and individuals subjected to the consequences of neoliberal development are naturally inclined against market values and that they will embrace alternatives if given the opportunity.

What much of this literature fails to consider or glosses over is how neoliberalization works as a cultural discourse. Political ecology provides a framework to understand culture as a dynamic process through which identities, values, and interests are produced in relation to changing political economic conditions. What I demonstrate in this book is that many communities that are threatened by neoliberal policies and ideologies also believe that market reforms and market relationships offer possibilities for political, economic, and social gains. Maasai community leaders and activists in Loliondo do not see investors simply as drivers of resource appropriation. Rather, they view them as potential collaborators in an ongoing historical struggle between a nationalist development project and one in which different marginalized groups, like the Maasai, can determine their own development trajectory. Such ideas are based on the hope of articulating local and global agendas as a way to challenge state-led planning.

The "global land grab" is shorthand for an emergent assessment and critique of current economic and political policies that advocate for the privatization of land and resources in the name of economic growth, job creation, and food security. Advocates of neoliberal economic policies describe these strategies as creating new value where an absence of capital, expertise, or "modern" management techniques have presented a barrier to the commodification and marketing of resources, goods, and services. Although certain groups and individuals are benefiting from this massive transfer of wealth and resources, the majority of residents in formerly colonized countries is losing access to resources and is more vulnerable as a consequence.[71] Much of the literature and debate about the global land grab has revolved around large tracts of arable land being acquired in underdeveloped countries and regions to grow crops to feed distant populations.[72] Another area of concern is the accumulation of land for biofuel production or climate-change mitigation that restricts local access to vital land and resources for essential food and livelihood production. Much less attention has been paid to the role of tourism and conservation as a site of resource concentration and dispossession in this context. This is especially true of community conservation, which depends on a large degree of consent and collaboration as opposed to earlier modes of conservation that relied almost exclusively on enclosure and dispossession.

The current trends to accumulate land primarily for gain by distant populations or private individuals pose a great risk to myriad peoples and production systems that do not easily conform to neoliberal capitalist production, distribution, and consumption. By resisting these processes, Loliondo leaders and activists provide an important example of the possibilities and limits when a group chooses to challenge the current articulation of global capital and national interests. Understanding how neoliberal policies and ideologies transform the political economic context of land use and development is a critical task of scholars. Many commentators and researchers studying globalization argue that national boundaries are no longer relevant or play a severely diminished role in economic investment and development. My research shows that for groups like the Maasai global development is always articulated to national boundaries and projects.

Any analysis of neoliberalization and its effects must take seriously how histories of postcolonial nationalism and state-building efforts interact with current economic thinking.[73] For the Maasai in Loliondo, the central feature distinguishing the political meanings and possibilities of neoliberalism in terms of privatization, investment, and political reorganization is how the "global legitimacy" of foreign investment determines the scale of struggle.[74] Rather than thinking about local power as always "nested" within a spatial hierarchy where the nation-state subsumes all other cultural and political groups, Maasai leaders and activists have come to understand their ability to negotiate directly with foreign investors, as well as other transnational actors and organizations, as a way to challenge the scale of development and the primacy of the state as the organizing principle of society.[75]

Using Villages to Reorganize the Social Relations of the State

In Tanzania, the village is not an inherently local institution. Maasai villages in Loliondo were created in the context of African nationalism and decolonization. They were shaped during a period of fierce nationalism, when Julius Nyerere and his Tanganyika African National Union (TANU) government of anti-imperialists attempted to create a new African institution to combat the forces of global capitalism and the cold war. Struggles over the meaning and character of the village and the state would play out largely within the boundaries of the nation of Tanzania, but they were born from a cold-war paradigm, in which newly independent nations like Tanzania were forced to demonstrate their economic vitality and perform development strategies that would give them standing in the community of modern nations. With the introduction of SAPs and austerity measures in the late 1980s, powerful global actors, including the International Monetary Fund, the World Bank, and the World Trade Organization, challenged the centrality of the nation-state as the focal point of society. One of the aims of decentralization policies was to identify the actual owners and stakeholders of resources in order to foster public-private partnerships to more efficiently and equitably exploit natural resources.

In Loliondo, the commodification of land and conservation hinge on a series of discursive tactics that attempt to link the globally determined value of nature with a clear owner of the resource. Whereas the state has maintained its hegemonic position as proprietor of national resources, the remaking of Loliondo turns on an assumption that the value of nature is produced by the activities of local stewards and their ongoing ability to practice forms of resource management compatible with conservation. As Neumann (1998) has shown, the state has used the commonsense idea of biodiversity as a universal value to exclude local claims and assert its territorial and political control over its subjects.

The current scramble to reorganize the Tanzanian landscape can be partly understood as an attempt by Maasai leaders and some tourism investors to harness the narrative of conservation and African nature as a global good and firmly attach it to local histories, resource management, and sustainable land use. Without Maasai stewardship, for example, much of the current wildlife habitat in many of the country's national parks, as well as in adjacent areas like Loliondo, would not exist. Once vilified as a destructive land use, since the late 1980s pastoralism has come to be understood as the livelihood system most compatible with wildlife. Unlike agriculturalists, who directly compete with wildlife habitat for productive land, pastoralists typically manage their rangelands in ways that support both wildlife and livestock. Community conservation projects that did not rely on enclosing pastoralist land created the possibility for disseminating this view of nature, in which Maasai interests could coexist with wildlife. This approach contrasted with the OBC hunting corridor and the Thomson Safaris/TCL lease, which both relied on the direct appropriation of Maasai village land and positioned Maasai pastoralists in direct conflict with authentic African nature.

Through these encounters, the village has become an increasingly meaningful instrument for representing the interests of Maasai communities in northern Tanzania. The emergence of the village as an important institution for regulating transnational investors as well as local livelihoods emerged out of the articulation of village rights as a way to defend Maasai rangelands from "development" in the 1970s and 1980s. By 1990 villages in Loliondo had participated in a village-titling program to help them shore up their collective land rights through village governance (see chapter 3). In the 1990s, those legacies were mobilized to assure ecotourism investors of the legitimacy of local land rights. The village is an elusive and shifting site. The Maasai organized their cultural understandings and identities through their villages. Treating their land as a commodity to be rented provided not only revenue to the village but also the political and ecological rationale for protecting a lifestyle and culture threatened by the state and certain types of outside capital investment. The cooperation of the ecotourism companies in this process provided an unanticipated mechanism to legitimize local control of village land.

Questions, Methods, and Stakes of the Research

Throughout this book I raise important questions about the politics of representation and commodification that characterize contemporary development and neoliberalization of nature in Africa. For example, who gets to represent the meanings and values associated with transnational exchanges, and how do those function simultaneously as sites of exploitation and opportunity? Specifically, I ask the following questions: (1) What happens when the state, which depends on the image of Maasai people and their "indigenous landscapes" to promote Tanzania's unique value in a crowded tourist marketplace, pursues policies and practices that threaten the very existence of Maasai people? (2) How do the Maasai people use their iconic status to challenge global patterns of accumulation and dispossession? (3) In what ways does the global tourist economy present opportunities for communities to resist and confront dominant representations that have historically been used against them? These questions all turn on one overarching question: Does the dominant neoliberal discourse of decentralization and discrete property rights create openings to challenge the political economic structure of tourism that relies on the framing of African nature as a global commodity that can best be managed by national and international experts?

I combine ethnographic research methods, including participant observation, interviews, attendance at policy-making meetings, textual and image analysis, and oral history with archival research, to illuminate the deep connections between resource struggles, landscapes, and the changing meanings of community. I argue that contemporary resource struggles like the ones in

Loliondo reshape space and society and produce lasting cultural-political trans-formations in ways that are not readily apparent. I am not interested in simply reinterpreting meanings and demonstrating that there are multiple moderni-ties or ways of being. I am concerned with how these altered meanings inform and redirect material political struggles. The key question is not whether global markets for tourism are good or bad, but how they are restructuring meanings of place, community, and rights.[76] I argue that the crucible for these encounters in the Loliondo area is the Maasai village.

I have been traveling to Tanzania for the past twenty years working closely with Maasai individuals and organizations, studying their relationships with NGOs, the state, and foreign investors. My research was carried out primarily over thirty months, from May 2000 to November 2004 and then again in June and July 2010. I have followed the unfolding events in Loliondo through regular correspondence with area leaders and residents. Many of my questions grow out of my longer history of tracing this complex relationship between communities, the state, and investors throughout the 1990s. During my research trips, I di-vided my time between Arusha town, where many of the Maasai NGOs, tourism investors, and regional government offices are located, and Loliondo, the main site of my research.

My research involved long periods of living in Loliondo, where I observed and interviewed residents, elected officials, NGO staff, tour operators, students, and some of the leading activists on the front lines of struggles over tourism and conservation. I was constantly struck by my informants' critique of conserva-tion and development, on the one hand, and, on the other, the hope and prom-ise associated with direct village-based investment as a path to radical social change. From the start of my research, I was skeptical that market relationships between the Maasai and private investors could be used as a long-term solution to land insecurity and political marginalization. To my surprise, over the past twenty years, and despite some obvious setbacks, Maasai leaders have contin-ued to express their faith in market relationships over state policy prescriptions. One of the interesting findings of this study is that more often than not the Maa-sai in Loliondo believed that they shared more in common with foreign tourism investors than they did with Tanzanian government officials and institutions.

Persistent Questions about Tourism Geographies

As a scholar and practitioner working in Loliondo over the past two decades, I followed the Avaaz campaign with enthusiasm and concern. The message was accurate; the Maasai faced impending threats from tourism investors who could provide the state a compelling reason to dispossess them of the resources necessary for their livelihoods and radically alter their future. But I also wondered if the antiglobalization message would ultimately limit the political choices available to the Maasai as they fight threats to their land and livelihoods on multiple fronts. The framing of tourism investment in Loliondo as fulfilling market opportunities simplifies the narrative of global capitalism as an essentialized force bearing down on helpless communities.

I draw on Gilliam Hart's formulation of geography to understand Loliondo as a part of a dynamic network of places: "First, a conception of place as nodal points of connection in socially produced space moves us beyond 'case studies' to make broader claims—it enables, in other words, a non-positivist understanding of generality. In this conception, particularities or specificities arise through interrelations between objects, events, places, and identities; and it is through clarifying how these relations are produced and changed in practice that close study of a particular part can generate broader claims and understandings. Such an approach decisively rejects formulations of the impact of 'the global' on 'the local'" (2006, 995–96).

Foreign investment is both a material and a symbolic site that wields the discursive and financial authority of transnational capital. Since the late 1980s, when economic liberalization opened Maasai village lands to commodification as a tourist space, the Maasai in Loliondo have reimagined and represented the village as a culturally meaningful site that also signifies political legitimacy within the nation-state. With the village now considered an identifiable territory valued as a tourist attraction, Maasai leaders have tried to renovate it from an external imposition with limited local legitimacy into a place indistinguishable from the idea of Maasai community. Whether the Maasai can harness this new image to actively govern their land remains an open question. It is, however, a question worth asking if we are to understand the stakes of neoliberal conservation and development in Tanzania and beyond.

CHAPTER 2

Loliondo

Making a Modern Pastoral Landscape

In 1992 the only car regularly traveling between Arusha and Loliondo was that of Lazaro Parkipuny, influential and trusted Maasai leader and director of the newly created Maasai NGO KIPOC. The acronym KIPOC stands for Korongoro Integrated People Oriented to Conservation and means "we will recover" in the Maasai language. Parkipuny left national politics in 1990 to start KIPOC, believing that NGOs would provide an important platform to challenge a state apparatus that he considered biased against pastoralists. He told me, "You have to have organizations to mobilize people to take action to solve problems instead of relying on the state. . . . People have the right to get correct information to counter state propaganda." Registered in 1990, KIPOC was the first NGO in Tanzania dedicated to pastoralists and defending their land rights.

Parkipuny was one of the first Tanzanian Maasai to graduate from the University of Dar es Salaam and earn his master's degree in sociology. He had also been the first MP for Ngorongoro District, which included the political divisions of Ngorongoro, Loliondo, and Sale. With his experience working on the USAID-funded Maasai Range Project in the 1970s and as MP from 1980 to 1990, Parkipuny had become especially aware of the potential for discord between the different Maasai ethnic groups with distinct territorial affiliations called *olosho* (described later in this chapter).

One of Parkipuny's aims for KIPOC was that it advocate for all pastoralists, including all Maasai clans and sections regardless of internal differences—not a straightforward or easy task. The Maasai origin story says that God chose the Maasai and gave them all the cattle in the world.[1] Livestock held by others, therefore, was considered stolen property, and the Maasai understood it as well within their rights to take it back. This meant that Maasai were not likely to peacefully coexist with other pastoralists, who they believed a priori had stolen their cattle. The ways in which this origin story was mobilized to justify cattle raids varied at different points in history. Parkipuny believed that the common threat of national land appropriation of rangelands for conservation and agriculture could unite pastoralists and hunter-gatherers, both of which he understood as indigenous people. He knew that mainstream African society misunderstood these groups and that their flexible property regimes, as well as their customs, made these societies easy targets for land dispossession. KIPOC therefore was devoted to "actively participating, through networking, in the worldwide movement of indigenous peoples to make states and mainstream populations respect the fundamental human rights to: (i) maintain their distinct cultural identity, land tenure and benefit from the natural resources that constitute the base of indigenous cultural and environmental integrity."[2] Parkipuny believed that NGOs could help unite the interests of different Maasai groups by focusing on common interests. "Our greatest asset is to realize we are all facing the same problem," he told me.

I met Parkipuny at the start of my field research, when a friend helped arrange a meeting with him in Arusha. Parkipuny agreed to help me with my study on tourism in Loliondo; if I met him in a month, he would take me to Loliondo. When I met him for the ride in late April 1992 at the Arusha hotel, he told me, "We will have to make one stop on the way." The stop turned out to be a four-day conference, the Second Annual Pastoralist Rights Conference, where the founding members of KIPOC and other pastoralist leaders from across Tanzania discussed how best to protect their land and natural resources from development schemes aimed at making pastoral land more profitable for the state and foreign investors. Pastoralist leaders were organizing themselves to confront both state-sponsored and privately funded development projects that threatened their land and livelihoods.

At the time I did not grasp the significance of pastoralist leaders from across Tanzania gathering to collectively organize their political tactics. I was just happy to get a ride to the notoriously inaccessible Loliondo area. But after a few days I began to realize that this meeting was a new space for Maasai and other pastoralists to organize and act together. One participant noted that the government-owned technical college where they were meeting, located in the largely pastoralist area of Monduli, had previously trained mostly experts who were not themselves pastoralists experts to facilitate national development plans and priorities. This conference was different. For four days the college was the site of efforts to remake development to serve the interests of pastoralists and other historically marginalized groups. None of the participant's naively believed that they would be successful overnight. But they were encouraged by the strong showing of pastoralist leaders from across the country and neighboring Kenya and the growing interest from donors to support their efforts.

For me the conference was a crash course in pastoralist history and politics. I quickly learned that the Maasai faced a number of threats to their land. Participants discussed efforts in the 1970s and 1980s by Serengeti National Park and the park's chief international conservation partner, the Frankfurt Zoological Society (FZS), to expand their control of Maasai land by mandating conservation buffer zones on village lands bordering the park. Maasai and Barabaig leaders also discussed the Tanzania Canada Wheat Program, a project located in the Basotu Plains of Hanang District that alienated forty thousand hectares of prime Barabaig pastureland.[3] Between 1978 and 1981, the National Farm and Agriculture Corporation, in collaboration with the Canadian International Development Agency (CIDA), took this land to grow wheat as part of a national development scheme—another example of state officials seeing pastoralist land as empty and open.

The Hanang case generated considerable attention from human rights organizations (see Lane 1996), and Parkipuny himself played an important role in connecting the case to a pattern of state-pastoralist relationships.[4] Parkipuny was not afraid to make his position known. Barabaig leader Charles Tano told me that Parkipuny and a Barabaig leader named Mrumbi had used their connections with the Canadian volunteer service organization CUSO to get invited to a dinner party hosted at the Canadian embassy in Dar es Salaam a few weeks after the Canadian government had finalized plans to fund the wheat project.[5] During the dinner, Parkipuny confronted a Canadian diplomat, asking why no one at the party had discussed the conflict between CIDA and the Barabaig people. Parkipuny was known for his confrontational style. In front of Canadian diplomats and senior Tanzanian officials, he turned his private conversation into a public address and accused the Canadian government of financing the "extermination" of the Barabaig people. Soon after the outburst, Parkipuny and Mrumbi were escorted out of the embassy. The next day they were called into the Tanzanian prime minister's office. The prime minister, familiar with Parkipuny from his time as an MP, warned him to stop harassing guests of the government. Whether Parkipuny's outburst had any specific effect on the project is not known. However, less than three months after the incident, the Canadian government announced that it was pulling its funding for the Tanzania Canada Wheat Program.[6] Perhaps more significantly, Parkipuny made explicit that he saw the connections among foreign donors, investors, and Tanzanian officials as working together to unfairly exploit pastoralists and their lands.

A group of interested scholars and Barabaig leaders also pressured CIDA, working with local and international journalists as well as NGOs, in what became an early example of leveraging the growing strength of civil society to pressure the Tanzanian state. During the conference in 1992, Barabaig leaders spoke about their experiences opposing the state-led development project, giving fellow pastoralist leaders confidence in their ability to challenge the state and win. The meeting participants reflected on their victory and promoted the importance of working with international human rights groups.[7]

Parkipuny had publicly linked the struggles for pastoral land rights and indigenous rights a few years prior, in a speech given to the International Working Group on Indigenous Affairs (IWGIA) in Geneva:

> The process of alienation of our land and its resources was launched by European colonial authorities at the beginning of this century and has been carried on, to date, after the attainment of national independence. Our cultures and way of life are viewed as outmoded, inimical to national pride and a hindrance to progress. What is more, access to education and other basic services are minimal relative to the mainstream of the population of the countries to which we are citizens in common with other peoples. . . . We do not advocate separatism, but assert the fundamental human right to maintain our cultural identity within the framework of United Nations of Africa. (Parkipuny 1989b)

He gave the speech on August 3, 1989, just two months after the United Nations adopted the International Labor Organization (ILO) Convention 169 concerning indigenous and tribal peoples—the first international convention urging governments to recognize the rights of indigenous people living within the borders of sovereign nation-states.

Parkipuny's speech was significant for arguing that international rights and protections granted to indigenous people in places like North and South America should extend to pastoralists and hunter-gatherers in Africa.[8] For the Maasai to be considered indigenous people, they had to distinguish themselves from other Tanzanians who were also technically indigenous. Unable to claim the position as a "First Nation," the Maasai people had to illustrate that they were a historically and geographically distinct cultural group and that they were specifically marginalized during Tanzania's colonial and postcolonial periods. Parkipuny's success in framing the Maasai as indigenous Africans influenced international human rights organizations, which began to regularly describe the Maasai as indigenous people in the 1990s.[9] The international recognition of the Maasai as an indigenous group helped attract funding for Maasai NGOs like KIPOC.

In this chapter, I move between illustrating how ideas about parks, ranches, and villages were imposed on Maasai communities and how those impositions were interpreted, understood, and translated into popular understandings among Maasai from Loliondo. Parkipuny played a critical role in this process as a leading Maasai intellectual who was actively engaging with and representing nationalist policies to international and local audiences. Not only was Parkipuny a national leader and international figure; he was also a significant local leader from Loliondo. His various writings, speeches, and informal conversations left an indelible mark on the symbolic meanings and the material form of Maasai landscapes in Tanzania and particularly in Loliondo.

Part of the challenge of telling any story is to convey not only what is unique about a place but also how those specific qualities have been produced through encounters and interactions with other places, people, and ideas. Such a view of place troubles the binary of the local and the global and the idea that places have natural boundaries. Parkipuny's own biography illustrates how ideas about what it means to be indigenous or local are formed in relation to other people and places. This chapter frames the histories and geographies of Loliondo that compose the context for the struggles over conservation, development, and social change discussed in later chapters.

Loliondo: The Last Frontier or Postcolonial Artifact

The Loliondo division in Tanzania is the northernmost region of Ngorongoro District, in the Arusha region bordered by Kenya to the north, the Ngorongoro Conservation Area (NCA) to the south, Serengeti National Park to the west, and Lake Natron in the Rift Valley to the east (see map 1). Loliondo covers 289,800 hectares (2,898 sq km) and has a population of 37,714 according to the 2002 census. Until 2010 Loliondo was made up of eight rural villages that were created under Tanzania's villagization program between 1974 and 1976 (Århem 1985a; Coulson 1979). Loliondo, Sakala, and Wasso are the more densely populated villages, clustered around the district headquarters and trading centers. They are classified as urban areas and are commonly referred to collectively as Loliondo town. Loliondo's rural villages are populated almost exclusively by Maasai pastoralists. Six of those villages share a border with Serengeti National Park and overlap with the Loliondo Game Controlled Area (LGCA). The LGCA describes a legal category of land management designating the area as a state-sanctioned space for trophy hunting. Resident hunting is prohibited in GCAs. The area's two hunting blocks, Loliondo north and south, span the entire LGCA and overlap with six rural Maasai villages. From north to south these villages are Ololosokwan, Soitsambu, Oloipiri, Olorien/Magaiduru, Losoito/Maaloney, and Arash.

References to Loliondo conjure up a particular vision of an African landscape: one of vast acacia-savannah grasslands where Maasai herders graze their cattle surrounded by abundant wildlife that move in and out of the nearby Serengeti National Park. Both pastoralists and wildlife have adapted to the semiarid landscape, with its unpredictable rainfall and frequent droughts. The lack of reliable rainfall, ranging from four hundred to fifteen hundred millimeters annually, makes it difficult to rely solely on agriculture for one's livelihood. Pastoralists move their herds according to large weather patterns, including the short rains (November–December) and the long rains (March–June), as well as the availability of seasonal water sources and semipermanent rivers. They also must be careful to avoid large wildlife migrations, as many species carry diseases that are easily transmitted to livestock. In particular, Maasai in Loliondo must avoid the short-grass plains in the western extent of their village lands from late January to early March. During that period hundreds of thousands of wildebeest depend on Loliondo's short-grass plains for giving birth to their calves. Wildebeest carry a lifelong infection that is harmless to them but causes bovine malignant catarrhal fever, a fatal disease for cattle. Livestock are susceptible to the deadly disease when they come in contact with the nasal secretions of wildebeest calves.

Many people first learn of the Maasai from coffee-table books. These heavy tomes, with their glossy images, portray tall Maasai in their vibrant red blankets living in open grasslands dotted with mud huts. The Maasai are revered in the West for their independence and perceived resistance to Western norms and values. Ironically, the Maasai have often resisted this representation, which situates them out of place and out of time. It is precisely the idea that the Maasai lack history and modern forms of agency that often enables others to speak for them. If coffee-table books are the Holy Grail of documenting indigenous cultures for popular consumption, then Loliondo is the taken-for-granted or "natural" setting of such exotic cultures within Tanzania. Invariably, when I told people I was doing research in Loliondo, their reactions reflected these stereotypes:

Loliondo is where the last real Maasai are.
They have not been polluted like other Maasai.
They still live on milk and blood.
They respect their elders.
They don't send their children to school. The boys just want to be
  warriors.
They don't farm or eat wild animals. They respect their culture.[10]

These descriptions came from urban and rural Tanzanians, foreign expatriates, researchers, tourists, government officials, and even Maasai people from outside Loliondo. I was intrigued by the consistent description of Loliondo as an authentic pastoral landscape and of the Maasai who live there as examples of iconic pastoralists.

After sharing their impressions with me, people usually took the time to expand on why Loliondo was such a unique place. It was unfailingly described as frontier-like in its culture, economy, and politics. I was told over and over that Loliondo's qualities were the result of its isolated location and its residents' limited exposure to the modern world. For most of the people I spoke with, Loliondo represented a place that had been relatively unchanged by history.

Despite the problematic notion that a landscape spanning what are now two separate nations, Kenya and Tanzania, and including much of the territory that today is inside Serengeti National Park and the Ngorongoro Conservation Area could have escaped the profound influence of colonialism, nationalism, and the global reach of conservation, I wasn't surprised by the stories I heard. Indeed, I was initially attracted to Loliondo precisely because of its remote location and the opportunity it offered to spend time with pastoralists who still practiced their traditional ways of life.

Rather than the final frontier passively awaiting colonization, however, Loliondo's history is one of intensive involvement and action in local, national, and international politics. For decades, the Maasai resisted colonization and investment that would have divided their land. Conforming to their own national development policies, the Maasai living in Kenya to the north had already divided their land into group ranches. Pastoralists in central and southern Tanzania had lost much of their land to peasant farmers and to industrial agriculture. It is difficult to understand Loliondo today without recognizing how the Maasai have interacted with national and transnational policies and practices of conservation, nationalism, and development.

As a cultural geographer and political ecologist, I am interested in the ways that history shapes the meanings of places and how those places in turn structure social relationships. Political ecologists are interested in how struggles over property rights and land use remake the meanings of landscapes and the cultural understandings and practices of subjects. Building on Dennis Cosgrove's (1984) pioneering work on landscape and ideology, Rod Neumann explains that "struggles over meaning are simultaneously struggles over social identity, belonging and exclusion, and land rights and use" (2011, 845). Such a focus on the discursive production of landscapes in no way averts attention from the material conditions produced through contests over meaning and value. As Neumann puts it, "what is at stake in struggles over landscape meaning are people's livelihoods in place" (2011, 845). Neumann's book on the history and politics of conservation in Tanzania, *Imposing Wilderness* (1998), helped define the field of political ecology. By historicizing the creation of national parks in Tanzania, he showed how Western conservation ideas and ideologies had literally remade landscapes and subjects. He built on classic work in political ecology that sought to locate rural land users in larger historical and political economic structures.[11] He demonstrated how representations of rural Tanzanians had shifted from portrayals as land managers to land degraders and poachers. My work builds on Neumann and other political ecologists by looking specifically at the material and ideological context of neoliberalization, in which the longer struggles over conservation, land rights, and citizenship have recently unfolded.

Without Fences

When I arrived in Loliondo in May 1992, it did appear in many ways like a remnant from the past. It took most of the afternoon and night to get there, and the final few hours of the drive were across the dusty tracks carved into the grass plains. Zebras, gazelles, hartebeest, impala, and hyenas were a few of the animals I saw roaming the plains that first night from the back of Parkipuny's Land Cruiser. Without fences, large-scale agriculture, or ranches, the boundaries of Serengeti National Park and the Ngorongoro Conservation Area seemed to blur seamlessly into the rangelands and Maasai villages in Loliondo.

At the time of my visit, more Maasai in Loliondo maintained their livelihoods through livestock production than in any other area in the country. The vast majority of village land was dedicated to rangelands for pastoralism, and relatively little land was used for agriculture.[12] The Loliondo Maasai continued to prioritize ceremonial activities and coming-of-age celebrations that could occupy weeks and months with preparations and festivities. Traditional leaders maintained a strong voice in decisions about marriages, conflicts, and regulating access to natural resources across different villages and Maasai ethnic groups. Communal livestock ownership among elder men and their sons, strict control of marriage customs by elders, and a relatively low level of migration to other areas were practices often deemed by state officials, development experts, and other Tanzanian citizens to be culturally and politically backward. But despite these perceptions, Loliondo was as modern a place as any other.

Loliondo anchored an important regional livestock trade, linking markets in Kenya and Tanzania (Letara, MacGregor, and Hesse 2006). The robust livestock economy provided opportunities for Maasai youth to engage in livestock-related businesses, which paid for the elaborate ceremonial activities that were associated with tradition and backward-looking attachments to the past. The political, economic, and cultural makeup of Loliondo was largely a product of efforts to protect pastoral resources from alienation, rather than of isolation or irrational attachments to tradition.[13] Loliondo has long been one of the most organized and active regions advocating for the rights of pastoralists.[14] It is through political leadership and social mobilization, and not by chance, that Loliondo has endured as a viable pastoral economy and community.

KIPOC is often credited with being the first Maasai NGO and leading a trend in the rapid development of Maasai NGOs.[15] Place-based and ethnic-oriented NGOs were new to Tanzania when KIPOC was founded in 1990, and the group represented a new institutional arrangement for a pastoralist social movement. Many of the founding members of KIPOC had been instrumental in fighting against government policies in the 1970s and 1980s that sought to alienate land from pastoralists for large-scale agricultural schemes, as well as for smaller-scale migrant farmers seeking new land. They built KIPOC to continue to fight against government plans to take pastoral rangeland for national parks, conservation areas, and agriculture.[16] Despite the loss of important grazing and watering resources that had been appropriated within the restricted boundaries of Serengeti National Park, Loliondo leaders were perhaps the most successful group of pastoralists in East Africa at protecting large areas of communal village grazing land.

"Conservation Are the People Who Stole Our Land": Framing Loliondo as a Conservation Enclave

The Second Annual Pastoralist Rights Conference held in May 1992 ended late on a Wednesday afternoon. Rather than spend one more night at the technical college, Parkipuny declared, "It is time to go." Along with twelve Maasai men and two women, I squeezed into the back of Parkipuny's white Land Cruiser. The road from Arusha to Loliondo passes through the Ngorongoro Conservation Area, a national protected area created along with Serengeti National Park in 1951. All vehicles—those carrying tourists, cargo, and less frequently Tanzanian nationals in buses or private vehicles—are required to pass through the NCA gate before 6:00 p.m., when the park rangers close the gate for the night. There was no way we could make it by then. We arrived at the gate at 7:30 p.m. A ranger immediately recognized Parkipuny, and the two men exchanged a few words. This was not the first time Parkipuny had arrived after the official curfew. Another guard lifted the iron bar to let us through. As we passed, Parkipuny yelled back to me in perfect English, "This is my home. No one can tell me when I can or can't go home."

After nine months in Tanzania, my Kiswahili was improving. My understanding of Maa, the Maasai language, however, was limited to a few basic greetings and words. As the conversation in the car grew louder and more animated, I could make out only one word: "conservation." I asked the man sitting next to me what they were saying about conservation. As the car hit a particularly wet patch in the road, he grabbed my arm for support and said to me, "Conservation are the people who stole our land." In the car that night, everyone was referring to the NCA, one of Tanzania's most important conservation areas and tourism destinations, as "conservation." I would later learn that Maasai frequently use the English word "conservation" to describe the Ngorongoro Conservation Area Authority (NCAA), the governmental agency responsible for managing the NCA.[17] The reference to "conservation" in that night's animated talk extended to all government agencies and their employees responsible for conservation programs such as the Tanzania National Parks Association (TANAPA), which oversees the country's park system, and the Wildlife Division (WD), which is responsible for managing safari and resident hunting.

Loliondo has been significantly shaped by colonial and postcolonial conservation ideologies and practices.[18] Just prior to independence in 1961, colonial officers convinced Maasai leaders to exchange all rights to the Serengeti plains for secure access to the Ngorongoro highlands and crater. In 1959 Serengeti National Park was created, paving the way for the "fortress conservation" model of wildlife management that promoted the idea that firm boundaries were necessary to separate land for conservation from land for people and their livelihood activities.[19]

The creation of Serengeti National Park and the NCA has been chronicled elsewhere.[20] My aim here is to highlight how promises to Maasai communities have been consistently broken in the name of conservation (map 5). This history has not only made the Maasai skeptical of conservation agencies and agendas but has also shaped how they see current conservation reforms aimed at incorporating communities into conservation management and planning.

The First Maasai Land Grab

During my field research, I often started interviews by asking Maasai in Loliondo to tell me about Serengeti National Park. Invariably I was told a version of the popular origin story for the park, which goes like this: There was a German man who wanted to keep lions. He asked Maasai elders if they would give him some land to keep his lions. They agreed and gave him some land near an area east of Ololosokwan village called Lobo. When a group of elders went to visit the man, they discovered that he had taken more land for his lions. Each time the elders went to visit him, he had expanded the area for his lions. Eventually the government used this as an excuse to create Serengeti National Park.

Anyone familiar with the history of conservation in northern Tanzania will recognize the central characters in this story. The popular version shares several important elements with the actual creation of the park. In the story, the Maasai agree to give up land for something they don't necessarily value: protecting lions.[21] They find that the European man with his curious interest in lions continues to take more and more land without permission. The state steps in on behalf of the German man and his lions to fix the arrangement with laws and guns. The Maasai lose access to their land and important resources for their livestock, while others, often foreigners, pay the government to see the man's lions. While many Maasai are well aware of other forces at work in the creation of the park, they continue to tell this origin story, believing that it captures the

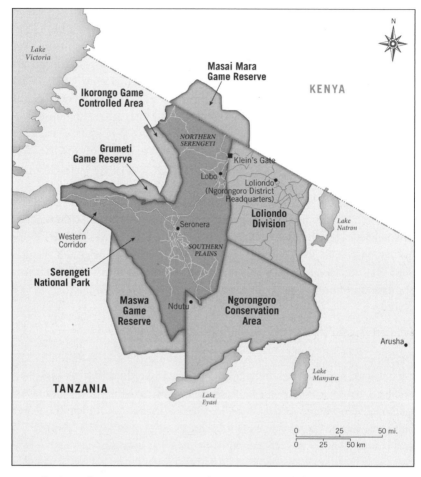

MAP 5. Designated conservation areas in northeast Tanzania, including Serengeti National Park, Ngorongoro Conservation Area, game reserves, and game controlled areas. XNR Productions.

injustices and ongoing threats posed by conservation. The region has a long history of conservation and the creation of a network of national protected areas that have gradually eroded customary land-use practices and rights.

In the late 1840s and then again the 1880s, a rinderpest epizootic killed up to 90 percent of wildlife and livestock in what is now northern Tanzania. When the Germans took control of Tanganyika in 1885—the former East African country that together with the island of Zanzibar would become Tanzania after independence—one of the resources they were interested in was the valuable commercial by-product of hunting, ivory. Soon after colonizing the country, the Germans created regulations to protect the remaining wildlife and regulate its use for hunting.[22] Colonial laws effectively banned customary hunting, requiring local people to apply for a license to hunt. According to historians, "the result of these measures was to convert, within the first decade of colonial rule, wildlife from a locally used and customarily managed component of the natural resource base, to a resource which Europeans largely possessed exclusive legal access to."[23] Beyond controlling the choices and behaviors of individuals, the German rulers reorganized the nation's territory, demarcating specific places of high value for wild game. By 1913 German authorities had created fourteen game reserves for hunting. The areas spanned some thirty thousand square kilometers, or 3 percent of Tanganyika's territory.[24] Local people were not prevented from living in the reserves, but their rights to use wildlife in the areas were severely limited. This was an early attempt to assert centralized control over what had previously been under local customary authority.

After World War I, the British took control of Tanganyika from Germany as a League of Nations protectorate. The Land Ordinance of 1923 gave the British Crown control over all property and severely weakened customary property rights and local institutions that regulated access to resources.[25] The British built on the German efforts to regulate and manage wildlife, adding specific rules governing who could hunt and where. They implemented game ordinances in 1921, 1940, and 1951, adding to the German-created network of protected areas by demarcating several additional game reserves throughout the country. In 1928 the Ngorongoro Crater was declared a hunting reserve, and in 1929 an area encompassing much of the present-day Serengeti National Park was declared the Serengeti Closed Reserve (see Shetler 2007). These policies reinforced the idea that in order to protect nature, it needed to be identified as valuable and separated from people who could do it harm.[26] However, up until 1930, strict separation of people and wildlife was not enforced.

By 1930 the British government had established a network of game reserves with more-substantial restrictions on settlement, cultivation, and hunting. These included reserves in the Selous, Mount Meru, Mount Kilimanjaro, the Serengeti, and Ngorongoro Crater. Neumann (1998) has shown that colonial officers, whose primary mandate was bureaucratic administration and tax collection, faced a challenge in balancing conservation interests and local agrarian production. As the direct liaisons with native communities, these officers wanted to avoid policies that would generate local hostility toward them. However, by the 1930s pressure from European conservation organizations was beginning to outweigh the concerns of colonial officers in outposts like Loliondo. In 1933 the British government passed the Convention for the Protection of the Flora and Fauna of Africa, which called for the creation of national parks in Africa. For the first time in Tanganyika's history, wildlife preservation would take precedent over local livelihoods.

The Game Ordinance of 1940, which declared much of the present-day Serengeti National Park and the Ngorongoro Conservation Area a single park, marked a new period of conservation legislation and management. Despite the ordinance, local people maintained some customary land rights to the protected area and in many instances limited rights to hunt and gather. The Maasai living in the Serengeti, Ngorongoro, and Loliondo were also becoming wary of what they saw as excessive colonial power over their lives. After expressing concerns through their leaders and representatives, the Maasai were repeatedly assured that the creation of a park covering both the Serengeti plains and the Ngorongoro highlands would not impinge on their land use or rights.[27] Over the next decade, however, government actions would provide ample evidence that conservation and national economic interests would supersede Maasai interests in the Serengeti and the NCA.[28] Restrictions on movement and settlement, as well as on burning and hunting, were eventually followed by a ban on all agriculture in the area in 1954.[29] Although the Maasai depended mainly on livestock for their livelihoods, small-scale agriculture was becoming an important aspect of their household production,[30] and the ban caused significant unrest and protest. British policies promoting conservation over pastoralism in the NCA created significant tension in the relationship between the Maasai and the colonial authorities. These local conflicts and the growing independence movement in the country pushed the colonial government to act.[31]

In 1959, during the waning years of British rule in Tanganyika, the colonial authorities negotiated a treaty with Maasai leaders.[32] The British proposed two protected areas, promising that in one of them Maasai pastoralist livelihoods would take precedence over wildlife conservation. The original Serengeti reserve was divided into two areas: Serengeti National Park, previously the Western Serengeti of the original reserve, including the Serengeti plains and several key permanent water sources; and the NCA, including the Ngorongoro highlands and crater. Under the arrangement, Maasai leaders agreed that the Maasai people would leave the new Serengeti Park, giving up all their rights to the area in exchange for permanent residence in the NCA.[33]

The NCA was designated as a mixed-use conservation area where pastoralism and conservation would coexist, with Maasai rights superseding wildlife conservation. Colonial authorities assured Maasai leaders that they would be "permitted to continue to follow or modify their traditional way of life subject only to close control of hunting" in the area.[34] One of the selling points of the deal was that the government would invest in social programs such as health care, veterinary services, and transportation, as well as subsidizing the costs of basic provisions like maize, sugar, and tea. The government also promised to develop new water sources to compensate for the lost access to water in the Serengeti.[35] Exchanging selected land-use access for the promise of much-needed services appealed to some Maasai leaders at the time.

In a speech to the Maasai Federal Council in August 1959, the governor of Tanganyika reiterated the centrality of Maasai land rights in the new area: "I should like to make it clear to you all that it is the intention of the Government to develop the Crater [NCA] in the interests of the people who use it. At the same time, the Government intends to protect the game animals in the area, but should there be any conflict between the interests of the game and the human inhabitants, those of the latter must take precedence."[36] Proposing the NCA as a place where the interests of the Maasai, wildlife, and the state were fused together was an attempt to reframe the relationship between the Maasai and nature.

However, by 1975 the Ngorongoro Conservation Area Authority had banned all agriculture in the NCA. In two decades, the Maasai living near the Serengeti and in the NCA saw their ability to practice pastoralism significantly reduced, which brought increased poverty and called into question the Maasai future in northern Tanzania. According to Kaj Århem, in *Pastoral Man in the Garden of Eden: The Maasai of the Ngorongoro Conservation Area, Tanzania* (1985b), cattle per capita declined from thirteen in 1960 to seven in 1977. This decline was met with an increase in the number of small stock per family, including sheep and goats, from eight to fifteen during the same period. The shift to small stock was one strategy used by the Ngorongoro Maasai to maintain the necessary milk supply to feed their families. The practice reflected an overall decline in available milk for each household, as well as a reduced market value of a family's overall livestock holdings.

The intensifying restrictions on pastoralist land use in the NCA became a touchstone for the newly independent nation of Tanzania. Research on the Maasai living in the NCA in the mid-1980s drew international attention and established a growing literature linking the NCA with calls to more thoroughly incorporate local and indigenous people into conservation planning and management. As the projects and literature involving community-based conservation (CBC) expanded throughout the 1990s, the NCA became an often-cited example of the need for integrated conservation and development.[37] Internationally, the NCA became a recognized model of a multiple-use conservation area supporting wildlife and rural people. Locally, in the Loliondo region, it came to symbolize the loss of pastoralist land and rights through state-led conservation. The creation of Serengeti National Park and the NCA influenced a regional understanding of power that fused international conservation, a discourse of modernization, and the emerging state interests.

As a UNESCO World Heritage Site and primary tourist destination in Tanzania, the NCA continues to be seen as a model of integrated conservation and development. But for many Maasai it is a failed experiment that only proves that the power of state and conservation interests override those of cultural groups like the Maasai. The Maasai often characterize the allocation of land for conservation and the eventual creation of Serengeti National Park and the NCA as a callous effort by the state to dispossess them of their land, and any conservation effort launched in northern Tanzania must confront this ongoing legacy. For many Maasai in Loliondo, the struggle over the NCA continues to define their marginal position as citizens and their lack of trust in state institutions to promote and protect their rights.

Making Pastoralists into Ranchers

One government strategy to curtail Maasai land use was to replace the seminomadic Maasai system of grazing with ranching associations. This idea was first posed in a report published by the USAID mission to Tanganyika in 1963.[38] The report suggested that "Ranching Associations" could serve as a useful "device for creating units with whom the Government could deal, and in whom title to land could be vested."[39] The report, written by Leland Fallon, a range scientist working for the USAID mission to East Africa, was vague on the details of establishing or managing the ranching associations but suggested radical transformations for Maasai pastoralists and rangelands. It recommended that the Maasai transition from subsistence to commercial producers, with the hopeful prediction that "someday undoubtedly, the Masai rangelands, [would] be supplying high quality fresh meat to European and other world markets."[40]

The U.S. range scientists working under the USAID mission used a popular model for measuring carrying capacity of rangelands at the time. The model was based on the carrying capacity of livestock units, and the scientists equated the impact of one bull to two heifers to five sheep, and so on. The research made assumptions about the relationship between pastoralists and land based on models that assumed an open-access system of grazing. Fallon (1963), for example, argued that common pool management—which was mistakenly assumed to be the Maasai system—was inefficient and environmentally destructive.[41] A similar critique of pastoralists was codified in ecologist Garret Hardin's (1968) article in the journal *Science*, "The Tragedy of the Commons" (1968). The tragedy that Hardin described was the inevitable depletion and destruction of resources when a lack of property rights undermine incentives to manage resources sustainably for future use. Ironically, this critique of market rationality was misused to characterize the Maasai grazing system, which was highly dependent on negotiated social arrangements governing access to territory and property rights. Hardin's proposed solution to the tragedy of the commons was to impose private-property rights, in order to solve what he saw as the "free rider" problem.

In 1964, the same year that Tanganyika formed its union with Zanzibar to become the United Republic of Tanzania, the newly independent government established the Range Development and Management Act. The legislation, based largely on the Fallon report's recommendations, spelled out a plan to transform pastoralists into modern ranchers by creating ranching associations. The first pilot ranching association in Kolomonik was started in 1966, near the Maasai district headquarters in Monduli, about 320 kilometers south of Loliondo. The Ministry of Agriculture was responsible for the project, and the initial government investment of one hundred thousand dollars was used to build two cattle dips and a pipeline to carry water to the area.

After less than one year, the new ranch faced many challenges. Ironically, the project exacerbated many of the problems it was meant to solve.[42] The new facilities allowed cattle to graze on arid areas longer than previously possible in the seminomadic system. The drilling of boreholes and development of other water sources enabled more-concentrated grazing for the ranch members. The water sources also attracted cattle from outside the ranching associations, contributing to high concentrations of cattle and considerable overgrazing. The government was unable or unwilling to invest more resources in expanding the water development further afield to prevent the overgrazing. Most association members abandoned the project within the first year.[43]

Foreign and national development experts saw the failure of Kolomonik as a problem of capacity, resources, and training. In 1970 the USAID agreed to take over the financing and managing of Kolomonik and to expand the "promising" development model to form other ranching associations.[44] The USAID signed an agreement with the Tanzanian government for a ten-year project called the Maasai Livestock Development and Range Management Project (MLDRMP). The goals of the project included establishing new ranching associations and helping the members plan and build water and cattle dip infrastructure, as well as market their livestock. Five range development experts from the United States were hired to oversee the project, which initially consisted of managing technical construction projects requiring heavy machinery imported from the United States. They constructed dams, dug boreholes, cleared bush, and built roads. They also provided funding for thirty Tanzanians to obtain bachelor's and master's degrees in the United States and then to return home to take over the project.[45]

The stated goal of the MLDRMP was "to assist the Government of Tanzania to achieve its objective of self-sufficiency and an exportable surplus to earn foreign exchange in the livestock sector."[46] The project had two primary objectives: create better infrastructure such as wells, pipes, and troughs to manage and distribute water; and establish cooperative ranching associations, which would be responsible for implementing and managing the new infrastructure. Technology was a prerequisite for change, but according to Allan Hoben, so-called cultural factors were the biggest impediment: "The primary factors inhibiting changing and delaying the transformation are basically cultural and sociological rather than technical" (1976, 29). The report went on to discuss how the MLDRMP had to be sensitive to the social and cultural context to allow the Maasai to adapt to the new technology "at minimum social costs and outside interference." Evaluations of the project repeatedly called for adapting to the local context. Adaptation, however, mostly meant the Maasai adapting to the program, not the other way around. The inability of the ranching associations to maintain their target quotas of livestock levels was a constant source of frustration for the USAID technical staff.

Parkipuny studied the project for his master's thesis at the University of Dar es Salaam and observed, "The associations have not been able to regulate livestock numbers to the quotas that the rangeland can support. This is because no Maasai will really lend a hand in keeping out the livestock of his kinsmen or neighbors from using water or dips simply because he happens to possess a title."[47] Parkipuny believed that the MLDRMP was out of sync with Maasai society and that no amount of material resources could compensate for its flawed design. The project faced numerous challenges, including a delay in the development of water systems and cattle dip facilities. Though the project had gained initial support from Maasai leaders, the lack of water made the grazing plans untenable.

A divide emerged within the project staff between technical versus social priorities and strategies. The range scientists were concerned mainly with developing the livestock industry and, unlike the social scientists, did not grasp the overall social context or pastoralists' dependence on livestock as a livelihood and not simply as income. Such a split "implied that any kind of work on the human aspects was to be handled by the project sociologist and was merely in order to clear the ground for the principle objective, the development of the livestock industry."[48] The focus on developing a national industry versus local livelihoods would continue to cause problems for the MLDRMP. Even after convincing several ranching associations that equipment delays were not deliberate acts but rather bureaucratic mishaps, the foreign experts' failure to grasp the ecological, economic, and social relations that sustained pastoralism led to antagonism between project staff and Maasai residents.

After ten years, the MLDRMP ran its course, and the ranching associations were disbanded. In the end, the project failed miserably to achieve its goals, but like many development interventions it did have lasting if unintended effects on Maasai development. The legacy of ranching associations and the MLDRMP led many Maasai to associate development with false promises and the veiled attempt to appropriate local resources for national goals. One of the reasons the ranching associations struggled was their ambiguous relation to the government's villagization campaign.

Villages: Progressive African Communalism

In 1967 the president of Tanzania, Julius Nyerere, spelled out his vision for development in the Arusha Declaration. According to the plan, Tanzania was compelled to overcome dependence on foreign capital and industry by producing food crops. "This is in fact the only road through which we can develop our country," Nyerere noted. "In other words, only by increasing our production of these things can we get more food and more money for every Tanzanian."[49] How would an agrarian country, which had been brought into the international order of trade as a primary commodity producer of such crops as sisal, cotton, coffee, and tea, become self-sufficient? Nyerere believed that the country had to scale up its production by organizing agrarian collectives as central sites of state-controlled production. These collectives would be known as "villages," invoking his own nostalgic belief in an authentic African community that was destroyed during colonialism. Villages would provide shared labor and collective property for more-efficient production. They would also become access points for state extension services, marketing infrastructure, and government regulation. The village was the centerpiece of Nyerere's plan to build an independent agrarian nation.[50]

Based on this one-size-fits-all policy, villages were created throughout the country. The program was controversial for a number of reasons, including its forcible relocation of people to concentrate populations even if it meant moving them to less productive areas. Notwithstanding the problems of implementation throughout the country, the abstract model of planned villages was especially incompatible with pastoralist production. Pastoralists depended on dispersed population centers to maximize unpredictable and unevenly distributed resources like grass, salt, and water for their livestock. The disparities between the national village model and the realities of pastoral livelihoods in semiarid rangelands looked like a disaster before ever getting off the ground. Nevertheless, convinced that pastoralism was an outdated cultural system of production, many government officials and expert development advisors believed that concentrating pastoralists into villages would facilitate a transition to agriculture and intensive livestock keeping.

In another speech that same year, 1967, called "Socialism and Rural Development," Nyerere explained the theoretical underpinnings of village-based national development. He described three guiding principles, which were also his basic assumptions about traditional African life. These were respect, common property, and work. Discussing respect, he observed, "There was a minimum below which no one could exist without disgrace to the whole family."[51] He then described how common property formed the base of the moral African community: "No-one could go hungry while others hoarded food, and no-one could be denied shelter if others had space to spare. . . . Inequalities existed, but they were tempered by comparable family or social responsibilities, and they could never become gross and offensive to the social equality which was at the basis of the communal life."[52] Collective labor, for Nyerere, was the foundation for development. "Everyone had an obligation to work," he noted. "Every member of the family, and every guest who shared in the right to eat and have shelter, took it for granted that he had to join in whatever work had to be done."[53]

To these strengths of traditional African communalism, Nyerere added what he believed were the key impediments of the traditional system that prevented society from reaching its potential. These were the role of women and poverty. Nyerere recognized the role of women as the core inequality in most Tanzanian households and communities. His recognition of social inequality represented a radical break with maintaining colonial systems of indirect rule as a path toward independent national development. He asserted, "It is impossible to deny that women did, and still do, more than their fair share of the work in the fields and in the homes. By virtue of their sex they suffered from inequalities which had nothing to do with their contribution to the family welfare."[54] Changing this situation, however, would prove difficult to legislate.

The self-sufficient village would not only overcome inequalities based on race, sex, and age, according to Nyerere it would reverse the cycle of poverty all too common in African societies. At odds with many of Nyerere's other writings on imperialism and the impoverishing forces of international trade and primary commodities export, his analysis of village poverty targeted more-local forces. He noted, "Certainly there was an attractive degree of economic equality [in traditional peasant African societies], but it was equality at a low level. For there was nothing inherent in the traditional system, which caused this poverty; it was the result of two things only. The first was ignorance, and the second was the scale of operations."[55] By establishing individual ignorance and inefficient scale of production as the primary impediments to development, Nyerere could advocate for achievable goals to reverse Tanzania's poverty. He concluded by saying that "the three principles of mutual respect, sharing of joint production, and work by all . . . can also be a basis for economic development if modern knowledge and modern techniques of production are used."[56]

Along with his moral analysis of African social change, Nyerere added a spatial argument for achieving development. The village was the organizing principle that would allow socialism to flourish by providing needed services to localities, as well as functioning as the center of democratic political participation. He explained how the relation between proximity and politics would ideally work:

> National defence, education, marketing, health, communications, large industries—for all these things and many more, all of Tanzania has to work together. The job of Government would therefore be to help these self-reliant communities and to organize their co-operation with others.
>
> An agricultural field worker, for example, would be teaching new techniques to about 40 people together, instead of one family at a time; he could thus spend more time and give more expert help to the village farm than he could ever to any individual farmer. Or, again, Government could not hope to give a water pump to every separate house in a scattered community, nor provide the miles of pipes which might be necessary in order to service one isolated house.
>
> The country would also become more democratic through the organization of ujamaa communities. The Members of Parliament, or of the Local Council, would more easily be able to keep informed of the people's wishes and their ideas on national issues if they were living together than if the people did not get a daily opportunity to discuss important issues together.[57]

Nyerere's plans often turned on the ability of state officials to transform the abstract space of development plans into the lived realities of Tanzanians.

As of 2012, there were ten thousand registered villages in Tanzania. None of them existed before 1975, when the policy creating villages as legal governmental authorities was enacted.[58] Villages were created under a variety of circumstances, with the nuclei of many of them coming from social or geographical units that had persisted from precolonial times. Villagization ignored that colonial administration had rarely been organized around these small settlements (rather colonial authorities had governed through district administrators).[59]

Tanzania's program of villagization has received considerable criticism for its heavy-handed tactics to forcibly move rural people, alienating them from their lands and the ecological contexts they knew best.[60] At the time, however, many believed that villagization would help Tanzania overcome almost a century of

colonial rule. But despite the initial enthusiasm for villagization among government officials and national intellectuals, the task of transforming pastoralists
into villagers remained one of the more complicated challenges for the government. Could pastoralists be worked into a national program designed primarily
for agricultural communities? This question would become a source of struggle
for the Maasai throughout Tanzania.

Villagization in Maasailand: Operation Imparnati

Maasailand was not included in the original phase of villagization. Pastoralists
were considered too problematic to warrant concentrated government efforts,
and resources were deemed better spent on more compliant agricultural communities. However, in the second phase of villagization the program became
mandatory, and regional administrations controlled implementation. In September 1974, Operation Imparnati, or "permanent settlements," was launched
in Monduli District, an area with a large population of Maasai pastoralists just
north of Arusha. By the middle of 1975, there were nine registered villages with a
total population of approximately two thousand people. A year later, 36 percent
of the residents of Kiteto District (south of Arusha) and 31 percent of Monduli
residents had been resettled in twenty-seven villages. Unlike the majority of
villages created under the Ujamaa program, the government specifically designated villages in Maasailand as either livestock or agricultural development villages. Distinguishing a dominant village mode of production can be interpreted
as a way for the government to limit the area dedicated to livestock production.[61]

There was little resistance to the initial stages of villagization. The Maasai did
not fear that the village would prevent them from carrying out their economic
activities across the new village boundary. They believed that once the government officials left, they would be able to carry out their activities as they had
previously. One of the Arusha regional officials noted, "The pastoralists were
easier to deal with than the cultivators."[62] For many Maasai the main incentive
to participate was the belief that they would gain clear land title by doing so.

It took four years for Operation Imparnati to reach Loliondo. In 1978 regional officials arrived to demarcate new villages. Most of the newly created villages were based on existing localities and their boundaries (map 6). Unlike the
Monduli Maasai, who thought that the villages might help them defend grazing
land from agricultural immigrants, Loliondo residents associated the program
with the government's strong-arm efforts to take away resources. Only three
years earlier, in 1975, the government had imposed an agricultural ban on the
Maasai living in the Ngorongoro Conservation Area, restricting their ability to
supplement their livestock economy with increasingly vital food crops such as

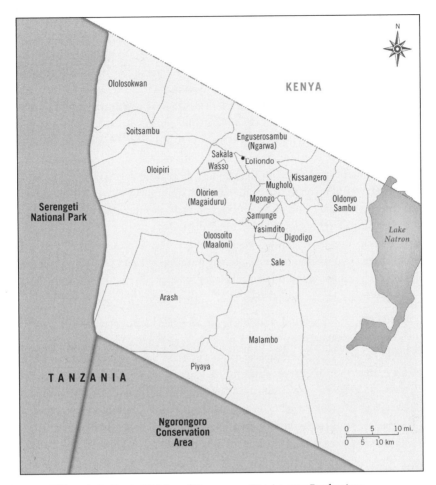

MAP 6. Villages in Loliondo Division of Ngorongoro District. xnr Productions.

maize and beans. This contributed to an ongoing pattern of false promises and pastoralist disenfranchisement. However, like other Maasai, Loliondo residents accepted the villagization program as inevitable and waited for officials to leave in order to resume their normal activities.

Parkipuny and Villagization

Reflecting on villagization almost thirty years later, in 2003, Parkipuny expressed his belief that it was one of many misguided state development schemes. He believes that Operation Imparnati was unsuccessful because national political leaders and state bureaucrats were ineffective. But despite his resentment, he does not credit the program with radically altering Maasai life in Loliondo. Although the Maasai were forced to create villages in Loliondo, as elsewhere, Parkipuny told me that the program had minimal influence on people's lives: "Villagization was a national policy, and it would have been futile to try to resist it. But what does it really mean in terms of land use?" He then turned and gestured toward an imaginary map. "If you look at a map, this *mbuga* [plain] has been divided into villages. Each village stretches to Serengeti, but when it comes to land use, grazing rights, the division separating one village from another is a formality. When it comes to salt licks like here, these village boundaries disappear."

Parkipuny put forward two arguments explaining why Operation Imparnati had minimal influence on Maasai production and social relations. First, villages failed to supplant traditional forms of regulating access to resources. And second, even if some government officials had the best interests of the Maasai in mind when creating the policy, the overly bureaucratic and inflexible structure of the program prevented it from achieving its goals. In his article "Some Crucial Aspects of the Maasai Predicament," Parkipuny writes,

> Beyond the drawing board stage, the implementation of the operation was not a mass transformation campaign. It was precisely an "Operation"—a programme implemented by the government and ruling party officials—and not a systematic programme to enable the people, be they in Maasailand or elsewhere in the country, to undertake their own all-round development. . . . Thus even those villages like Upper Monduli established nearly three years ago . . . have to await the time when everybody else in the district has moved into a village before the next undefined step is taken by the officials at the district headquarters. (1979, 154)

Parkipuny goes on to note that the project failed to achieve any of its goals not only because of misguided bureaucrats but also due to government planners' misunderstanding of the pastoralist mode of production.

> Finally there is a gross failure to comprehend the essential need to separate two basic requirements: the need to concentrate human population to facilitate the procurement of social services and provide viable units of production and cooperation, on the one hand, and, on the other, the need to spread out the livestock population to safeguard the range land from the destructive power of large herds (Parkipuny 1979, 155).

His experience with implementing villagization policies gave Parkipuny firsthand knowledge of the inner workings of government. Rather than give him hope of transforming the system from within, the episode strengthened his antinationalist leanings. In place of the abstract model of the village, Parkipuny advocated formalizing the role for traditional institutions to govern land, resources, and rights in Maasai areas. Parkipuny (1979) invoked a populist vision of socialism to challenge a scientific nationalist socialism and advocate for what today we might call indigenous rights. At the time he advocated Maasai rights through his particular understanding of populist socialism.

In Parkipuny's article, which reads like a pastoralist manifesto of sorts, we can see the seeds of an argument linking the village as a state institution with a transnational understanding of Maasai rights: "The people should not be made to sit back and let the government do whatever it wants. Since the well-being of the people must be the purpose of development, they must take control of the situation by creating their own socialist institutions for local management of the process of production, without being overpowered by the centre's requirements of uniformity."[63] Whether Maasai villages could someday become a new "socialist institution" is still an open question and is in many ways at the heart of this book's inquiry.

Did Villagization Remake Pastoralism?

What lasting effects did villagization have on Maasai social and ecological relations? Experts disagree on the significance of villagization in shaping Maasai social, economic, and ecological relations. Daniel Ndagala argues that villagization was the final act in an ongoing effort to settle pastoralists and bring them in line with the goals of a modern African nation:

> Unlike other districts in which [villagization] was known under individual district names such as Operation Mbulu, Operation Hanang, etc; the resettlement program in Maasailand was termed "Operation Imparnati." The Maasai word *imparnati* (sing. *emparnat*) means "permanent habitations." Permanence of habitation was emphasized here probably because of the belief in several quarters that one of the main snags in Maasai development then was nomadism. This, of course . . . is a misconception of pastoral problems. The Maasai have been undergoing sedentarization for several decades so that Operation Imparnati was just an acceleration and completion of that process. (1982, 29)

In contrast, Katherine Homewood and Alan Rodgers assert that although people may live, grind their maize, or go to school in particular villages, as an institution for regulating people's economic relations and social activities, the village is rather insignificant:

> Overall, these "villages" have had little lasting impact on patterns of settlement and seasonal movement, nor do they correspond with traditional economic or leadership structures. Individual families still live in widely dispersed bomas

[homesteads where several families live together with their livestock]. Seasonal movements crosscut village boundaries and different families using the same village in the dry season may move to different wet season pastures. . . . Alongside the imposed village structure, the traditional social systems of section, clan, age-set and boma still govern NCA [Ngorongoro Conservation Authority] Maasai access to resources and form the basis of their risk avoidance strategies and of their efficient livestock management in an unpredictable environment. (1991, 56)

Perhaps the discrete regional focus of each study influenced the authors' perspectives. Ndagala (1982) was writing primarily about Maasai villages in Monduli District, whereas Homewood and Rodgers (1991) were focusing on Ngorongoro District, and the NCA in particular. There is evidence to support the claim that villages had a more significant impact on regulating the movements and activities of Maasai in Monduli than in Loliondo.[64] Little evidence, however, supports the argument that villagization radically changed the seasonal movements of livestock from wet- to dry-season grazing areas or altered access to water or mineral deposits dispersed across the landscape in Loliondo. The democratically elected village assembly did not replace the authority of lineage, sectional or clan affiliations, or age sets in managing the complex sociospatial arrangements of pastoralists in Loliondo.

Chief among the lasting effects of villagization was the construction of several primary schools, encouraging Maasai to keep their permanent homesteads relatively close to the new village centers. Extension agents also promoted the cultivation of small plots of maize and beans, which became an increasingly significant part of the Maasai diet from the 1970s onward. Despite these important influences, the Maasai in Loliondo saw the village as an instantiation of state management separate from internal Maasai social relations and governance.

State efforts to settle pastoralists through villages and ranching associations throughout the 1970s and 1980s did little to turn Maasai pastoralists into Maasai villagers. However, neoliberal policies and ideologies together with the changing meaning of indigeneity led to new political tactics in which the Maasai were in a better position to wage their struggle as villagers than they were as an ethnic group. My argument is that from the 1990s onward the village emerged as a central institution for managing access to resources, organizing cultural values and interests, and claiming local land rights.

Territory and Identity

Maasai history is one of dynamic processes of competition and struggle for territory with neighboring groups of agriculturalists, semipastoralists, and other pastoralists. Richard Waller (1985) describes how the interaction of forces—including trade, drought, stock raiding, and intermarriage—shaped the current configurations of Maasai identity and territory. He conveys a sense of how the history of the Maasai is one of relational production of identity and territory, where "different Maa-speaking groups competed for control of stock, grazing, and water, absorbing some of their defeated opponents in the process and forcing others onwards onto the periphery, where they settled or merged with the surrounding populations, adjusting their economy and identity accordingly" (1985, 358).

One of the main differences between pastoralist expansion and agricultural expansion is that "herding groups commonly appropriate the resources of areas much larger than those which they effectively occupy" (Waller 1985, 365). Because of the lack of physical occupation and relatively small military force, pastoral territorial expansion does not mean either complete occupation of land or conquest of people. Another factor limiting the ability of pastoralist groups from effectively controlling large territories is their relatively small-scale political organization. Maasai territorial control operates largely through sectional affinities, known as *olosho* (pl. *iloshon*).

Along with clan membership, Maasai ethnic sections are the primary way that ethnicity is locally understood and mobilized. This is especially true in Loliondo, where a number of sections share overlapping territories. A council of elders is responsible for sectional political decisions. Identification with a particular section is based on lineage and territory, but in times of peace, boundaries between sections remain fluid. Intermarriage between sections is common and an important source of territorial alliances between them. The majority of Tanzanian Maasai belong to the Kisongo section. For example, most of the Maasai in Monduli and Kiteto Districts are from the Kisongo section. In contrast, Loliondo Maasai include Maasai from three dominant sections: Laitayok, Loita, and Purko (described in more detail in chapter 5).

Conclusion

Rather than simply being left out of the development process, Loliondo leaders have actively promoted pastoral livelihoods and organized communities to resist the efforts by state agencies and officials to fix their identities and rights to a given territory. My own initial nostalgic view of finding the most authentic place for pastoralists made me question how landscapes that appeared so timeless and natural were actually produced through cultural struggle. The commonsense truth that Loliondo was the "last place with real pastoralists" was due more to Maasai engagement with national and international actors and interests—including conservationists, foreign experts, hunters, farmers, and state officials—than to Maasai remoteness from them. Rather than the isolated periphery of Tanzania, Loliondo is in many ways the core of East African pastoralism. Maintaining a regional economy capable of supporting pastoralism was the result of a political project. Liberalization in the form of structural-adjustment policies and deregulation opened tourism in Maasai villages as a new economic activity. This posed new risks of land dispossession in the name of conservation. The persistent power of "the myth of wild Africa" created obstacles for the Maasai to represent their villages as sites of both pastoralism and conservation. But with the ability to attract direct partnerships with safari tourism operators, many Maasai leaders used the new historical moment to translate the meaning of the village as the best place to achieve conservation goals. Rather than reproduce the dominant idea that nature must be kept separate from people, the Maasai represented the village as a site of both pastoral production and wildlife conservation.

I have illustrated how the people of Loliondo are bound together not only by customary relations but also by their collective political action to successfully defend their land from encroachment by the state, settlers from other regions, and investors. Despite the appearance of an unchanged landscape, the history of Loliondo reveals the importance of social mobilization and struggle in producing the meanings and values that give the place its particular shape. By reimagining the village as a property-holding, authentic community, Maasai leaders drew directly on neoliberal discourses of privatized property rights and decentralized natural-resource governance to challenge the nation-state's authority over Loliondo as a global conservation area.

CHAPTER 3

Community Conservation
The Globalization of Maasailand

Wildlife and Land Reform: Collectivization or Privatization?

The WMA Regulations of 2002 were supposed to help reconcile conflicts between Tanzanian communities and the central government by legally empowering villages collectively to manage the conservation activities on their land. With years of experience working with foreign-owned tourist companies and abundant wildlife habitat including dispersal areas for Serengeti National Park, Loliondo seemed the perfect location for a model WMA. For over five years, the African Wildlife Foundation (AWF) and the Frankfurt Zoological Society (FZS), with funding from the USAID and the World Wildlife Fund (WWF), promoted the WMA with village leaders and local youth, who, they argued, would benefit from the new opportunities to increase safari tourism on their land and reap multiple benefits including employment opportunities for their residents. They sponsored workshops and study tours to promote the project. Leaders were given daily stipends of approximately fifty dollars, the equivalent of the average monthly salary for a Tanzanian citizen. They were shown successful projects in both Tanzania and Kenya and told that they too could become rich through conservation.[1]

While the WMA enjoyed some local support among leaders in Loliondo, the majority of leaders and residents associated the WMA with a government scheme to take their land. As far back as January 2001, six village chairmen and three ward councilors from Loliondo sent a letter to the director of wildlife requesting that all government efforts to demarcate and establish a WMA on their village lands cease immediately.[2] This was an uncertain time for rural citizens of Tanzania as the new land legislation was taking effect in that year, 2001. The new land acts divided land into three categories: general land, reserved land, and village land. General land was a new legal category describing public lands including "unoccupied or unused village land."[3] Loliondo leaders were concerned that the new land acts would be used against pastoralists to argue that they were not efficiently using their land and hence justify state seizure of pastoral village land and resources. Village governments were uncertain if this ambiguity meant that they must reestablish village boundaries to demonstrate ownership, regardless of previous land titles or certificates.[4]

Since WMAs are established on village land that is set aside explicitly for the purposes of conservation, demarcating a WMA may guarantee local authorities secure rights over the area. However, many Loliondo leaders believed that creating a WMA could weaken their claim that land managed for both conservation and livestock remains village land. As opposition to the WMA grew in Loliondo, supporters of the WMA began to promote it as the only way for pastoralist communities to retain their land rights under the new land legislation. They argued that resisting the reform would lead the government to designate the entire area as general land, which would make it vulnerable to being auctioned off to foreign investors. Pastoralist rights organizations did their best to debunk this as deceptive politics and to assure communities that they could challenge the government's claim to their resources by drawing on the new land acts. Pastoralist rights NGOs contended that accepting the WMA would make it harder to assert local claims to land. These NGOs helped villages build the argument that the Land Act of 1999 and the Village Land Acts of 1999 provided villages with "statutory rights" over land, even if the central government retained authority over wildlife. Village leaders used this to argue that they could legally lease their land to tourism investors who were not directly "consuming" or interfering with wildlife.

Community Conservation

What we now know as community conservation became key to the Tanzanian state's policy toward wildlife management and safari tourism in the late 1980s. Moving away from earlier conservation strategies to exclude pastoralists, community conservation initiatives in the 1980s and 1990s sought to incorporate pastoralists and other rural communities into their projects. They did this by using tourism as the driving incentive for communities to accept conservation as an economic activity. Dan Brockington argues that such tourism revenue was promoted as the best way for conservation to "pay its own way."[5]

Many of Tanzania's conservation areas were in semiarid savannah grassland ecosystems that supported both wildlife and livestock populations. The new projects were established as community-based conservation (CBC) projects in the hope that both pastoralists and conservationists would recognize their common interest in preserving the rangelands. The sponsors of these projects promoted CBC as a way to unite the pastoralists and conservationists against the encroachment of "degrading" land uses, in this case large-scale agriculture, which threatened both pastoralism and the conservation of wildlife habitat. CBC was largely born out of the idea that rural communities and conservationists shared certain interests in preserving specific landscapes that were also valuable in a globally commoditized tourism industry. Many policy initiatives try to build new coalitions by posing their objectives as a win-win scenario for multiple groups. The success of CBC in Tanzania was always tenuous because the different participating groups had conflicting agendas and goals alongside their shared interests.[6] CBC proponents believed that economic benefits from tourism would supersede and remake all other interests and transform groups skeptical of conservation into productive environmental subjects. Building a broad and deep coalition in support of CBC was difficult for many reasons, not least of which were the range of actors who had differing ideas of the meaning of conservation.

Tanzania was not alone in experiencing problems achieving this wishful win-win scenario; such tensions have steadily played themselves out across the globe, and CBC has fallen out of favor with many groups who initially promoted the idea.[7] Yet in Tanzania several groups in the conservation community, especially ecotourism safari companies, hoped that this idea could serve as a platform for their interests in the short term and perhaps create new openings and alliances in the longer term. Some of the larger conservation organizations in East Africa, such as the AWF, the FZS, and the WWF, which were most closely associated with command-and-control approaches to conservation, began CBC projects in the 1990s.[8] Although none of these organizations gave up on their core conservation efforts that depended on excluding pastoralists and other rural producers from protected areas, they did experiment with CBC by engaging community groups in wildlife management and use on their village lands. This approach had several potential benefits for the conservation organizations including gaining access to community lands that were previously the domain of the Wildlife Division (WD), which managed the areas exclusively for hunting. CBC offered the prospect of replacing hunting-safari tourism with photographic-safari tourism, which was much preferred by most of the mainstream conservation groups. Although hunting and conservation are not mutually exclusive, organizations like the AWF, the FZS, and the WWF were deeply committed to the existing system of protected areas and saw CBC as a way to expand buffer zones around national parks free from hunting.

Conservation Crisis

Poaching significantly increased throughout the 1980s, and antipoaching efforts were costly and mostly ineffective.[9] In 1989 the government sponsored the violent Operation Uhai, an unparalleled effort led by the WD to send military and police officers into rural areas to stop poaching. The program, meaning "Operation Life," lasted two years and essentially treated every rural Tanzanian as a poacher.[10] While villagers were arrested, harassed, and killed over the two-year period (1989–91), the often well-connected and influential actors behind the poaching activities and their lucrative markets were rarely charged or implicated.[11] Under the leadership of the country's second president, Ali Hassan Mwinyi, Operation Uhai reiterated the centrality of wildlife management to national sovereignty and development and also signaled heightened conflict between rural livelihoods and a national conservation agenda.[12] In an attempt to reestablish some trust with villagers, the Tanzanian government approached the German development agency Gesellschaft für Technische Zusammenarbeit (GTZ) in 1990 and asked it to help establish a community-based wildlife management project with villages around the Selous Game Reserve. The Selous Conservation Program was one of the first efforts to involve villagers in wildlife management in Tanzania. The village wildlife management initiative in the villages surrounding the Selous Game Reserve became an initial model of community conservation in the country.[13]

Increased poaching was not the only threat to wildlife conservation in Tanzania. The high costs associated with the popular "fences and fines" approach to national park management were also becoming prohibitive, especially in light of structural adjustment policies (SAPs) that cut state budgets across the board.[14] Despite the large amount of land dedicated to conservation in Tanzania, important wildlife habitat extended beyond the boundaries of national parks and protected areas: 70 percent of wildlife populations depended on some habitat outside core protected areas.[15] Because of these factors, conservationists turned their attention to protecting wildlife habitat outside national parks. Specifically they focused on preventing the conversion of rangelands suitable for both live-stock and wildlife to farmland. With the realization that much of the critical wildlife habitat was in existing savannah ecosystems outside protected areas, many conservationists turned to pastoralists as partners. Although many pastoralists also farmed, protecting rangelands was often their top priority.[16]

Tanzania's oversight of wildlife conservation activities is divided between the TANAPA and the NCA, which are responsible for national parks and conservation areas, and the WD, which is responsible for wildlife management in game reserves, game controlled areas (GCAs), and open areas (OAs). The main difference between GCAs and OAs is that hunting by Tanzanian residents is illegal in GCAs and legal in OAs. The WD's primary function is to regulate the country's resident hunting and trophy-hunting industry in over 140 designated hunting blocks, the majority of which are located adjacent to national parks and conservation areas. Because of this jurisdictional legacy, the WD became the primary government agency responsible for implementing the WMA policy reform, with its focus on wildlife tourism and trophy hunting on village lands.

Development advocates, including human rights groups, proposed CBC, and mainstream conservation organizations often joined the policy process only after it had gained significant support and momentum. It was hard for these groups to completely oppose or ignore what was being described as a new, "friendlier" approach to conservation. It was meant to address the crisis in the popular "fences and fines" approach to conservation, which was too costly and antagonistic to local people, by involving rural communities in conservation planning and management and to share benefits more equitably (see chapter 1).[17] CBC advocates argued that making ecological and financial benefits more tangible to rural communities would change their attitudes and influence their values in favor of conservation. By the early to middle 1990s, the idea of involving local communities in both conservation management and benefit sharing was becoming widely accepted by some donors, policy makers, and conservation organizations.[18]

These projects were often met with skepticism and have had mixed results. The reluctance of these groups and other high-profile international conservation organizations to abandon their close relations with and substantial support of state agencies that promote more traditional forms of exclusionary conservation has posed a major challenge to their legitimacy in the eyes of communities.[19]

In March 2004, I attended and observed a workshop at the Ngorongoro District headquarters in Loliondo.[20] The district executive director sent letters requesting that all village and district leaders, CBOs, and conservation NGOs working in the area attend the meeting to learn more about the proposed establishment of a WMA in Loliondo. WMAs were Tanzania's official policy approach to CBC. Sixteen areas across the country with large and valuable wildlife populations suitable for safari tourism and trophy hunting were chosen to establish the new "community-based protected areas." Almost half of these were in pastoralist areas. In exchange for setting aside part of their village lands for wildlife habitat, the government would transfer to local institutions some management authority and the ability to collect revenue from tourism and hunting-related investments.

By 2004 communities throughout Tanzania had been experimenting with a variety of CBC-type approaches, including village-based tourism joint ventures, for over a decade. However, with the creation of the WMA the state declared only one sanctioned CBC pathway and policy to involve local communities in wildlife management and safari tourism.[21] The WD was the department of the Ministry of Natural Resources and Tourism (MNRT) responsible for managing wildlife outside national parks. Up until this time, the WD's primary focus had been regulation of the lucrative trophy-hunting industry. The WD's interactions with community groups and leaders were minimal, and it had developed a reputation as one of the government agencies that was most antagonistic toward rural communities. Having total legal domain over all wildlife in the country often led to the impression that the WD ruled these lands completely. Rural communities were rarely consulted about safari hunting that took place on their lands, and many of them came to resent the WD. As the agency chosen to oversee wildlife management on village lands, the WD was now the central government body responsible for implementing the new WMA policy. Many of the people involved in the early stages of CBC in Tanzania described to me the resistance of the WD to take on such a role, which it too considered outside its mandate and core mission. Eventually, with significant support from the German GTZ, the WD agreed to assume this new role. With its own history and bureaucratic culture, the WD's management style shaped the implementation of the WMA policy. One of the effects of this style was to apply a one-size-fits-all process regardless of the specific ecological or social dynamics in different places proposed to pilot the WMA process.

To comply with the mandate, the WD established sixteen pilot WMAs throughout the country. The meeting that day was to discuss the new WMA guidelines and regulations, educate the community about the new policy, and lead a planning exercise to establish a WMA in Loliondo.[22] Once a WMA had been identified by consultants and approved by the WD, no one thought to ask the designated communities if they wanted to participate in this new pilot project. Because WMA's were the country's new policy, the WD assumed that any community interested in participating in tourism in any way would simply embrace the opportunity to create a WMA. It organized a series of meetings, seminars, and workshops to educate communities on how to participate in the new policy.

Despite the new rhetoric of a friendlier approach to conservation, many people familiar with CBC reforms in Tanzania, including a large number of the people attending the meetings in Loliondo that day, did not believe that the WD officials were willing to entrust significant authority over wildlife use and management to local people. A provision in the WMA guidelines giving the director of wildlife final authority over all decisions concerning WMAs did not instill confidence in many Maasai people I interviewed, who were already skeptical of the WD and other state wildlife authorities (see chapter 2). It was only after years of pressure by international donors like the USAID and international NGOs such as the WWF that the WD had reluctantly accepted its new charge to include local representation in managing wildlife on village lands.[23] The skepticism of many in Loliondo notwithstanding, the WMAs did offer for the first time a mechanism for the central government to authorize local communities to participate directly in wildlife management and to benefit from its utilization.

To establish a wma, villages need to follow the elaborate procedures laid out by the wd. After being "sensitized on the importance and cost benefits of conserving wildlife resources," villages are told to identify "an area fit to be designated as a wma." In most cases this means pooling village land together with other villages. If all the adjacent villages agree to participate, they begin an eleven-step process to register a new cbo to be able to legally participate in managing tourism and hunting activities on their land. To establish a cbo, representatives from each participating village must draft a constitution and develop a strategic plan. At each step, the cbo should seek the endorsement of all the participating villages. The cbo must then prepare a land-use plan recommending to the participating villages "land to be set-aside as communal village land for the purpose of establishing a wma." The cbo then creates a "general management plan" for the wma.

Once these steps are complete and approved by the wd, the cbo applies to the director of wildlife to become an "authorized association" (aa), capable of managing the wma. The application should include the following:

- Minutes of the Village Assembly meeting that approved the formation of the wma;
- A completed Wildlife Management Area Data Sheet in the format provided for in the Second Schedule to the Regulations;
- A certified copy of the cbo's Certificate of Registration;
- A copy of the cbos Constitution;
- A Land Use Plan approved by the respective Village Assembly(ies);
- A sketch map of the proposed wma in relation to the Village Land Use Plan(s);
- Boundary description of the proposed wma, its name and size;
- A copy of the General Management Plan or a Resource Management Zone Plan.[24]

If the director of wildlife approves the cbo's application, the director will grant it status as an aa, which enables it to apply for "User Rights" to be able to "enter into an investment agreement with investors for the purpose of utilizing wildlife resources in the wma." Although "the primary beneficiary of the wmas shall be the villager in the village(s) forming the Authorized Association," revenue from all contracts is divided 35 percent for the wd and 65 percent for the aa representing the wma.[25] The aa's revenues are further divided in half, with 50 percent going directly to member villages and 50 percent being reinvested in WMA administrative costs and conservation activities such as hiring village game scouts.[26] Loliondo was one of the few areas in the country that had already attracted significant tourism investment without much state oversight. For the architects and supporters of the WMA policy, government involvement was necessary to protect the interests and rights of all Tanzanian citizens, as well as to ensure a fair system for tourism and hunting investors. In 2002 the WMA policy seemed like a late addition to the ongoing experiment with CBC in Tanzania. For example, villages in Loliondo had been working directly with tourism companies for over a decade, and accepting the WD's new management style and oversight was not a very welcome prospect.

A Singular Approach to Community-Based Conservation

At the Wildlife Management Areas meeting in 2004, the WD representatives told the mostly Maasai audience that, together with district officials including the district natural resources officer and the district game officer, they would use their expertise to advise communities on how best to use their village land for conservation and wildlife management. They would also help villagers negotiate agreements with tourism and trophy-hunting investors who would lease rights to land and wildlife within the WMA. One of the WD speakers at the meeting depicted his agency's new role as that of a benefactor looking out for the interests of the villagers, who, he asserted, were "certain to be swindled without [the WD's] protection."[27] With the WMA as the only legal mechanism for communities to participate in wildlife management, WD officials believed that Loliondo residents would appreciatively embrace the new opportunities presented to them, as they claimed most of the communities in the other sixteen designated pilot WMAs had.

Had WD officials paid more attention to the actions and words of Loliondo leaders over the previous several years, dating to the release of the new Wildlife Policy of 1998, in which the framework for WMAs was first proposed, they should not have been surprised to encounter a skeptical audience. As described in chapter 6, by 2004 five of the seven rural villages bordering Serengeti National Park had formed joint-venture tourism agreements with private safari ecotourism operators. Villages in Loliondo had already been overseeing tourism on their village lands and earning between ten thousand and sixty thousand dollars annually without directly partnering with, ceding control over their land to, or directly sharing revenue with the central government. They had attracted investors and negotiated contracts without the help of state officials. While not perfect, the village-based joint ventures had succeeded in generating enthusiasm for the broader CBC goals by showing that conservation could pay its own way.[28]

One of the WD facilitators challenged this alternative view of CBC in Loliondo head on, declaring that the "villagers were being taken advantage of [by private tour operators]." Speaking into a microphone, he stated, "The private companies bring many tourists and give the village chairman a little something in exchange." Coercion and bribery were not infrequent in foreign investment schemes or development projects. However, as one of the elected village representatives I was sitting next to explained to me, nor were they the exclusive domain of the private sector. "I prefer to take my chances with a tourism company over a WD official," he whispered and then grinned.

When the Maasai villagers in attendance were finally given a chance to speak, they asked several questions about the WMA. They inquired about the lack of clarity over revenue sharing, whether the director of wildlife had ultimate authority over all management decisions, and why a single village could not apply to become a WMA by itself. It quickly became apparent to the WD and district officials that this meeting to establish a WMA in Loliondo was not going as planned. After the question period was abruptly ended, another WD representative took a more forceful approach. Shifting from promoting the virtues of community involvement in wildlife management, the official made clear that refusing the WMA was not an option. If villagers wanted any say in managing tourism on their lands, then establishing a WMA was their only choice. Standing on the makeshift stage in the conference room at the district headquarters in his brown suit and silver tie, the official stressed his agency's authority.

> We hear there are so many tourist camps [in Loliondo], and they pay directly to the villages. Right? Yes. These are all against the law. Wildlife is all state property. Natural resources are all state property. These contracts that you all have are illegal. The only person who can license tourist activities is the minister [of natural resources and tourism]. . . . We have taken many [of the companies] to court. So you will decide if you want game controlled areas [the current system] or wildlife management areas [the newly proposed system].

The threat was the latest in a series of declarations by the WD that the existing tourism projects in Loliondo, in which ecotourism investors signed contracts directly with villages, were illegal.[29] Despite the WDs assertion that there was no choice in the matter, Loliondo leaders attending the meeting clearly believed that there were other possible paths to fulfill the promises of CBC.

This meeting was one of dozens between national officials and Loliondo leaders between 2000 and 2011. It is just one of many encounters in which different actors articulated their interests in a particular vision of CBC. Rather than a coherent set of policies, CBC, like other economic and political reforms, came to Tanzania as a mix of promises and goals. Different actors inserted themselves in the process to influence the outcomes. These actors included the Tanzanian state and in particular the government agency responsible for implementing CBC, the WD; conservation NGOs; civil-society groups; private companies; and finally the rural Tanzanians whose livelihoods, landscapes, and interests were the object of these interventions.

In this chapter, I describe how these different actors interacted with the changing policy landscape and attempted to influence the meanings and possibilities of CBC in Tanzania. I do not advocate for or against the WMA. Rather I want to show how the WMA represented a particular CBC intervention and why communities in Loliondo saw the WMA largely as a continuation of colonial and nationalist conservation policies. I cannot evaluate whether WMAs are a good-faith effort to involve communities in conservation. Instead, I want to situate the WMA policy in a broader historical and geographical context. This chapter situates the history of CBC efforts in Loliondo, illustrating the emerging context for safari tourism and hunting on village lands, and the way that Maasai villagers experienced the contradictions of decentralization, community participation, and neoliberal conservation. The policy and political context of wildlife management in Loliondo informs the three ethnographic chapters that follow.

The Crisis of National Game

Along with mining and agriculture, tourism is one of Tanzania's three leading economic activities.[30] According to the Tanzania Tourism Sector Survey, Tanzania earned approximately $1.3 billion, or 33 percent of its GDP, from tourism activities in 2008. This was an increase from 1995, when the country earned $740 million, or 16 percent of its GDP from tourism. The majority of Tanzania's 770,000 visitors come for "leisure and holidays." Although Zanzibar is a popular beach destination, wildlife in general and visits to national parks and the NCA in particular form the cornerstone of the tourism industry in Tanzania.[31] Emphasizing nonconsumptive photographic tourism within national parks and the NCA and trophy hunting in game reserves and game controlled areas, Tanzania's central government has developed a highly regulated industry centered on the country's world-famous wildlife populations and natural landscapes.

The growth of Tanzania's tourist economy since independence in 1961 has coincided with the expansion of the country's network of national parks and the NCA. Tanzania is known for its commitment to conservation, with almost 40 percent of the country's land dedicated to some form of protected status, approximately 14 percent as national parks and conservation areas.[32] Tanzania's extensive network of protected areas and its large bureaucratic infrastructure reinforce the importance of wildlife and their habitats for the country's economic prosperity. The WMA policy to increase conservation and tourism on village lands was one of several initiatives to promote and expand wildlife-based tourism.

In one of political ecology's landmark texts, Rod Neumann (1998) documents the important role of Western ideas, colonial policies, and the government's desire to be recognized as a modern nation-state in the emerging postcolonial order, to establish the significance of conservation for Tanzania's economic and political stability. Despite the newly independent government's socialist critique of many colonial policies and programs, it not only embraced conservation as a strategy; it also promoted it aggressively. Before independence the Serengeti was the country's only national park. From independence in 1961 to 1992, the state created fourteen national parks.[33]

Although the first independent government of Tanzania replaced the Fauna Conservation Ordinance of 1951 with the Wildlife Conservation Act (WCA) of 1974, it largely reproduced colonial ideas valuing wildlife as a national commodity over its value as a local livelihood resource. If anything, the WCA of 1974 made it even clearer that wildlife was a national resource and that local rights to resources that had been largely criminalized under colonial policies would remain in place.[34] The WCA of 1974 coincided with Tanzania's radical rural development program known as villagization (described in chapter 2).

Hunting was illegal in national parks and the NCA but allowed in the country's game reserves. Game reserves were a category of land under central government control and managed by the Wildlife Division primarily for trophy hunting. Tanzanians were forbidden to live in game reserves but could get permission for resident hunting if the resident owned an appropriate and licensed firearm. People often imagine trophy-safari hunting taking place in special reserves set aside solely for hunting. However, many of the country's hunting areas were located on village land. These lands are designated as GCAs and OAs, demarcating them as areas with abundant wildlife populations suitable for hunting, as well as areas of human settlement and production.

Enlisting Pastoralists in Conservation

In 1985 the Norwegian Agency for International Development provided a grant to the Tanzanian MNRT to develop a regional conservation strategy for the Serengeti, known as the Serengeti Regional Conservation Strategy (SRCS). Staff from the FZS, the International Union for Conservation of Nature (IUCN), and the Serengeti Wildlife Research Institute helped plan and facilitate the initial organizational meeting of the SRCS. The goal of the SRCS was to address what it described as "the growing conflicts between the needs of people and those of conservation in the Serengeti region."[35] The SRCS also signaled the conservation community's recognition that the future of Serengeti wildlife depended on the management of the entire ecosystem, including large areas outside the core national park.

One of the recommendations of the SRCS was to ensure compatible land use in adjacent areas referred to as "buffer zones." Although buffer zone was not an official land category, Serengeti National Park officials had used the term to describe the Loliondo GCA in the past. The SRCS report recommended changing the primary use of GCAs surrounding national parks from hunting areas to conservation buffer zones. It noted, "The game controlled areas . . . limit [resident] hunting but do not otherwise prescribe land-uses; as such they have often been the site of unrestricted settlement and cultivation. The situation has been exacerbated by the fact that buffer zones per se are not presently recognized as a category of land-use under existing Tanzanian legislation."[36] The SRCS report went on to say that Loliondo "presents a particularly valuable opportunity to develop the buffer zone concept in the Serengeti region."[37]

The SRCS leaders believed that helping to address threats to pastoral livelihoods, including cattle theft and lack of reliable grain markets, could be the foundation for cooperation between the park and local populations. Despite the antagonistic history between Serengeti National Park officials and the Loliondo Maasai, the insecure livelihood of pastoralists appeared to present an interesting opportunity for collaboration. Having a strong state partner like the TANAPA to address livestock raiding from the Sukuma and Kuria people living in the western Serengeti, as well as the multiple threats to convert pasture into large-scale farms, was an appealing prospect to many Maasai leaders.

For the TANAPA and its NGO partners, the AWF and the FZS, the SRCS was an opportunity to build better relationships with neighboring Maasai and to solidify the importance of conservation in the Loliondo area. The SRCS report recommended creating "an experimental zone, ten kilometers in width, . . . along the eastern boundary of Serengeti National Park."[38] It continued, "The wildlife authorities should initiate a dialogue with the relevant regional authorities and representatives of the local people, in order to obtain their cooperation in the establishment and management of such an area. As an immediate first step, an agreement should be reached on preventing the establishment of agriculture in the vicinity of the park boundaries."[39] To this end, the TANAPA established a "parks as good neighbors" program (*ujirani mwema* in Kiswahili), also known as the Community Conservation Service (CCS). The CCS provided social services to rural communities adjacent to the park. CCS efforts in Loliondo included the construction of primary-school classrooms and a health clinic and laying water pipes.[40]

The SRCS architects believed that strengthening pastoralists' rights through secure village land tenure would create a legal framework enabling their buffer-zone proposal to work. To that end, they proposed assisting district and national officials to survey and title Loliondo villages. If the promise of the park outreach program worked as planned, the TANAPA believed that investing revenues from Serengeti National Park into village development projects like school classrooms, water infrastructure, and medical dispensaries would encourage the Maasai to accept the buffer-zone concept and embrace managing their village land for wildlife conservation. A village titling program created the conditions for the TANAPA to distribute benefits to identifiable communities. The SRCS joined together with KIPOC, the IUCN, and the Arusha Catholic Diocese Development Organization (ADDO) in their village registration campaign to survey and demarcate villages in Loliondo. With financial support from the Ford Foundation and other donors, ADDO had already worked with NGOs and government agencies in Kiteto, Simanjiro, and Monduli Districts. These groups worked together with the regional land office to demarcate boundaries between villages. By 1990, nine villages in Loliondo had received official title deeds. Maasai village leaders and SRCS representatives believed that these title deeds were more significant than the standard certificate of occupancy. Maasai leaders saw village titles as a way to protect Maasai collective land rights. Conservationists saw the titles as a way to create a framework for a buffer zone that covered the entire boundary of Serengeti National Park, spanning multiple villages.[41]

The Multiple Meanings of Conservation

Although the SRCS identified possibilities for collaboration, pastoralists and conservationists did not share a history of overlapping interests. Building on the Loliondo Pilot Community Conservation Project, the AWF applied for a grant of one hundred thousand dollars from the Royal Netherlands Embassy in 1991. The proposal would allow the AWF to continue its work in Loliondo as part of its "Neighbors as Partners" program. In the initial proposal, the AWF identified the Loliondo-based NGO described in chapter 2, KIPOC, as its local partner. One of the chief objectives of the project was "to strengthen the institutional capabilities of a truly indigenous and independent NGO, KIPOC, which [would] act as a mechanism to address conservation issues in the local communities in the Loliondo Division."[42]

KIPOC means "we shall recover" in the Maasai language. One of the reasons the name was chosen was to challenge Western conceptions of conservation. The name signified that conservation was a discourse that the Maasai must both participate in and overcome. Ironically, in their documents and reports the AWF staff translated the meaning of KIPOC as "we will survive," drawing on a more recognizable framing of conservation as preservation of nature, which cast the Maasai in a fixed and anachronistic relationship with their land.

After a few meetings between KIPOC and the AWF, the AWF staff changed their plans. The AWF requested dropping KIPOC as its partner in a revised proposal submitted some months later. In a brief paragraph, the AWF officials wrote, "While AWF wholeheartedly supports the concept of local people organizing into a non-governmental body to promote development and conservation, it appears it will not be possible to utilize KIPOC to the extent anticipated."[43] AWF officials had hoped that the community conservation efforts under the TANAPA's good-neighbors program had influenced the development of KIPOC and its stance toward conservation. KIPOC's agenda, however, was built around a crucible of land and cultural rights, in which the AWF, the FZS and the TANAPA were seen more as obstacles to pastoralist development than as potential allies. KIPOC and other Loliondo leaders joined with international conservationists in the village-titling project to restrict large-scale agricultural development and defend rangelands. They did not, however, support the associated goals of conservation groups to turn Loliondo villages into a buffer zone for Serengeti National Park.

Safari Hunting, the Wildlife Division, and Community Conservation

The SRCS focused on relations between Serengeti National Park and the surrounding communities. It also had another goal, to advocate against hunting in the region. It might not seem unusual for conservation NGOs or private tourism companies to oppose hunting. For many advocates of CBC in Africa, hunting was not anathema to conservation goals. Drawing lessons from the well-regarded CAMPFIRE (Communal Areas Management Program for Indigenous Resources) in Zimbabwe, where hunting was the key economic activity, many CBC advocates believed that Tanzania's lucrative hunting industry could be key in helping rural communities earn substantial revenue from local wildlife. This dynamic helped establish opposing camps on how CBC would be run in Tanzania, pitting groups like FZS and AWF, which saw CBC as a way to promote a nonconsumptive form of conservation, against groups like GTZ and the WD, which largely wanted to reduce poaching and promote conservation for hunting. These differing positions relied on an understanding of safari tourism as either nonconsumptive ecotourism or trophy-hunting tourism.

As part of the economic reform process that came along with SAPs and austerity measures, the MNRT established the Wildlife Sector Review Task Force (WSRTF) in 1994. It was made up of government officials and foreign technical advisors and was tasked with providing recommendations for wildlife reform. One of the WSRTF's (1995) conclusions was that tourist hunting, given its lucrative nature, had the greatest potential to provide concrete benefits to local communities and create meaningful incentives for conservation. This belief was soon codified in the Tanzanian Government's *Policy and Management Plan for Tourist Hunting* published in 1995. The policy called for "widen[ing] opportunities for rural people . . . to participate in the tourist hunting industry and . . . ensur[ing] more equitable distribution of revenue."[44]

The task force recommendations were incorporated into the country's first policy specifically aimed at conservation activities outside national parks and game reserves. The Wildlife Policy of 1998 created the legal framework for privatizing the hunting industry that had already been under way since the desertion of the national hunting company, Tanzania Wildlife Corporation (TAWICO), in the late 1980s. With wildlife the property of the state no matter where it was found, the Wildlife Policy of 1998 provided the first framework for local communities to legally participate in wildlife management on community lands. The process was for communities to establish WMAs in order to gain legal rights and joint-management authority with state agencies over wildlife. Signaling a new role for villages, the document reads, "It is the aim of this policy to allow rural communities and private landholders to manage wildlife on their land for their own benefit."[45]

The language of the policy left open many possibilities. WMAs could not be formed without the release of the guidelines and regulations that would come four years later, in 2002. Still, the policy signaled a change in the relationship between communities, the state, and wildlife on village lands. Tanzania's wildlife bureaucracy, however, was not well prepared to receive the reforms. The WD had only recently reorganized the hunting industry, in 1988, and was loath to relinquish its authority over this lucrative activity.[46] Debate about the efficacy of CBC in Tanzania would largely hinge on the question of community participation and the competing roles of hunting and ecotourism in rearticulating conservation to a specific form of safari tourism.

Despite the rhetoric of WMAs and greater community participation in conservation, Maasai communities in Loliondo were skeptical that the WD and the MNRT were truly willing to devolve rights to local communities. For example, before releasing the WMA guidelines and regulations in 2002, the MNRT cracked down on all existing village tourism arrangements. The government released the Wildlife Conservation (Tourist Hunting) Regulations of 2000, essentially declaring all existing contracts between villages and ecotourism companies illegal.[47] The regulations stated, "No person shall conduct tourist hunting, game viewing, photographic safari, walking safari or any wildlife based tourist safari within a hunting block . . . except . . . with the written authority of the Director of Wildlife. . . . Provided that this sub regulation shall not apply where such activities are carried out in gazetted Wildlife Management Areas." Communities often turned to NGOs to assist them in navigating the often contradictory and complex terrain of wildlife reform. As I discuss in the next section, the NGO sector was also divided on how best to approach CBC in northern Tanzania.

Conservation NGOs and WMAs

While NGOs have different goals, donors, and agendas, several well-funded conservation NGOs played a central role in promoting and maintaining support for conservation in Tanzania. The two NGOs that dominated the Serengeti ecosystem, including Loliondo, were the U.S.-based AWF and the German-based FZS. Both of these NGOs were very influential in the SRCS, working with the TANAPA in its attempt to promote the value of national parks to bordering communities in the 1980s. One of the key provisions of the WMA policy was to involve an international NGO to partner with the government to help fund and implement the WMA. The AWF and the FZS were the two primary NGO partners in northern Tanzania. These NGOs were deeply invested in the core system of protected areas in northern Tanzania and saw community conservation as a new approach to fulfill long-standing desires to conserve land in Loliondo for conservation.[48] Both NGOs dedicated funding and resources, including staff and time, to CBC. However, for both the AWF and the FZS, CBC remained a relatively small part of their overall operations. As a U.S.-based NGO and a large recipient of USAID funding, the AWF embraced market approaches to conservation. It established a business development office in its Arusha headquarters to help communities start tourism-related enterprises. The FZS remained more committed to a parks-based approach to conservation. It saw CBC as a way to extend goodwill between parks and people and to finally establish the long-sought-after buffer zones around Serengeti National Park. The FZS's approach looked very similar to the one laid out in the SRCS, in which it played a prominent role.

At the same time that the AWF and the FZS captured funding and influence in the development of CBC in northern Tanzania, a group of newer NGOs, less well funded and with significantly lower profiles, emerged. This group of international NGOs saw the emerging market for ecotourism outside protected areas as the driver of new revenue that could fund more innovative and successful approaches to CBC. Advocates of this more market-based approach to conservation believed that to achieve genuine participation and enthusiasm from community partners, CBC had to address the problematic legacies of colonial conservation and decenter state authorities as the only viable conservation experts.

For these groups and the individuals who staffed them, their critique of state power and interests served as an effective connection with rural communities living in wildlife-rich areas.

These new voices for neoliberal conservation approaches saw liberalizing the wildlife sector and tourism on village lands as a win-win for conservation and poverty reduction. Rather than seeing state institutions like the WD or the TANAPA as their primary partners, these NGOs considered private ecotourism companies their key partners to fulfill the promise of CBC. Supporters of this free-market approach to conservation believed that community conservation would not only reduce poverty and generate new support for conservation; they also saw it as a moral project that would begin to reverse the colonial legacies associated with conservation. With large and influential conservation NGOs like the AWF and the FZS already entrenched with state interests and institutions, newer NGOs took leadership roles in this brave new world of conservation politics.

One of the groups to promote this new conservation agenda in northern Tanzania was the Sand County Foundation (SCF). The SCF was a relatively small NGO led by Fred Nelson, an expatriate researcher and development worker from the United States. Nelson had spent time in southern Africa working with CAMPFIRE in Zimbabwe. He was a passionate advocate for harnessing tourism revenues to support community conservation initiatives. When he first arrived in Tanzania, Nelson tried to work directly with the conservation establishment but was largely turned away by the AWF and other influential NGOs. The SCF had no history in Tanzania, and Nelson operated with an unusual degree of freedom, picking and choosing the projects he wanted to support. As an outsider to the influential foreign conservation community, Nelson worked directly with CBOs and private tourism operators, whom he found shared many of his ideas and beliefs.

In 2000 Nelson helped to start the Tanzania Natural Resources Forum (TNRF), a nonprofit group formed to promote community natural-resource management in Tanzania. Nelson and others believed that to compete with groups like the AWF and the FZS for policy influence, they needed to form their own organization that would articulate their positions and lobby for specific political change and reform. The mission of the TNRF is "to bring about improved natural resource governance in Tanzania by being a demand-driven network of members and partners that helps people to bridge the gap between people's local natural resource management needs and practices, and national natural resource management priorities, policies, laws and programs."[49] The TNRF recognized that international NGOs dominated the conservation agenda and believed that a robust civil-society organization needed to include local NGOs and private companies. TNRF founders and directors believed that these groups shared interest in using market-based approaches to managing landscapes, and that these approaches would best address both sustainable conservation and livelihood security. The idea was to create a forum where differing opinions could be discussed and negotiated by the members, rather than by outside experts and donors. As discussed in chapter 6, support from groups like the SCF and the TNRF lent legitimacy to private sector–initiated projects. In fact, the TNRF and its members helped promote the idea that many projects initiated by private companies were more ethical and just than those initiated either by state agencies or mainstream international conservation organizations.

This history is important in understanding how Maasai communities in Loliondo understood conservation and the NGOs that promoted it. In 2002 the government passed the Wildlife Conservation Regulations, giving the WMAs legal status and setting a three-year period to establish the sixteen pilot WMAs throughout the country.[50] Given the significant costs and complex structure of establishing a WMA, substantial funding and expertise were necessary. The policy approach was to pair each WMA with a sponsoring NGO that would both fund and provide technical support to the AA overseeing the WMA. In partnership with influential donors like the USAID and the GTZ, the WD selected these "strategic" partners and chose the FZS to help finance and facilitate the WMA in Loliondo. By choosing the most iconic NGO associated with the creation and administration of Serengeti National Park, the FZS, the WD faced an uphill battle to convince Loliondo leaders that this was a truly community-based project.

It took almost ten years, but by 2011 there were fourteen registered AA's participating in the WMA program. Loliondo was not among them. From the start, WMAS were promoted as decentralized business ventures that would give communities legal rights to wildlife in exchange for a commitment to managing a portion of village lands for conservation. In November 2011 the TNRF hosted a workshop to assess the first decade of WMAS. The workshop, "Wildlife for Communities in Tanzania: Taking Stock of Governance of Wildlife by Communities," brought together researchers, government officials, nonprofit organizations, CBOs, foreign donors, international conservation organizations, and tourism investors.

The overall conclusion of the meeting was that after a decade the WMAS had not lived up to their promise. A summary of research included the observation that "there is often little genuine community participation and evidence that communities have sometimes been forced to accept WMAS." One researcher concluded, "There are often high conservation-induced costs—crop damage, livestock depredation, opportunity costs of land and related resources. Benefits are often very limited, or absent altogether." Another study found that "business investors [were] frustrated with the lack of clarity and consistency in policy, changing regulations and fees, lack of security of the investments, and other issues." Yet another study noted that "there [were] emerging conflicts between member villages in WMAS. Some villages [had] contributed more land for WMAS than others."[51]

These findings, while provisional, supported the fears that Loliondo leaders expressed in the late 1990s when their area was designated as one of the pilot WMAS. Their refusal to participate, making Loliondo the only area to do so, sparked the growing tension between Maasai villages in Loliondo and state officials over how best to manage wildlife on village lands.

Legislating Land Rights

The Land Acts of 1999 divide all Tanzanian land into three legal categories or recognized classes. (For a brief overview of this and other major wildlife and land legislation, see the appendix.) These are general land, reserved land, and village land. Reserved land refers to lands set aside for special purposes such as forest reserves and game reserves and are governed by nine different laws. Village land refers to that land managed by each village council. General land is all land that is neither reserved land nor village land. This new class of land is the most controversial and contentious category, one that has created uncertainties in establishing firm village land rights.[52] "The ambiguity stems from the definition of General Land which is provided in the Land Act: 'general land' means all public land which is not reserved land or village land and includes unoccupied or unused village land" (Sundet 2005, 3). This clause has caused obvious concern on the part of village authorities, which must reestablish village boundaries by demarcating and registering village boundaries based on new land surveys, bylaws, and land-use plans to demonstrate ownership, regardless of previous titles or certificates. Many Maasai believe that the ambiguity of this clause was designed to help the government to identify "surplus" land for investors. The long history of public land seizures, especially for conservation areas and large-scale agriculture, has contributed to pastoralists' skepticism toward the land reforms and the bureaucratic complexity involved in re-securing village land tenure.[53]

While the specific language of the new laws may seem outside the scope of everyday conversations about land rights, the entanglement of conservation reforms and land reforms has led to heightened awareness and discussion of the new laws and their implications for pastoral land security. Specifically, the recent wildlife reforms to create WMAS outside the core protected areas of national parks and game reserves have left the many pastoralist communities with limited choices. Advocates, including international conservation organizations like the AWF, the WWF, the FZS; international donors like the USAID and the GTZ; the WD; and some local government bodies such as village and district councils, have argued that establishing a WMA will guarantee its status as village land, despite the need to gazette the WMA as reserved land. Detractors, including community organizers and NGOS, argue that anxieties over land tenure contribute to a misinformation campaign, and that gazetting land as a WMA jeopardizes long-term village access to and control of the land. Groups on both sides of the WMA debate have sponsored workshops and training sessions regarding the new legislation.[54] In 2002 the Government of Tanzania proposed to allow fifteen areas to create pilot WMAS and gain for the first time legal rights to negotiate contracts with tourism and hunting companies. Of the fifteen designated pilot areas, Loliondo is the only one to have so far rejected and resisted the implementation of the WMA.

The WMA was supposed to create a new mechanism for allocating safari tourism concessions on village lands for both hunting and ecotourism. This would replace the current system in which the central government leases hunting concessions on village land to private, largely foreign-owned hunting companies. Village leaders have complained that they do not benefit from these activities and have argued for greater control over wildlife on their land. The WMA aims to address this by devolving certain rights and management responsibilities to village leaders in exchange for guarantees of land management practices that promote conservation and limit permanent agriculture and settlement. Some village leaders across Tanzania have accepted the terms of the WMA, seeing it as the best way to shore up their land rights in these uncertain times and to have a more direct say in the type of safari tourism activities on their land. The village leaders in Loliondo and their supporters have not accepted the WMAS and see them as a way to destabilize pastoralist tenure by setting aside even more resources exclusively for conservation. Community leaders have connected the WMA policy with past efforts to extend park boundaries such as the SRCS. They have also drawn on their recent history working with ecotourism companies, signing contracts, and collecting use fees for access to wildlife on village land.

Conclusion

While Loliondo's opposition to the WMA cannot be reduced to a single factor, it is clear that a few key areas of agreement about the WMA emerged at community meetings in Loliondo. One was the history of suspicion of anything that seemed like a state-led conservation effort. The FZS and the AWF tried to distance themselves from state wildlife management agencies and prove their new bona fides, but their participation only further jeopardized the notion that the WMA was a community-based initiative. Another key concern was how resources were to be divided and managed between villages themselves. The WMA was to be managed jointly by several villages. This model was designed to spread revenue across villages that had disproportionate resource wealth but which formed a viable habitat for wildlife. It should be noted that while Loliondo's shared boundary with Serengeti National Park linked six villages as an important dispersal area for Serengeti wildlife, each village had been able to attract its own investment without ceding any property rights or management authority to neighboring communities (see chapter 6). The legacies of the village titling program codifying discrete Maasai villages as distinct communities would continue to influence wildlife management and tourism in Loliondo.

Resisting the WMA required more than just antagonism and mistrust of the government's commitment to balance conservation and development. It also depended on the ability of local communities to find alternative ways to articulate and defend their property rights. Loliondo residents and their fellow Maasai in Simanjiro were the only group of people in the country to resist the implementation of the WMA policy, and their leaders often drew on their belief that there were alternatives to the WMA. Although the WD continued to insist that the WMA was the only choice, the ecotourism contracts and joint ventures represented an alternative for "home grown" CBC in which the villages felt that they had more control over the terms of the relationships with investors, which were negotiated at a "very local level."

As long as groups do not trust state institutions to safeguard their interests, communities like those in Loliondo will look for alternative means to assert and legitimize their claims. By the early twenty-first century, the market, however tainted in the eyes of communities and state institutions, possessed magical qualities. To proponents of the WMA, the market holds the promise of transforming the value of Tanzanian nature and harnessing it for local and national development. For Loliondo residents, the market appears capable of validating long-standing Maasai claims to territory in their ongoing struggle to find a legitimate place in the national community of Tanzania without having to submit their land to extensive bureaucratic oversight and uncertain land-use restrictions by accepting the terms of the WMA.

CHAPTER 4

"The Lion Is in the *Boma*"

Making Maasai Landscapes for Safari Trophy Hunting

Typically, the long rainy season arrives in northern Tanzania in mid-March and extends through late May or early June. During this period, the Maasai and their livestock disperse across their village lands, taking advantage of grasses far from permanent water sources. This annual ritual is a critical aspect of semi-nomadic pastoralism and is one of the primary reasons the Maasai and other pastoralists are able to sustain themselves in low-rainfall areas that are unsuitable for permanent agriculture. Maasai movements are relatively predictable these days, with herds traveling farther from their homesteads the longer the dry season lasts. Every few years, the spring rains do not come as scheduled. With water and grass hard to find, the Maasai and other pastoralists adjust their seasonal movements. They must travel farther to find food and water for their livestock and stay longer when they do. The spring of 2009 was one of northern Tanzania's worst droughts in a decade. Because of the extended dry conditions, the Maasai from several villages in Loliondo congregated near the Serengeti National Park boundary. The Maasai typically used this area in such conditions. This was village land but not permanently settled because of the high concentration of wildlife, which spread disease to livestock and pose risks as predators. The Maasai who had lived here permanently in the 1960s and 1970s had moved farther east in the 1980s to avoid threats from wildlife and cattle theft by armed groups from western Tanzania. These groups would ambush Maasai, steal their livestock, and then flee through Serengeti National Park, making it difficult for the Maasai to retrieve their cattle. Thus by the 1980s and early 1990s, there were few permanent homesteads in the area, but it was common to find temporary cattle camps, called *ronjos*, where young men spent weeks or months tending their families' livestock before returning home with the rain.

During the 2009 drought, the Maasai had little choice but to seek grass and water in what was clearly the most nourishing extent of their territory at the time. The larger-than-usual concentration of Maasai and their livestock raised concerns for district officials, who saw a conflict brewing with the scheduled arrival in July of the Ortello Business Corporation (OBC), the Dubai-based company that had held the hunting rights in Loliondo since 1992. The Maasai retained their land rights to the OBC hunting grounds but usually avoided the area when the OBC was using it. For the first ten to fifteen years of their operation, this meant staying away from late September to early November, as the OBC only used the area for a short portion of the July-thru-March designated hunting season. Hunting tourism was largely tolerated in Loliondo. It did not radically alter the land as would a large hotel, farm, or a conservation buffer zone that prohibited livestock use. After the OBC dismantled its elaborate encampment of massive tents and loaded its fleet of vehicles back onto airplanes bound for Dubai, there was little trace of the company's presence. A few permanent buildings and cement platforms, along with an unknown reduction in the wildlife population, were all that remained. As the Maasai did not eat wild animals and only rarely hunted (for lions), the loss of game was of little concern to most local residents. As long as the Maasai had access to their rangelands they put up with the OBC as the company posed no imminent threat to Maasai land use and rights. That all changed during the drought of 2009.

On July 4, 2009, Maasai pastoralists from villages throughout Loliondo woke to a frantic scene of state police officers shouting through bullhorns from atop their vehicles, telling residents to leave the village areas adjacent to Serengeti National Park immediately. The select group of police known as the Field Force Unit (FFU) arrived in dark green Land Rovers and proceeded to evict hundreds of Maasai and thousands of cattle from traditional village lands.[1] Over the next two days, the FFU threatened, harassed, and jailed Maasai for grazing their cattle in the OBC's hunting area, never mentioning that it was also Maasai village land. The government had sent letters to district councilors and village leaders telling them to remove people from the area prior to the OBC's arrival, this time close to the beginning of the hunting season in July. Seeing no just cause and no historical precedent, the leaders unanimously refused to leave their land. The police burned between 100 and 150 *bomas*, or seasonal cattle camps and homesteads, sending people and cattle frantically searching for safety, pasture, and water. The evictions affected close to ten thousand pastoralists. More than thirty thousand head of cattle, sheep, and goats were displaced and forced to seek grasses and water elsewhere during the difficult drought. The evictions led to the widespread death of livestock.[2] One Maasai man in his mid-thirties told me that he lost more than one hundred cattle, a significant part of his family's household wealth.[3]

Evictions for conservation are not new phenomena. Mark Dowie (2009) has documented the significant impact of conservation on people whom he calls conservation refugees. Pinning down a number of people displaced by conservation is difficult. Dowie cites sociologist Charles Geisler, who believes that such refugees could number as many as fourteen million in Africa alone. "The true figure if it were ever known," writes Dowie,

> would depend on the semantics of words like *eviction*, *displacement*, and *refugee*, over which all parties on all sides of the issue argue endlessly. However, the point at issue is not the exact number of people who have lost their homeland to conservation, it is that conservation refugees, however defined, exist in large numbers on every continent but Antarctica, and by most accounts live far more difficult lives than they once did, banished from lands they thrived on, often for thousands of years, in ways that even some conservationists who looked aside while evictions took place have since admitted were sustainable. (2009, xxi)

Anthropologists Dan Brockington and James Igoe, like Dowie would a few years later, also found conservation to be responsible for large-scale displacement, documenting more than 170 separate incidences around the world. Summarizing the social and cultural effects of such displacement, they write, "Beyond material loss to livelihoods or dwellings, protesters fight their symbolic obliteration from the landscape—their removal from its history, memory, and representation. Other groups protest their loss of power and control over their environments, the interference of conservation regulations into their lives in ways over which they had little control. Else they protest the interference of different value systems into local economies, the commodification of wildlife and nature into things which tourists can purchase, but which locals can then no longer afford" (2006, 425). The authors argue that state institutions and interests, supported by domestic and international elites, play a large role in promoting the importance of protecting African nature, even at the expense of displaced and dispossessed people.[4]

In the past, states like Tanzania have justified evictions for protecting important wildlife habitat and promoting national security, especially when protected areas were near international borders. The state's defense of the OBC hunting concession and the Thomson Safaris nature refuge (discussed in chapter 5) relied on no such scientific or nationalistic appeal. With state-led development under attack under neoliberalization, the government's rationale was more pragmatic and market driven. If national conservation was a matter of economic efficiency, then land and wildlife resources in Loliondo were too valuable to be left under the control of naive villagers. Tourism and natural resources minister Shamsa Mwangunga commented, "We cannot allow villagers to control such important activities [tourism and hunting] because some dishonest businesspeople will utilise that as a loophole to unlawfully exploit our resources."[5] This statement raises important questions about land rights in Loliondo: What is the state's primary interest in managing wildlife and tourism on village lands? How do competing interests among different state agencies such as the TANAPA, the WD, and district governments influence the meaning of safari tourism on village lands? By what methods can state officials identify unscrupulous business people? Whose job is it to protect Tanzanian citizens from these investors? When are decentralization and participation appropriate? And who decides?

Many Maasai leaders and activists I interviewed believed that government officials initiated the evictions in Loliondo to prevent negotiations between villages and foreign investors fearing that such direct relationships would undermine the state's assumed monopoly on overseeing direct foreign investment. In order to understand policy decisions concerning safari tourism and wildlife management on village lands in Tanzania, it is necessary to understand how different actors understood foreign investors. Ultimately how different actors imagined the interests of foreign investors helped determine the degree to which those investors could shape the future meanings of conservation in Tanzania. Could state actors use their partnerships with foreign investors to solidify and legitimate national claims to territory? Could local people like the Maasai harness their direct relationships with foreign investors to force the state to recognize their rights to their land? Ultimately, how these relationships interacted with and transformed national myths, geographies, and identities would help determine whose interests were represented through neoliberal conservation.

Codifying State Interests

Three weeks before the July 4, 2009, evictions, the Ngorongoro District commissioner sent legal notice to Maasai residents to leave the hunting area immediately. Upon receiving the letter, the district executive director, the central government employee responsible for administering state policies in the district, sent a letter to locally elected village leaders and district councilors, ordering these representatives to evict their fellow pastoralists from the OBC hunting area.[6] The leaders received the letter but chose to ignore the order. They had never before been told to vacate their village land in anticipation of the annual hunting season. Between 1992 and 2009, the OBC—or the police acting on the company's behalf—had several times forced Loliondo residents to vacate part of their land to make way for OBC hunting parties. But this was the first widespread eviction of all the Maasai from an extensive expanse of their village lands.

Pressed to explain the evictions, government officials initially claimed that they were evicting Maasai who had illegally "invaded" the area from Kenya to take advantage of Tanzanian pasturelands during the prolonged regional drought. The argument that Kenyan Maasai were illegally coming to Tanzania had been used before and seemed a convenient way to save face and drum up national support. But although Kenyan Maasai did and do occasionally make arrangements with their Tanzanian kin to use their land, this was not a widespread occurrence in the 2009 drought. Rather, Kenyan Maasai for the most part relied on their own emergency plans, including transporting grain and water onto group ranches as well as heading north toward Nairobi to sell their livestock. There was no evidence to support the government's claim. Perhaps that was the point. State officials could assert that the Maasai being evicted were Kenyan, and possibly no one would notice. The Maasai from Tanzania and Kenya did, after all, look alike, speak the same language, and mostly wore the same iconic dress of red and blue cloth. However, when the government started specifying that certain Maasai individuals were Kenyan, its story crumbled. Two of the people accused of being from Kenya were in fact elected representatives of the Ngorongoro District Council, and another was a long-time member of the Soitsambu village government. The claims were further discredited when journalists failed to find a single Kenyan among the thousands of fleeing Maasai.[7]

Government officials shifted to another commonsense narrative, claiming that the evictions were necessary because the Maasai, regardless of where they were from, were destroying the nation's natural resources. The evictions, they said, were necessary to protect the important wildlife habitat bordering Serengeti National Park. In an interview conducted by an investigative team led by the NGO FemAct a month after the evictions, the Ngorongoro District commissioner, Wawa Lali, reported that he was obliged to enforce the law and to "protect the natural resources for the country's best interests." The Maasai population and its livestock had been increasing, he said, and this posed a danger "not only to the ecosystem" but also to the very existence of the "wild beasts" that inhabited the area. Indeed, it was true that more Maasai and livestock than usual were using the village areas bordering Serengeti National Park due to the drought conditions, but there was nothing unprecedented about this short-term concentration of pastoralists.

Lali assured the media and researchers that the evictions were legal and had been conducted in a manner that "paid attention" to the "human rights" of the evictees. He reiterated that the government had amply warned the communities, and when they did not respond, he had given what he described as "a legitimate command to evict the pastoralist[s] from the respective area." When asked about the violent tactics, Lali said that the police had ensured that all residents had left the area before the *bomas* were burned. He then stated, "The *bomas* were only burnt [to] prevent the communities from resettling . . . after the eviction."

The government's motivation to clear the land for the OBC and to assert the company's right to hunt over Maasai rights to graze was kept somewhat murky. In a videotaped interview, the Arusha regional commissioner, Isidori Shirima, explained the evictions this way: "This exercise was done in order to take people away and show them where to go back to; where they came from. . . . I want to assure you that those people who are removed are only those in the area that the OBC was given the right to hunt in."[8] It was unclear if he was referring to the false claim that the Maasai in the area were from neighboring Kenya, or if he was saying that Tanzanian Maasai did not belong in the hunting area, despite it being within their village lands. A journalist pressed Shirima about the OBC's involvement in the evictions. He responded, "Listen, the OBC does its activities according to the regulations and procedures of the government of Tanzania, not according to their own laws. They operate according to the way we instruct them. The issue of managing the hunting area under the law is a matter for the government."

Many of the Loliondo leaders and activists I spoke with saw this as a clear example of how the OBC and central government interests were aligned. Loliondo residents, leaders, and activists explicitly blamed the government for the evictions. In a recorded interview, a young Maasai man in his twenties stated, "Now the government seems to see that the Arabs have more value than those of us born here in Tanzania. We were born here in Tanzania. This foreigner has come from Dubai, invited into our home but now chasing us out of our home. We fail to know what to do. The Arab has given the government corrupt money to chase us from our homes, this place where we were born."[9] The Ololosokwan village chairman accused the government of breaking the law: "My village has a title deed showing it owns the land; it has done its land-use planning. My village has done this planning and the procedures as we have been instructed. But I am shocked that on the fourth of July, my village was burned, while we are using the land lawfully. I am surprised that our government does not follow the law, does not keep the law in mind. I don't know where we are headed."[10]

Community organizations and local leaders quickly planned a direct action response to the evictions. NGONET, a network of NGOs working in Loliondo and Ngorongoro, carried out its own investigation.[11] The NGOs' findings linked the government's support of the OBC with that for other regional tourism projects, arguing that the government was using investors to recast Loliondo as a "national conservation area" and to reconsolidate state control over Maasai territory. Officials acknowledged that they were enforcing the rights of the OBC to use the Loliondo area for trophy hunting. Lali, the district commissioner, stated explicitly that this land was especially important for its conservation value as a safari hunting area, reminding his audience that the local communities themselves had signed a contract with the OBC allowing the company access to village lands. "The respective contracts were valid and legally entered between the two parties by mutual consent and understanding," Lali said. "The villages benefitted from the contract and their annual income was duly paid by the company."[12] Villages were thus bound by the terms of the agreement, including abstaining from grazing in the area during the hunting season.

Most critical observers and media reports believed that the evictions were a direct response to pressure by the OBC to clear the land of the unusually large number of livestock before their upcoming hunting safari. But despite the clear interests of the foreign investors, the Maasai expressly framed the conflict as one between themselves and the government. This response is understandable, for the Maasai were constantly suspicious of a government strategy to take their land by expanding Serengeti National Park. State representatives like the regional and district commissioners cast their duties as protecting the national interest. They seemed to believe that other Tanzanian citizens would see the value in using Maasai lands for hunting tourism rather than subsistence livestock production.

The Agreement to "Bring Development to the Villages"

When the OBC first gained the lease to the Loliondo hunting concessions in 1992, central government officials together with Ngorongoro District officials recommended that the company propose community development initiatives to satisfy local communities and prevent international opposition. Such initiatives were eventually made into a "requirement" before the OBC could "enjoy and benefit from their hunting license." As part of the initial proposal, the company offered to pay two thousand dollars annually to each village whose land it used for safari hunting. Unlike the joint-venture contracts (described in chapter 6) negotiated between the village governments and private tourism investors, central government officials signed this so-called contract with the OBC "on behalf of the six villages identified in this proposal."[13] Several Maasai leaders I interviewed commented that a "real" contract involved negotiation between two parties. But in the OBC case, they were informed about the agreement and told to embrace "their good fortune." Many village leaders saw the OBC's annual payments "as a token fee to appease the villages."[14]

The *mkataba* (contract or agreement) was titled "For the protection and management of wildlife to bring development to the villages within the 'Loliondo Game Controlled Area' South & North."[15] The two parties named were Brigadier Mohammed Abdulrahim al-Ali (for the OBC) and the district government of Ngorongoro (for the Maasai villages). On November 20, 1992, an

OBC representative on behalf of the brigadier, the Ngorongoro District development officer, the Ngorongoro District MP, and the regional commissioner signed the contract. The regional commissioner signed on behalf of the central government. And underneath the MP's signature was a handwritten amendment stating that this signature was on behalf of the six villages in Loliondo. These villages, named on page 2 of the contract, were Ololosokwan, Soitsambu, Oloipiri, Olorien/Magaiduru, Loosoito, and Arash.[16]

Although several hunting companies had incorporated community development projects into their hunting operations, this "agreement" between the OBC and the village governments in Loliondo was the first official contract, with a set of binding obligations for all parties.[17] Typically, hunting companies were allocated exclusive rights to a hunting block every five years by the WD, which oversaw hunting activities in Tanzania under the MNRT. These arrangements were exclusively between the central government agency based in Dar es Salaam and the private safari hunting investors, mostly foreign-owned companies. With numerous questions about the legality and ethics of the OBC deal, government officials advised the company to present a development plan to go along with its hunting block lease.

The original OBC agreement includes several statements, assumptions, and proposals. It begins, "Wildlife is a natural resource with great potential to generate foreign currency and to provide employment to citizens raising their quality of life." It then states that wildlife has not generated the revenue that it could or should for "the economy of the district, its citizens, or the nation in general." The agreement's opening section ends with a telling statement that captures the dominant ideology of the early 1990s when the global popularity of free-market capitalism coincided with dwindling state resources and power: "The brigadier and the [Ngorongoro] district are ready to live and work together for the purpose of bringing development to the citizens who live in the above-named villages." The OBC and the district agree to protect the area close to Serengeti National Park to make sure that the plants and animals are preserved for future generations. The parties also agree to increase opportunities for local citizens to "make money" and to benefit the community through community services such as "clean water" and "education." Another expressed purpose of the partnership is to "give a new face" to the activities of countries from "Uarabuni" (the Arab world/Middle East) to protect and manage wildlife as a way to bring development to resource-dependent communities.

The proposal stipulates that the OBC agrees to pay 25 percent of the national tax and fees for use of the hunting area to the district government. "The money is to be deposited into the bank annually before each hunting season, on the first day of July each year." The agreement essentially delegates regulatory authority to the brigadier: "The brigadier will ensure that he himself, his friends, and guests will not destroy the environment . . . while hunting. Whenever they are hunting, they will seek expert advice from government wildlife officials." Along with the vague responsibility to "protect the environment," the agreement says that the brigadier will provide "aid" to bring water and build primary schools and health clinics as well as to "purchase medicine" for each of the named villages. To implement this elaborate development agenda, the brigadier is to submit his plans annually along with a budget. The agreement essentially asks the brigadier to finance and implement a variety of endeavors that were historically assumed to be the responsibility of the state. No state official opposed the OBC's role in the contract as conservator or benevolent administrator. This somewhat absurd idea was self-legitimized by the historical precedent and commonsense understanding of outsiders as better able to appreciate, understand, and conserve African nature.[18]

In between the promised development assistance and the request for the brigadier to provide salaries, stipends, and vehicles for antipoaching rangers is the statement that "the brigadier will allow the villagers to continue to graze their livestock within the hunting area as long as they do not commit crimes of any sort." Section 4 states that the contract is good for ten years and can be terminated if the brigadier and the district government determine that it is no longer in their "collective interests" (*kwa faida yao wote* in Kiswahili). There is no mention of Maasai villages or villagers in this section of the agreement, raising questions about who owns the resources in question and who the accountable parties involved are.

"Wildlife Is Our Oil": A Brief History of the Politics of Trophy Hunting in Tanzania

Tanzania is one of fourteen African countries that allow tourist hunting, commonly referred to as trophy or safari hunting. Both Kenya and Uganda used to host trophy hunting but have since halted the practice in favor of other forms of nonconsumptive tourism activities. Because of this, Tanzania is the preferred safari-hunting destination within East Africa, offering seventy different species of wildlife that can be hunted.[19] In 2008 it cost $3,800 for a tourist license to hunt and kill a lion in Tanzania. This "trophy fee" charged by the WD had risen from $2,500 in 2007, $2,000 in 1993, and $1,400 in 1988. A typical twenty-one-day hunting safari in 2010 cost between $50,000 and $150,000.[20] Lion, buffalo, and leopard are the most valuable species for the hunting industry, generating close to 42 percent of the trophy fees for the WD. These trophy fees are but one way that Tanzania benefits from the hunting industry. Estimates suggest that a single visiting hunter brings in anywhere from fifty to one hundred times more revenue than a nonhunting tourist. Hunters and outfitters also pay permit fees, conservation fees, observer fees, trophy-handling fees, an annual rent called a concession or block fee, as well as the license fee of an accompanying professional hunter. Recent estimates claim that revenue earned from the hunting industry is approximately $30 million dollars, with the WD earning about $10 million directly from trophy fees.

Tanzania is well known as a tourist destination. It is worth restating the remarkable statistic that Tanzania has dedicated more than 25 percent of its national territory to some form of conservation; 14 percent of that land is dedicated to national parks and the NCA, and the remaining 11 percent is managed as forest reserves, game reserves, or GCAS. Tanzania has more than 140 hunting blocks, the actual territories allocated to hunting companies, covering 250,000 square kilometers that are leased to approximately sixty hunting companies, the majority of which are owned by investors from the United States, South Africa, and Europe. These hunting concessions are located throughout the country in game reserves, GCAS, or state-designated open areas.

One of the far-reaching policies of German and British colonialism was limiting Africans' traditional hunting rights while promoting recreational safari hunting for Europeans. From the first years of German occupation and rule in the 1890s up until the 1920s, European hunters could shoot game without a license almost anywhere they pleased. Licenses were introduced in the early 1920s, when the government granted sport hunters a large quota per license and allowed them to hunt anywhere in the country except in game reserves; this lasted until the 1950s.[21] Big-game hunting has long been a controversial practice around the world, with strong feelings both in support and against. The influential German conservationist and Frankfurt Zoo director Bernhard Grzimek cast aspersions on hunting in his 1956 documentary *No Room for Wild Animals* when he stated, "All one has to do is go into Nairobi and hire oneself a 'safari' from one of the agencies. Everything is then laid on—a hot bath every evening in the city of tents in the middle of the bush, ice-cold drinks, an excellent cuisine—and the wild animals brought to just the right distance from the gun to ensure that they can be shot dead without any danger."[22]

In an unpublished 1983 essay, Maasai leader Lazaro Parkipuny described hunting more graphically and bluntly:

> Indeed the excitement of the whites, colonial civil servants, missionaries and settlers alike was not climaxed in watching, photographing and describing the scenery and wealth of wildlife they found here. Their pleasure was only recorded and hearts fulfilled at sights such as the heaviest ivory from the biggest horn of

a ferocious rhino that took a bullet in his brain, the display of the biggest horns of a sable antelope shot; the distance at which an eland was killed with a small caliber rifle, etc. . . .

The main attraction of the Serengeti to Europeans at the time, up until the 1930s, was *shooting lions* [that were] helpless in the extended [plains].[23]

Hunting remains an emotional and contested issue in conservation circles. Many conservation and animal welfare groups passionately advocate against hunting. Others argue that well-managed big-game trophy hunting is an effective conservation tool for regulating species that might otherwise destroy their habitats. Proponents also claim that hunting is one of the most lucrative forms of safari tourism to generate revenue for conservation.[24]

In the early 1950s, the Tanganyika Game Department began to regulate hunting more tightly, attaching specific fees to each animal and demarcating ninety GCAs to protect important wildlife areas. After independence, the Game Department increased its revenue by using game reserves and GCAs for hunting. In an effort to reorganize control over the hunting industry, the socialist government banned all sport hunting from 1970 to 1978. Then in 1978 the Tanzanian government created a parastatal company, TAWICO, to oversee and manage hunting throughout the country. Although the intent was to nationalize hunting, as the socialist government was doing with most sectors of the economy, TAWICO regularly subleased many of the hunting blocks to private companies, mainly from Europe.

Accusations of corruption and mismanagement burdened TAWICO, and by 1988 the government had placed control of the hunting industry under the WD of the MNRT. The WD significantly expanded hunting areas, almost doubling the number of available hunting blocks to 130, covering approximately 180,000 square kilometers, or 25 percent of Tanzania's land surface. The hunting areas were almost evenly distributed between unoccupied game reserves and GCAs and open areas, which were both occupied by both people and wildlife. In the late 1980s, the WD established the current fee structure and model of leasing individual hunting blocks to private hunting outfitters.

Situating the OBC in Loliondo

Relations between Loliondo communities and the OBC have become increasingly tense and hostile over the past two decades. This does not mean, however, that communities are necessarily against hunting or even against the OBC's use of the area. The OBC's strange and sensational arrival onto the hunting scene in Tanzania introduced a number of new norms and practices. Not only was the OBC the first company to build its own international airstrip in a remote region of the country, but the company also used the area exclusively as a private reserve for its guests rather than as a profit-generating hunting enterprise. Because of this, the OBC often used the area less intensively than other companies and in the early years only set up hunting camps for approximately two months, in September and October. Over time, OBC parties stayed longer, leading to more conflict with Maasai residents and ecotourism companies who also used the area for their own safari activities. The OBC was also different in the way it engaged with local communities. OBC officials hired a local manager who was responsible for representing the company's interests. The manager dealt primarily with district officials but initially hired area youth to work in the hunting camps. Many of these jobs were low-paying temporary positions, clearing grass and setting up tents. However, the OBC did employ a number of Loliondo youth who had attended secondary-school and spoke English as drivers and higher-level camp staff. In the first decade the OBC made a concerted effort to hire local people and build strong ties to local leaders. This changed after the OBC hired a new manager in 2002 and began hiring the majority of its staff from other parts of Tanzania and from Kenya.

The OBC's exclusive rights to both of Loliondo's hunting blocks was not a foregone conclusion. When the OBC first applied for both of the Loliondo hunting blocks in 1991, another influential group from the United Arab Emirates was also applying to use the area. The head of that group, a man known as Malala, had formed close relationships with several Maasai leaders including Parkipuny. At the same time that the OBC was solidifying its position with the central government by, for example, donating vehicles to the WD, Malala was working with Maasai leaders to gain their support. Malala donated four two-way radios, a large generator, and approximately five thousand dollars to support the Emanyatta secondary school, a community school established for students from the region. Not only were Maasai leaders contrasting the OBC with the ecotourism safari companies operating in the area; they were also comparing the OBC to this different United Arab Emirates–based hunting company that seemed to work more closely and openly with local representatives. In 1995 the OBC was granted exclusive hunting rights to the area. Local leaders believe that they used their influence to have Malala deported.[25]

Despite their skepticism about the OBC, Maasai leaders in Loliondo did not strongly resist the OBC lease for several reasons. First, there was a history of insecurity near the border of Serengeti National Park; Kuria and Sukuma people crossed the park to steal Maasai cattle. Many Maasai thought that the OBC's presence, with its many vehicles and police presence, would secure the area from cattle rustling. They believed that the OBC's presence might actually enable

Maasai to reestablish territorial control of their village land near the Serengeti. Second, the OBC initially employed several local Maasai as camp managers, construction foremen, camp guards, and porters, as well as seasonally employing a number of young Maasai men. Finally, the OBC promises of development assistance, including the drilling of several boreholes for water and the construction of a new secondary school, were seen as benefits in contrast with previous hunting companies that had simply used the area and left the villagers with nothing to show for it.[26] As one Loliondo leader told me, describing his early support of the OBC agreement, "I encouraged people to re-sign the contract with the OBC. We didn't have a problem with the investor, but he must fulfill his promises to employ youth until the projects are finished. At least we could hold him accountable to the contract."[27]

By 2000, however, local impressions had changed. A series of droughts had made the seasonal grazing available near the park boundary more essential to the pastoral land-use patterns of most residents. Being excluded from the area when the OBC was hunting began to pose a serious threat to Maasai livelihoods. A young Maasai man from Soitsambu village told me, "The OBC has started to change. In the past the OBC didn't stop livestock. Now they stop livestock. They try to build a positive relationship but now tell people to get rid of livestock."[28] A new camp manager hired in 2002 was hostile to many local Maasai and began employing young men from other regions instead of local youth. By the early twenty-first century, only a handful of Maasai remained employed by the OBC, and they were mostly performing menial jobs as guards or grass cutters, which paid very low day wages. After almost a decade, very few of the development projects initially promised by the OBC had been realized. Finally, the government began to aggressively defend the OBC's exclusive rights to use the Loliondo hunting area outlined in the contract. As one male elder told me in 2004, "To have them [the OBC] here is like a thorn in your leg that you can't take out."[29]

An elder Maasai man living near the OBC hunting area told me, "He [the OBC] is a giant [and] we failed to move him. Without this wildlife and this good land, he will move without even saying good-bye."[30] The man was referring to a widely discussed plan to poison water sources in the hunting area. Residents reasoned that if the OBC wouldn't leave their land, they would take away what the company found valuable by killing the wildlife. I asked if this strategy would harm other tourists using the area. He said, "We love all other tourist companies except [the OBC]." When I asked if the OBC harassed Maasai for being in the company's hunting area, he replied, "No! They can't. They sometimes come to *ronjos* [temporary cattle camps] near their camp and say, please give us space to hunt. One day we put trees on the [airstrip] to stop their plane. They are afraid of us. They are afraid of us because this land is not theirs." Whether or not this show of confidence and bravery was put on for my behalf, the people I interviewed in this one particular homestead and across Loliondo seemed emboldened by the idea that they were defending what was rightfully theirs. The belief that the land was theirs and that it must be recognized as such was a powerful narrative, capable of mobilizing the Maasai throughout Loliondo. As I will discuss at the end of this chapter, this discourse of Maasai land rights was critical in helping leaders organize Maasai interests across villages and different Maasai ethnic groups.

In 2001 several Maasai families reestablished permanent homesteads near the Serengeti National Park border and close to the area used by the OBC. Their move was widely supported by traditional leaders who saw the OBC's presence as a means of permanently dispossessing the Maasai of their land. Many of the Maasai I interviewed expressed a desire not only to remove the OBC but also to regain the land they had lost to the national park. The idea of regaining land was not so far-fetched: in 2005 the Kenyan government degazetted Amboseli National Park. The Kenyan government took management of the area away from the Kenya Wildlife Service and turned it over to the Olkejuado County Council and the local Maasai people. Although few Maasai believed they would repossess Serengeti National Park, most Maasai in Loliondo were determined not to lose any more land to conservation.

The OBC and State Revenue

When Brigadier Mohammed Abdulrahim al-Ali began high-level talks with government officials in late 1991, Tanzania had just recently deregulated tourist hunting, shifting oversight and management from the state-owned TAWICO to the WD. Beginning in 1988, the WD began to allocate hunting blocks to private outfitters for five-year periods. Hunting advocates pushed for longer lease terms to encourage sustainable management of wildlife by private companies and outfitters. Many companies saw the five-year allocations as a step in the right direction, even if they preferred even longer leases. At the time, two private local outfitters were using the two Loliondo hunting blocks (Loliondo was divided into a southern block A and a northern block B) through a sublease from TAWICO. The two local outfitters had been preparing to bid for the hunting concession when they came up for lease in 1994. But instead, the government transferred the hunting rights directly from TAWICO to the OBC in 1992.

From early on, the OBC was an important source of revenue for the state. The OBC paid game fees, observer fees, conservation fees, permit fees, and trophy-handling fees. And to maintain good relations with the government, it paid fees based on 100 percent of its hunting quota, regardless of what OBC guests actually killed.[31] For example, in 2009 the OBC paid $560,000 to the central government and $109,000 to the Ngorongoro District council; in 2008 it paid $150,000 to the six Maasai villages stipulated in its contract.[32] The amount paid to the central and district governments was a fivefold increase over revenues earned from the hunting blocks prior to the OBC's arrival in 1992.[33]

Beyond direct payments, the OBC donated at least thirty new vehicles, sophisticated radio equipment, and other unspecified "field gear" to the WD.[34] The company also paid the state police to escort its guests and funded the construction of a government secondary school in Loliondo. The OBC also helped to repair and maintain the road network in Loliondo, using road crews and equipment that the company had brought in to build a private landing strip and develop a network of roads in its hunting blocks.[35]

In 1992 the WD changed its process for allocating hunting revenues: 75 percent of profits went into the state treasury, and 25 percent went toward the Tanzania Wildlife Protection Fund (TWPF). This fund was established to provide "rural people with revenue from tourist hunting."[36] Although the TWPF is intended to channel revenue directly to rural people living in proximity to hunting activities, the funds are in practice dispersed to district governments. There is little evidence to show that this money has been given directly to rural people or villages or that it has been used for local development activities.[37] There are no public records pertaining to the TWPF, which is internally audited by the government. In 2010 an anonymous report was circulated to private tour operators and journalists. The exposé, titled simply "Inside the WD (Wildlife Division)," was written by someone with intimate knowledge of the agency's inner workings. The report alleges that the Tanzanian Hunting Operators Association (TAHOA) uses the funds generated from the TWPF to influence the director of the WD, who in turn uses the money to influence elected officials and government officers. While this is one perspective on corruption within the WD, there is widespread belief that the WD benefits disproportionately from hunting activities.

Renewing the OBC Contract

In sharp contrast to the state's policy declaring ecotourism investors and the village-based tourism contracts illegal (see chapter 6), in 2002 government officials encouraged the OBC to renew its contract with the villages and to substantially increase its direct payments. The district commissioner strongly encouraged the village governments to enter into a new "development cooperation contract" with the OBC. Although skeptical, some village leaders hoped this renewal would provide a genuine opportunity to negotiate the terms of an agreement and to seek recognition for their village land rights. What they found, however, was an agreement that lacked basic information, such as a timeframe or mechanisms for increasing fees. The new contract also stipulated that the OBC would coordinate grazing patterns in collaboration with the villages. It proposed establishing a joint management committee that would include village and company representatives, to ensure that hunting and grazing activities did not "collide."

Unsatisfied, Maasai leaders drafted their own alternative contract to present to the OBC. This contract shared core elements with the OBC proposal but reinforced village land rights. The Maasai version also included a stipulation to allow other nonhunting tourism, which provided 80 percent of village income, on village lands. The district commissioner rejected this alternative proposal and presented village leaders with a "take it or leave it" proposition.

Despite complaints by village leaders and the refusal of elected officials from two villages to sign, the OBC contract was renewed in 2007, with the OBC increasing its annual payment to each village from two thousand to twenty-five thousand dollars. One of the new stipulations was that the Maasai not bring their livestock into the OBC's hunting area when the OBC was present. This language was similar to the village-based joint-venture contracts, which included similar stipulations to avoid bringing livestock into the core tourism areas during the tourist season, but in these cases there were exceptions for granting access when necessary. There were no such provisions with the OBC contract.

Loliondo leaders were unhappy with the policy changes and the lack of village representation in determining the new contract with the OBC. In a meeting on December 18, 2007, village leaders from all six villages that overlapped with the OBC hunting area expressed their objections.[38] They stated that the OBC had not fulfilled its promises to provide social services; that OBC employees had harassed community members; that the OBC had illegally built permanent structures, including two cement houses and an airstrip, which interfered with regional grazing patterns; and that the OBC's presence was "disturbing the tour operators who provide reasonable money for villages' development projects." Finally, the village leaders expressed their fear that the OBC's ongoing presence would lead to "changing Loliondo grazing land into [a] game reserve to serve the interest of the Hunting Arab Company [sic]."[39] These fears were reinforced in a meeting between village representatives and the Ngorongoro District commissioner in which he "ordered" village leaders to set aside areas for hunting within their village lands. He told them not to farm or build any grazing camps in the hunting areas. Maasai leaders' fears that the new contract was a tool to turn village land into a game reserve were coming to pass.

Despite these new restrictions, only one village, Arash, refused to accept the OBC payment. The other village leaders signed the contract. One village leader who signed the contract but opposed the OBC told me that "communities decided to accept the money but not the contract. The communities and NGOs proposed their own alternative contract [to the OBC], but the OBC refused."[40] Not one Maasai leader I interviewed saw the arrangement with the OBC as a legally binding contract. Maasai leaders consistently described the contract as an agreement that was open for some negotiation. One village leader told me that since he never had any say in drafting the OBC arrangement, it was not really an agreement. When I asked him what it was, he told me it was a way to get something from the hunting company. Without it they would get nothing. He explained that if the OBC wanted a real agreement, the company would have to invite the Maasai to negotiate. Until then, the arrangement was all on the government's terms, he told me. In taking the money for the OBC contract and hoping to renegotiate the terms later, many Maasai leaders apparently did not anticipate the possibility of strict enforcement. To their surprise, state officials chose to enforce the new contract, with its stronger language about restricting grazing during hunting season. And the method of enforcement was the eviction of the Maasai from their land.

The evictions of 2009 were an unprecedented event in Loliondo. Yet many Maasai leaders I spoke with saw them as simply the latest government effort to dominate Maasai people by controlling their land. For all the wealth and power of the OBC, and with a national critique of foreign ownership of Tanzania, many Maasai I interviewed saw the OBC primarily as the state's partner and not the driving force of their dispossession. They believed that the OBC deal was the best way for the state to reassert its control over Maasailand. Though companies like the OBC are often seen as the primary protagonists in the global land grab, the Maasai see them as the latest pawn in the state's plans to take their land. Many Maasai I spoke with expressed their belief that the OBC may gain short-term benefits but the state ultimately gains control over their land and natural resources.

Loliondogate: State Making in Neoliberal Times

The WD's granting of the Loliondo hunting blocks to the OBC in 1992 sparked a national scandal. The public representation of the OBC deal was as one in which the government had rewritten the rules to allocate land to wealthy investors from Dubai, an example of the government selling out its people to the highest bidder. Journalists dubbed the land allocation Loliondogate, and the story was invoked over and over in articles and reports to describe the status and role of foreign investors in the "new Tanzania."[41] Critics linked this apparent abuse of power by central authorities to the emerging neoliberal investment climate, portraying the government as desperate to attract capital and the OBC as being able to do whatever it pleased without oversight.[42] The OBC's presence coincided with an increasing number of land conflicts throughout the 1990s between rural Tanzanians and foreign investors in different economic sectors including agriculture, industry, and tourism. The highly publicized Tanzanian Land Commission inquiry headed by University of Dar es Salaam law professor Issa Shivji highlighted these struggles.[43]

Since the 1990s, Tanzanian civil society has used the OBC controversy to question the relationship between the state, foreign investors, and citizens and to raise a central question about neoliberal development: Who is it for? One 2009 newspaper editorial highlighted the contradictions of neoliberal development in the context of the OBC agreement:

> There is now a widespread feeling that investor rights in [Loliondo], which has been under the spotlight since 1993 [*sic*] when the government leased it to a senior UAE [United Arab Emirates] military officer, have been overblown and overprotected while compromising the interests of local people. It is time to call for a review of the [OBC] contract, in which the economic interests of having the investor in place are weighed against those of the local population, which should be given the first priority.[44]

There are several ways to interpret the OBC's presence and influence in Loliondo. One is through the lens of Maasai communities, which view the company as promoting the state's agenda of national development in spite of the desires and needs of local people. Another is from the vantage of critics of neoliberal development and, more specifically, critics of big-game safari hunting. These activists, journalists, and scholars see the OBC as buying access and rights and wielding their immense wealth and power to do whatever they please, to turn Loliondo into their private hunting reserve. From the perspective of state employees, bureaucrats, and administrators, however, the OBC was a tactical partner. For the Ngorongoro District government, the OBC, with its seemingly infinite wealth, could provide the resources for development that the district was charged with delivering. For these state actors, the OBC appeared to have the funds and expertise to finally "mine" the natural resources of the region, even if these resources were aboveground wildlife and not subterranean minerals and oil.[45]

Tanzania remains one of the world's poorest countries. The SAPs and other political and economic reforms of the mid-1980s have not created widespread employment or significantly increased the average annual earnings for the majority of citizens. In the throes of adapting to a free-market political and economic system in the early and mid-1990s, Tanzanian state agencies came to depend on partnerships with companies like the OBC; such arrangements became necessary for the state to adequately govern. In his book *On the Post-*

colony (2001), political scientist and philosopher Achille Mbembe describes the social formations arising from these emerging articulations among capital, civil society, and the state. He portrays such arrangements as "private indirect government." He says that a prominent feature of postcolonial states in Africa and other former colonies in Asia, Latin American, and the Caribbean is "the privatisation of sovereignty." He argues that historically weak African states, made even more vulnerable through SAPs, became dependent on outside support to carry out their everyday functions and maintain their legitimacy.

Neoliberal reforms opened up opportunities for state actors to work closely with private capital. Investors offered money and other external resources necessary to reproduce the basic functions of local government, creating a way to fund governance in such resource-poor contexts. In return, state actors offered private investors protections and assurances that they had the authority to defend investors' rights to resources. That is, state officials leveraged their authority in the form of national sovereignty to promote foreign investment and recruit investors as collaborators. Along with international NGOs and development agencies, foreign investors played a central role in supporting state functions. Government bureaucracies could largely manage the ways that NGO assistance and development aid were dispersed and implemented. Foreign investors were different: although dependent on state approval and support, they often wielded considerably more power than other development partners. State officials had to work hard to channel foreign investment in ways that explicitly helped the state. One way to understand government interests and actions in Loliondo is through the prism of a struggle over the privatization of sovereignty. Tanzania is a relatively weak state, competing with other weak states for private capital, and national sovereignty is one of the most valuable resources that state actors there have to offer investors.

In their article "Spatializing States: Toward an Ethnography of Neoliberal Governmentality," anthropologists James Ferguson and Akhil Gupta (2002) elaborate on this idea. They claim that a commonsense understanding of the state as a unified entity reinforces the appearance of encompassment, whereby the national interests are seen to incorporate and dominate all local interests. But, they say, such spatial metaphors obscure the fragility of such an image of the state: "The extent to which states are successful in establishing their claims to encompass the local is therefore not preordained, but is a contingent outcome of specific sociopolitical processes. And, as the precarious situation of many states in Africa today makes especially clear, the state has no automatic right to success in claiming the vertical heights of sovereignty."[46]

The village-based joint-venture contracts that the Maasai entered into in the 1990s (described in chapter 1 and discussed further in chapter 6) presented a direct challenge to the state's claims to encompassment and national sovereignty. Many Maasai believed that if they could negotiate directly with foreign investors, they would be able to channel the associated representational and material power to support their own claims over land and resources. Thus we can begin to comprehend why state actors ordered the evictions of its citizens in Loliondo in 2009 in the name of protecting the contractual rights of the OBC. Mbembe argues that new modes of governing such as the OBC agreement are not simply a matter of the state surrendering sovereignty to capital but rather an alliance between the state and capital based on mutual dependence. But as a close look at the initial agreement between the OBC and the Ngorongoro District government illustrates, it is unclear how much agency the state has when dealing with foreign investors. Rather than a strategic partnership based on mutual interests, these relationships often remake the interests and values of state institutions, aligning them closely to those of the investors.

Within the context of neoliberal development, where the reach of wealthy investors seems endless and peripheral landscapes like those in Loliondo appear all too ripe for the picking, companies like the OBC are often presented as the primary protagonists of the "global land grab." From this macro view, nation-states like Tanzania as well as marginalized cultural groups like the Maasai both appear as victims of neoliberalization. But this is not necessarily how state actors or Maasai people understand the politics of neoliberalism. For both of these groups, the current political and economic system offers opportunities as well as obstacles to redefining the state, its territorial authority, and the meaning of citizenship.

Neoliberal Territoriality

Demarcating lands for conservation has helped to secure the foundations of modern nation-states across the globe, especially in sub-Saharan Africa. Summarizing the link between conservation and state making, geographer Rod Neumann explains, "States come into being by asserting control over mosaics of commons, dispossessing local, non-state entities of pre-existing claims and rights in the process. States assert control through scientific and technical acts of surveying, inventorying, zoning and mapping the living resources of its territory. . . . These actions in effect enclose local commons and transfer ownership to the state, which then controls the allocation of benefits from the land and its biological resources" (2005, 121). In Tanzania almost 25 percent of the land base is under state protection and control as either a national park, a game reserve, a forest reserve, or a hunting concession.

When I first visited Loliondo in 1992, I heard stories of the government wanting to expand Serengeti National Park into Loliondo. On return visits over the past twenty years, I have heard references to the imminent creation of a new conservation area, be it a buffer zone, a corridor, a game reserve, or a WMA. On August 15, 2009, just weeks after the evictions and in the midst of a chaotic scene in Loliondo, the district commissioner used a very public ceremony to distribute checks from the OBC to nine villages in Loliondo.[47] Since then there have not been any further evictions, but the Loliondo Maasai have lived with much uncertainty as well as considerable fear of permanent dispossession.

Responding to the Loliondo leaders, state officials used the example of the violence of the 2009 evictions to justify a policy that would once and for all separate people and wildlife in Loliondo. They argued that such a separation was necessary to prevent future conflicts. The government proposed to turn the current village land that had supported thriving wildlife populations for several decades into a new protected area. In July 2010, the minister of natural resources and tourism, Shamsa Mwanguga, announced that the government had resolved the "Loliondo stand-off" by clearly defining the boundaries used by pastoralists and those used for conservation.[48] She stated, "That's why the government decided to demarcate the areas by putting boundaries between the areas used by pastoralists and the reserved areas."[49] This radical proposal to essentially dispossess the Maasai of a significant portion of their land was being justified in the name of national and regional security, and ultimately as protecting the interests of wildlife and local communities. Even before this action, government officials had been promoting a plan to demarcate the OBC hunting concession as a new conservation area for hunting. Many people I interviewed believe that the evictions were intended to create the appearance of instability and give the government an excuse to finally create a new protected area, which would effectively exclude all Maasai activity. The Maasai continue to aggressively oppose this effort. In 2013 the government backed down from its plans to create the wildlife corridor only to put it back in place in November 2014.

The Bureaucratic Spaces of Maasai Activism

On August 11, 2010, Maasai leaders from Loliondo and central government representatives participated in a meeting in Karatu to discuss land issues in Loliondo. The official premise was to discuss why villages in Loliondo were not participating in the new district land-use planning exercise. Loliondo villages had up until then resisted the new planning process because they feared that the government would use it to take their land for hunting.

The meeting was organized by regional NGOs and had taken more than a year to plan. It cost approximately 17 million Tanzanian shillings, or $17,000, for approximately one hundred people to meet for two days.[50] Given the high profile of the Loliondo evictions and land conflicts, the meeting was framed as a chance for regional and national leaders to discuss land-use planning in Loliondo to resolve conflicts. As a representative from one of the organizing NGOs said, "The point of this meeting is to plan land use in Loliondo that will bear good trust for the area."[51] The Ngorongoro District commissioner welcomed everyone and thanked the sponsoring organizations. He referred to these organizations as "our development partners" and said, "We can't bring development anywhere without these private-public partnerships." He stated that "better use of our land" was necessary to uplift the Tanzanian economy and community. Despite the efforts of a "small group of people who are trying to prevent us from developing," he contended, private groups like NGOs and investors "needed to work together with the government to bring development to our *Jamii* [society/family/community]."

He then summarized how he hoped the meeting would help resolve the conflicts in Loliondo: "It looks to others outside that we don't understand land issues like other districts. Let's use this seminar to join others who are benefiting from their land. . . . Let's use the policies and laws of this country to plan the best use of our land." Without naming names or being too specific, the district commissioner returned to the question of Loliondo residents resisting the government's attempts to create a new conservation area. He cast the resistance to district planning as the work of a few misguided individuals who were looking out for their own personal interests. He presented the government as looking out for the common good and those Maasai leaders opposing the planning effort as serving their own interests. "Let's put this individualism aside and work together as a community," he said, "as a village, as a ward, as a district, as a Jamii [community]."

While officially the meeting was organized to help villages demarcate their boundaries and create land-use plans, the village leaders and NGO organizers saw it as an opportunity to confront the government and openly discuss the OBC contract and evictions. The moderator asked participants to describe what they thought was the purpose of the meeting. There were several comments indicating that participants wanted to learn more about the planning process and implementing the new land laws. After about fifteen minutes, an older Maasai man rose and said, "I thought it would be a chance to discuss the conflict between the citizens of Ngorongoro [Loliondo] and the OBC. Given that everyone is here and the DC [district commissioner] is here, we would find out where the conflict with the OBC is." For most of the Loliondo residents in attendance, the two issues of land-use planning and conflict with the OBC were inextricably linked. The Maasai feared that the OBC's influence with district and regional authorities would unduly influence the district planning process. Two decades of the OBC's hunting in Loliondo had given the Maasai little confidence that any planning process would promote their interest. The meeting continued for several hours, methodically working through the technical aspects of village land-use planning. Having observed several similar meetings in the past, I felt that I was witnessing a game of cat and mouse with both sides staying just far enough away from the core issues to preclude any meaningful debate. Nonetheless, both sides made it clear that they were not backing down from their positions.

Later in the afternoon, one of the elected council members revealed that the government had already visited Loliondo to survey the land and demarcate a new conservation area for hunting. After heated comments, the Ngorongoro District lawyer, Clarence Kipobota, declared that the officials were only carrying out the minister's plan to divide village land and to create an *usharoba* (wildlife corridor): "1,500 square kilometers for the wildlife corridor and 2,500 square kilometers for village land." He followed this by saying, "The area was not very big." At this point the meeting erupted, with most of the men in the audience standing up and protesting. Once the meeting facilitators got everyone to calm down and take their seats, the lawyer continued explaining why this new district land-use plan made sense. He argued that creating the corridor—which would effectively dispossess the Maasai living in Loliondo of more than 37 percent of their land—was actually a way to protect residents from unscrupulous investors. "When there is a valuable resource, there is a conflict," he said. "Local people want to benefit, but now around the world investors are also looking for these valuable resources. Investors often have *sauti sana* [a lot of power] to be heard." He maintained that creating a *pori tengefu* (protected area) would limit the ability of investors to take advantage of innocent villagers: "This land-use plan is being proposed as a solution to the conflict that happened in July 2009." The cruel irony of taking Maasai land to resolve a conflict that had been instigated by the government on behalf of a foreign investor was not lost on the audience. Loliondo leaders convincingly insist that government plans for a new protected area illustrate how tourism investment that is solely accountable to central authorities legitimates a state territorial strategy to rule Maasailand. Such legal justifications proved to Maasai leaders that their fears were well founded.

To support his case further, the lawyer cited the Wildlife Act of 2009, which stated that hunting blocks needed to be separated from village areas. The village chairman from Arash contested the argument, telling the lawyer that this was still an unsettled clause in the law, as it conflicted with the country's Land Law of 1999: "If there are any conflicts between laws, then the land law is the mother law" and takes precedent. Village leaders and national officials utilized the ambiguities in new policies and laws written in support of neoliberal reforms to assert their claims to authority over their lands and resources and their rights. The village chairman asked the district lawyer if village land titles were still valid. They were, he replied. "Then why is the district trying to go around the villages to create this plan?" he asked. The lawyer had no direct answer. Instead, he invoked a classic trope that framed the Maasai as ignorant and backward: "Refusing development is no way to protect your land and have development." But as far as the Maasai in the room were concerned, development in this context meant state accumulation and not increased opportunity or prosperity for Maasai people. Resisting this kind of development in favor of another sort was precisely how the Maasai planned to protect their land.

The meeting laid bare the strong opposition to creating a new protected-area wildlife corridor in the heart of Loliondo rangelands. And because a new district land-use plan requires the approval of local representatives, the meeting achieved a temporary suspension of the planned protected area. During a tea break, one of the Maasai village representatives told me, "*Simba ameshaingia boma,*" the lion is already in the *boma*. This was the same as saying that the wolves were at the door. The Maasai have continued to use meetings like this, as well as legal action, national and international media coverage, demonstrations and protests, and working through the district political system to resist national efforts to create this new protected area in Loliondo. By preventing the government from implementing its plan for over five years, Loliondo leaders rank as some of the most successful activists in the country in protecting their land rights. Yet despite their efforts, the government appears committed to establishing the wildlife corridor. As of November 2014, the Tanzanian government had informed the Maasai community of its intent to enclose the 1,500-square-kilometer area.

Conclusion

In April 2002, the MNRT publicly defended the hunting practices of the OBC and the government's role in allocating the concession and overseeing the activities of the company.[52] Among the points raised were that the OBC adhered to all laws and regulations governing the tourist hunting industry, which included paying all appropriate fees and hunting only those animals allowed. The ministry also cited the OBC's contribution to district development, including building a primary and secondary school, drilling boreholes, procuring generators and water pumps, constructing cattle dips, and purchasing buses to enhance local transportation. The ministry pointed out that the company contributed revenue directly to six villages and paid school fees for twenty-one area children. After rebutting accusations of illegal hunting practices and the transport of live animals from Loliondo to the United Arab Emirates, the ministry made it perfectly clear to Kenyan organizations opposing hunting in Tanzania, and to anyone else who was listening, what wildlife meant to Tanzania:

> The wildlife found in Tanzania is the property of the Government of Tanzania. The notion that these animals belong to Kenya is not correct. The wild animals in Loliondo Game Controlled Area do not have dual citizenship. Since some animal species move back and forth between Tanzania and Kenya it is better understood that these animals would be recognised to belong to either party during the time they are in that particular country. Animals in Maasai Mara, Serengeti, Loliondo and Ngorongoro belong to one ecosystem namely, Serengeti ecosystem. However, Tanzania being a sovereign State with her own policies has the right by law to implement them.[53]

If we replace the word "Kenya" with the phrase "the villages of Loliondo," the ministry's explanation reveals more than an international dispute over resources: maintaining the government's rights over wildlife within national boundaries is critical to maintaining state sovereignty and authority. Claiming that Tanzanian villages had no more rights over Tanzanian wildlife than Kenyan citizens illuminates the importance of how the idea of private property is developing in Tanzania today. Proponents of neoliberal policies argue that tourism investment should strengthen private-property rights and minimize the central power of the nation state. Tanzania's efforts to turn Loliondo into a national hunting corridor indicate otherwise. Much like the Maasai themselves, Tanzanian government officials are translating the meanings and implications of neoliberal development to a number of audiences. Rather than submit to the idea that decentralization leads to more-efficient and effective environmental management, government officials draw on the current policy context to reassert the need for centralized state authority. Many public employees remain strongly attached to their belief in the validity of the nationalist project as the right way to govern resources and people. This notion is especially strong among civil servants in the conservation sector.[54] But beyond combining the still-persistent idea that African nature is too valuable to be managed by Africans, government officials are able to recast themselves as agents of neoliberal modernity, in which the market logics of efficiency replace the socialist beliefs in collective national interests. In Tanzania neoliberalism is actively reshaping the terrain on which the state reimagines and asserts its role as a sovereign power.

Area shared by livestock and wildlife and used as mobile
safari campsites, Loliondo. Photo by author.

Maasai woman preparing tea inside her home,
Soitsambu village, Loliondo. Photo by author.

Sheep and goats grazing on Maasai village land near boundary
of Serengeti National Park, Loliondo. Photo by author.

Mobile safari campsite, Loliondo. Photo by author.

Cattle grazing in
Soitsambu village,
Loliondo.
Photo by author.

Cut-out images of Julius
Nyerere, first president of
Tanzania, and Bernhard
Grzimek, veterinarian
and advocate for African
conservation and
specifically for creating
Serengeti National Park.
Photo taken by author
at Serengeti National
Park Visitors Center.

Photo of President Julius Nyerere granting a diploma to Maasai MP and
KIPOC founder Lazaro Moringe Parkipuny at the University of Dar es Salaam
in 1975. Photographer unknown, print in possession of the author.

Airplane of the Ortello Business
Corporation and airplane of
the Ngorongoro Conservation
Authority at the Arusha
Airport. Photo by author.

Avaaz campaign flyer protesting the eviction of Maasai from their village land in Loliondo for trophy hunting.

Contested property of Sukenya site of Thomson Safaris Enashiva Nature Refuge project, Loliondo. Photo by author.

Elected district representative and Maasai civil society leader. Photo by author.

Maasai village meeting to discuss impact of safari tourism
in Ololosokwan, Loliondo. Photo by author.

CHAPTER 5

Nature Refuge

Reconstructed Identity and the Cultural Politics of Tourism Investment

In 2006, the owners of the U.S. tourism company Thomson Safaris leased 12,617 acres of land in the heart of three Maasai villages in Loliondo. The lease granted a subsidiary company, Tanzania Conservation Limited (TCL), exclusive land rights for ninety-six years. The land, known to local people as "The Breweries" or "Sukenya Farm," was used as grazing land by Maasai residents and contained an important water source, the *oltimi* spring. The land had also been the site of a government-run barley farm from 1987 to 1989, under the state-owned company Tanzania Breweries Limited (TBL). After unsuccessfully trying to farm barley, TBL effectively abandoned the area in 1989, leaving the land to be used as it had for hundreds of years, for grazing and watering livestock. The land was particularly valuable as a grazing reserve, or *olakari*, for young calves, sick animals, and essential milking herds that needed to stay close to Maasai homesteads.

The Thomson Safaris owners created the company, TCL, a subsidiary of Thomson Safaris' parent company Wineland-Thomson Adventures, Inc., to facilitate the deal.[1] The owners of Thomson Safaris had been interested in starting a community conservation project in Tanzania for years, and this land, with no large-scale agriculture or significant permanent settlements, presented a perfect opportunity. As is the case throughout East Africa, wildlife largely coexist with pastoralists given their mutual need for rangeland, water, and minerals, including salt. Although most conservationists and ecologists recognize the compatibility of pastoralists and wildlife, representations of pastoralists degrading the land still abound. Historically, the belief that African pastoralism is an open-access grazing system that inevitably destroys rangelands contributed to the justifications for conservation lobbyists and state officials to appropriate vast pastoralist territories to create national parks and conservation areas. Conservation advocates argued that protecting these areas was the most effective way to protect African nature and would also promote national development through international safari tourism. More recently, with the rise of community conservation, donors and investors have seen pastoralist lands as promising places to conserve existing wildlife habitat outside core protected areas. Pastoralists understand current conservation projects through a historical lens of pastoral territories being taken in the name of conservation.

As the new owners of the old TBL farm, TCL promptly renamed the area Enashiva, a Maasai word for happiness that, according to the company, had been the Maasai name for the creek that ran through the property.[2] According to the company blog, "Enashiva represents the culmination of nearly 30 years of Thomson's commitment to Tanzania." Thomson Safaris hoped that Enashiva would be a "model for community development, conservation, and responsible tourism." Along with its goal to restore the Enashiva land to its natural state and increase wildlife numbers, the company planned "numerous local projects for the benefit of the community," including drilling a borehole and water well; establishing a controlled grazing program; providing ongoing support to local schools; funding a women's collaborative; and training local people to work for the company.[3] Enashiva was to be a place where Thomson Safaris' clients could see that their tourism experience was helping to preserve African nature and promote development in Maasai communities. On its face, the Enashiva Nature Refuge looked like an ideal community conservation project in Tanzania.

Much to the company's surprise, Maasai leaders in Loliondo immediately protested the sale and plans to turn the land into a conservation project. The way Enashiva came into being stood in stark contrast to the village-based joint-venture tourism projects described in chapter 6, in which village governments granted ecotourism companies access to village lands. It was also viewed differently than was the OBC hunting concession described in chapter 4. Although controversial, until the evictions in 2009 and the subsequent government attempts to enclose fifteen hundred square kilometers of Loliondo Maasai land as a new game reserve for hunting, the land on which the hunting block stood was still legally owned by the Maasai. In the Thomson Safaris case, the Tanzanian government granted a ninety-six-year lease to a foreign private investor to manage the land as it saw fit. With state-sanctioned property rights, Thomson Safaris/TCL could do what it pleased with the land. That it decided to create a private wildlife refuge was a major concern to the local community, who depended on the land for grazing and water for their livestock. Residents viewed Thomson Safaris/TCL owners' repeated statements that the project would bring benefits to the local community with more than a bit of skepticism—especially after their first actions were to burn all Maasai structures on the property and actively chase livestock from the land.

With a history of successful community tourism projects in Loliondo, the Thomson Safaris/TCL owners assumed that the Maasai villagers would be willing partners in their efforts to promote community conservation. In a promotional video, Thomson Safaris manager John Bearcroft explains, "We were trying to preserve a piece of heaven that we can share with our guests. . . . This was an opportunity . . . to give some value to the community for tourism."[4] Like many safari companies, the Thomson Safaris/TCL owners expressed their interest in bringing tourism revenue to local people as a way to encourage conservation and educate local people to value wildlife in new ways. But why then was there so much resistance to the project? Why didn't large numbers of community members embrace it? How did community members think about benefits from tourism? Was revenue and funding for local development projects a sufficient trade-off for losing access to twelve thousand acres of grazing land? Money earned from tourism over the previous decade had helped villages complete infrastructure projects, sponsor students to go to secondary school and university, as well as pay for village leaders to attend meetings and workshops related to tourism. But the village tourism joint ventures described in chapter 1 and discussed in detail in chapter 6 were fundamentally different from this project. Not only had they generated new sources of income, but they reinforced village land rights by giving the Maasai some leverage within the state in managing tourism in village lands. The Enashiva project looked like an altogether different thing. Monetary benefits were not enough to offset the political economic costs of losing land and authority, compromising long-term access to grazing resources.

Tracing the struggle over Enashiva reveals how interests are produced and represented through different tourism projects and the different ways that markets are made meaningful to groups like the Maasai, state agencies and officials, and tourism companies. The village-based joint ventures promoted the idea that villages and investors could use markets to recognize and amplify local ownership claims over natural resources. In contrast, the Enashiva project bound community conservation to state agendas for controlling territory and natural resources by centrally regulating foreign investment. To prevent Thomson Safaris/TCL from taking their land, the Maasai of Loliondo drew on their conviction, even if it lacked tangible evidence, that village land claims were equal to, if not more significant than, national claims. In partnership with ecotourism investors, Maasai villages used market forces to bolster collective claims. This chapter shows how the idea of privatizing nature is contingent on mobilizing certain understandings of community and making them legible to different audiences, including state officials, journalists, and tourists. It illustrates how private safari tourism companies, state officials, and community representatives work within a framework of free-market policies and ideologies to try to tilt the understanding and implementation of resource rights and control in their favor.

Buying Trouble

For Enashiva to work as a successful community conservation project, it needed to attract tourists who would generate revenue to channel back into managing the property as well as support development projects for the surrounding communities. To entice those tourists, Thomson Safaris promoted several tours at the "private nature refuge," including the twelve-day "Tanzania Discovery Safari" and "Wildlife & Cultural Safari." Similar to the exclusive opportunities offered through the tourism joint ventures described in chapter 6, Thomson Safaris offered a unique experience that promised to connect guests with real African landscapes and people. "The private nature refuge gives travelers the opportunity to explore the wilderness as well as the culture of the Maasai," according to Thomson Safaris promotional material.[5] "Travelers will have an unforgettable experience . . . when they visit a local women's group to witness how the women have started to plan for the future of their families. Later, the cultural exchange continues as your new Maasai friends gather around the campfire at your Nyumba [house] to share stories." The promise of Enashiva was that tourists could experience authentic landscapes and culture and that their presence and money would help to preserve them. Tanzania relies on investors like Thomson Safaris/TCL to bring money and expertise to generate revenue for the country and its citizens. Such a narrative of foreign investment frames investors as generous actors helping to bring development to poor and marginal people and places.

Thomson Safaris/TCL paid $1.2 million to TBL for the Enashiva land and invested more to manage the area for conservation and to bring new tourists. The company also helped establish a nonprofit foundation, Focus on Tanzanian Communities, which provides benefits to communities living near the company's tourism projects. As such, Thomson Safaris was in line with several ecotourism companies in Tanzania that were involved in funding and/or leading a separate NGO through which their clients could donate money for more philanthropic projects. Such affiliated NGOs further blurred the boundaries among the state, the market, and civil society and raised questions about the idea of a free market that operated independently. According to Thomson Safaris/TCL, purchasing land in Loliondo was not about making money for the company but rather about leaving a legacy for Tanzania. Even if profit was a secondary objective of the project, Thomson Safaris/TCL relied on free-market ideas to assert its legitimacy as a land manager and steward. Its reputation as a successful adventure tourism company gave it the credentials to promote safari tourism as a philanthropic development strategy.

For the Loliondo residents and leaders I interviewed, however, the Enashiva project delivered few real benefits. After TBL abandoned its property in 1989, the land reverted to a communal grazing area shared by Enadoshoke, Sukenya, and Monderosi, the three subvillages of Soitsambu village, where the land was located. The three Maasai ethnic sections or groups (*olosho*, pl. *iloshon*) that live in these villages, Laitayok, Loita, Purko, had come to agreement about using the land, which included a prohibition on large-scale agriculture. Managing wildlife was not an explicit goal of the communities' land use, but it was a subsidiary benefit of Maasai practices such as cultural taboos against hunting, no fences, and the use of fire and other techniques in managing the land for grasses that appeal to both livestock and wildlife. The villages' chief complaint against Thomson Safaris/TCL was that it was restricting grazing and water access on land that for hundreds of years had been a key pasture area and the primary dry-season water source for hundreds of families and thousands of livestock. For many Maasai, Enashiva was far from the "happy place" that Thomson Safaris planned to create.

Resistance to the Thomson Safaris project was largely associated with one charismatic leader, Lucy Asioki. Perhaps the most influential woman in Loliondo, Asioki was a Maasai from the Purko ethnic group, who grew up in the Monderosi subvillage of Soitsambu village. Maasai people come from a variety of ethnic sections and clans. Along with age-set groups, these social categories help regulate where people live, whom they marry, which traditional leaders they follow, and in times of conflict whom they organize with. Although it is increasingly common to marry across these categories, ethnic affiliation still has meaning, particularly in terms of political organization.

The Maasai are the majority ethnic group in Loliondo. As described earlier in the chapter, most Maasai in Loliondo come from one of three *iloshon* (sections). *Iloshon* are based on territorial and political affiliations that organize social relationships including access to grazing land and the selection of traditional age-set leaders. Like many categories of belonging, ethnic section is not a fixed identity but rather a cultural position that changes over time. The research for this book focuses on six villages in Loliondo that border Serengeti National Park. They are from north to south Ololosokwan, Soitsambu, Oloipiri, Olorien/Magaiduru, Losoito/Maaloni, and Arash. The Purko are the majority section in Ololosokwan and Soitsambu. The Loita are the majority in Olorien/Magaiduru, Losoito/Maaloni, and Arash. The Laitayok, who are the smallest group in the area, are the majority in Oloipiri.

As I discuss later in this chapter, the meaning of ethnicity was reworked in the struggle over Enashiva and became one of the project's most significant effects. Asioki worked closely with Lazaro Parkipuny in the early 1990s, starting women's groups throughout Loliondo under KIPOC, the NGO that Parkipuny had founded. In 1997, she founded the Pastoral Women's Council (PWC), which, with more than eight hundred active members, has grown into the largest member-driven civil-society organization in Loliondo and is a powerful advocacy group in the region.

The PWC focuses on "three main problems facing women in Ngorongoro District," including the Loliondo division, where the Thomson Safaris/TCL project is located: lack of property ownership rights; lack of participation in political decisions; and lack of education for Maasai girls.[6] Over the years, donors and various partners have called on the PWC to focus more directly on "women's rights" issues, especially female genital cutting or female genital mutilation.[7] But the PWC has maintained that in order to address a range of pastoral women's issues, it must first address education, political participation, and property rights. It is not surprising, then, that PWC members and other women throughout Loliondo have played a leading role in protesting land deals in the region. The organization consistently points out that the burden of land dispossession falls disproportionately on women. Loss of land and access to natural resources invariably means that women have to walk farther, work harder, and sacrifice more for the well-being of their children, husbands, and elders.

Asioki was one of the first people whom elected Soitsambu village council members went to when they heard about the Thomson Safaris/TCL land deal in 2006. Not only was the PWC active in all three subvillage areas of Soitsambu near the Enashiva project, but Asioki had also been elected as an at-large district councilor, a position created to promote women's participation on district councils throughout Tanzania. As a popular councilor, she was a trusted voice in the district, and she knew the former Sukenya Farm area well. Hers was one of the four hundred or so families that shared access to grazing land and water sources at Sukenya. The PWC, along with village leaders, district councilors, and other civil-society organizations, quickly organized meetings with residents to discuss the land deal.

Persepo Mathew was another leader involved in this early effort to stop the land deal. Mathew was an elected leader from Ololosokwan village, which bordered Soitsambu village and which had itself negotiated an agreement with tourism investors who had acquired land under circumstances similar to the Thomson Safaris/TCL deal.

Mathew explained to me what happened next: "I was in the meeting. That was the first day the whole community, the whole [village] government, the whole clans [Maasai ethnic groups] were together. We sat in the meeting and chose people to do three things: first, to confirm if the announcement was real or not; second, if it was real, to find a lawyer and a way to stop this land from being sold."[8] The third thing, he went on to explain, was that they decided to publicize their views as quickly as possible. "We needed to tell people that the village [Soitsambu] was against this sale. We wanted to write in the same gazette [where the land sale was advertised] to say that this land is in conflict, and nobody should purchase this land, and if they do, they have bought trouble."[9] By saying that this land is in conflict, Mathew was referencing the ongoing dispute between Soitsambu village and the Tanzanian state over the Sukenya Farm. To avoid dealing with the messy land struggle, Thomson Safaris/TCL quickly inserted itself into the conflict. Shortly after purchasing the land, the public relations staff of Thomson Safaris/TCL recast the conflict as one of internal ethnic rivalry. The company used such stories to raise questions about the legitimacy of the Maasai opposition to the Enashiva Nature Refuge.

Village representatives met with journalists and filed a court injunction to stop the sale. "We were surprised to learn that the land is for sale," Soitsambu village executive officer Saima Mbusia told the *Arusha Times* in February 2006. "The [former TBL] farm is a home of two Primary schools, a dispensary and a catchment for a number of local water sources. Whoever is going to buy the land, as advertised by the TBL, would have bought a row. . . . There are a lot of questions without answers. Most of us are asking how, when and who gave TBL our land that we inherited from our ancestors?" The paper cited TBL's Northern Zone director in response, who insisted "that his company ha[d] all legal rights to own the farm."[10]

The publicity notwithstanding, Thomson Safaris/TCL set up a campsite on the property in June 2006 and sent a manager to inform the village of the company's status as "owners and neighbors." In August 2006, the first Enashiva project manager, Peter Jones, arrived with the Ngorongoro District solicitor and other officials to announce at a meeting that Thomson Safaris/TCL had purchased the land. Regarding the villagers' complaints, the district solicitor sternly said, "That is over now."[11] Village leaders and residents responded that they did not accept the lease and that Thomson Safaris/TCL should "go away."

That Peter Jones was the Enashiva project manager did not help matters. Jones, a British expatriate who had lived in Tanzania since 1976, owned his own safari company, Tanganyika Film and Safari Outfitters. In a situation similar to that of Enashiva, in 1995 Jones purchased land in the Maasai area of West Kilimanjaro that was previously controlled by the state-owned National Farm and Agriculture Corporation. He bought the land in order to restore it as a wildlife area and created the Ndarakwai Ranch. Tourism companies, including his own, use the ranch, which the owners describe with the slogan "from wasteland to wildlife haven" for private safaris. In 2002, Jones helped to found the Kilimanjaro Conservancy to manage the area. The Thomson Safaris/TCL owners referenced Ndarakwai Ranch and the Kilimanjaro Conservancy as models for their own efforts to establish a nature refuge in the middle of Maasailand. In this context, the choice of Jones makes sense. However, most Maasai people did not share the Thomson Safari/TCL owners' perspective of Ndarakwai as a successful model of community conservation.

Among Maasai activists and leaders, Jones had a reputation for his ego and aggressive tactics. Despite promises that his project would deliver benefits to the nearby Maasai communities, one of his first acts was to deny the Maasai the right to graze on the farm, which they had used for decades, including when it was managed by the state. Ndarakwai Ranch was known throughout Maasailand as "taken land" (*ardhi ilichukiliwa* in Kiswahili). If Jones was the choice to manage the Enashiva property in Loliondo, regional leaders feared the worst. Those fears were confirmed within Jones's first few months in Loliondo. As manager of Enashiva, Jones ordered the destruction and burning of all structures on the property and prevented the Maasai from grazing and watering their livestock anywhere inside the Enashiva boundaries.

The Maasai living adjacent to Enashiva repeatedly told me that Thomson Safaris/TCL staff prevented them from grazing on their traditional lands. John ole Perseti, a Maasai man about thirty-five years old, lived in the Monderosi subvillage area bordering the Enashiva property.[12] He discussed his sentiments about the Enashiva project. He contrasted the state's previous effort to turn the area into a barley farm with the current effort to make it a nature refuge. We met in his house on a Sunday afternoon in July 2010. "The first time this land was taken by Tanzania Breweries [TBL], it was better," he said. "The breweries came and farmed a small area and didn't really give us any trouble and then they left." After Thomson Safaris/TCL arrived, however, company staff drove around and mapped the property. One day, they came close to Ole Perseti's homestead in Ilmasilik. He saw the vehicle in the distance, with a group of men "dressed like park rangers" walking around his family's *olakari* (reserve grazing area for calves and milk cows who are too small or fatigued to travel long distances with the rest of the herds). Eventually, the car drove up to his *boma*. The men got out and asked him his name. After giving his family name, he asked them what they were doing. The men told him that they were mapping the land to show people the boundaries. "Even your *boma* is in our land," they added. The men, who were all Tanzanians, went on, "You can no longer use this land. It is the land of a *mzungu* [Swahili for "white person"], not of Maasai."

The area that Thomson Safaris/TCL had purchased had "the water and the grass" his family, as well as those of about four hundred other families from three Maasai areas of Enadoshoke, Monderosi, Sukenya within the Soitsambu village, and three Maasai ethnic groups the Laitayok, the Loita, and the Purko, needed to survive as pastoralists. "They [Thomson Safaris/TCL staff] also closed the paths for livestock." And that, Ole Perseti said, is when the problems started. At first local residents did not heed the company's threats to stay off the Enashiva property. Despite declarations by the company that the land was theirs, Maasai residents were confident that Soitsambu village leaders would eventually win their dispute and get their land back from the company. Rather than just passively resist, Ole Perseti explained that he and about ten other men decided to graze their livestock herds together in the middle of the Enashiva property. Eventually, the new project manager who replaced Jones, a Marusha Maasai named Daniel Yamat, approached the group in his vehicle. He asked the men why they had brought their livestock onto "the farm." He then sped off in the direction of Loliondo town. About an hour or so later, Yamat returned with three vehicles filled with Tanzanian police officers. "They came close to our cows, honked their horns, and fired shots into the air to make [our] cows run," Ole Perseti told me.

The herders tried to stop their cattle from fleeing and asked the police to stop harassing them. In their eyes, they were only grazing livestock as they always had. Instead the police arrested five of the men and drove them to the nearest jail in Loliondo town. Word quickly spread about the arrests. Families had to travel to town and pay fines the equivalent of hundreds of dollars, a significant sum, to get the men released from jail. "Children can't herd livestock [currently]," Ole Perseti told me, because they "are afraid of the police." In 2009 police arrested people nearly every other week. According to several sources, almost every man from Ole Perseti's subvillage of Monderosi had been arrested. "I only know one man who has not been arrested, and that's because he was too scared to go [herding in the area]," a Maasai woman in her thirties from Monderosi told me.

Paulo Silas, a Maasai man in his late twenties from Enadoshoke, another subvillage area bordering the Enashiva property, told me, "We will never stop grazing, even if we are beaten and arrested. If we see a car, we will run to the mountain."[13] I asked what happens when they are caught grazing on the Enashiva land. "We are brought to the Thomson Safaris/TCL camp," he explained, and "beat .. with *rungus* [wood clubs]." Who beats you? I asked. Silas explained that Thomson Safaris/TCL hired Maasai from the Laitayok ethnic group, as well as members of the Sonjo tribe, as guards. The company has repeatedly denied employing guards, explaining that all its employees are game rangers. "The guards must have police [with them] to arrest herders," Silas told me. "Otherwise, they beat young herd boys when the police are not present."

As discussed in chapter 2, the Maasai in Loliondo come from one of three prominent subethnic groups, the Laitayok, the Loita, and the Purko. Such subethnic identity is one way that the Maasai distinguish themselves, but it does not necessarily mean there is division or conflict between the groups. The Maasai live together among different subethnic groups and marry across subethnic groups. These practices contribute to the blurring of ethnic boundaries and create a context of flexible ethnic identifications and understandings. However, ethnic affiliations do have material meaning and can be mobilized to create alliances, as well as encourage divisions.

Because the Purko and the Loita are the majority subethnic groups in Loliondo, many of the most outspoken challengers to the Thomson Safaris/TCL project were members of these ethnic groups. As the smallest subethnic group in the area, the Laitayok had fewer leaders in positions to oppose the project. The Laitayok—whom Thomson Safaris/TCL hired as rangers and camp staff—were a minority within Soitsambu village as a whole but the majority within Sukenya subvillage, the population center closest to the Thomson Safaris/TCL land. By hiring Maasai almost exclusively from the Laitayok ethnic group, Thomson Safaris/TCL created new leadership positions. The authority of these individuals was clearly tied to the legitimacy of the company and its claims over the land. One result of this tactic was that opposition to the Enashiva project was being divided along ethnic lines and creating conflict.

Empowering Individuals and Ethnic Groups

Complaints from village leaders and civil-society organizations led to a visit from the regional commissioner in late 2006 and from the president of Tanzania, Jakaya Kikwete, in 2007. It was after President Kikwete's visit that Judi Wineland, who along with her husband, Rick Thomson, co-owns Thomson Safaris, reached out to Lucy Asioki for help. Wineland knew that Asioki ran the largest Maasai women's organization in Loliondo and hoped to appeal to her by discussing their mutual concern for women's rights. In an August 2007 e-mail to Asioki, Wineland explained that Thomson Safaris was "currently working with the various village elders around Loliondo to begin a Community Based Tourism model."[14] She expressed to Asioki an interest in working with women: "If you and I are able to help these local women through tourism, then please let me know." Wineland never mentioned the contentious history the company faced and did not indicate any knowledge of the role played by Asioki in challenging the Enashiva project. I had met Lucy Asioki during my first visit to Loliondo in 1992 and had come to know her well. She told me that she did not appreciate this "deceptive" introduction, as she was certain that Wineland was well aware of the widespread opposition to the Thomson Safaris/TCL project, especially among women. Asioki saw the e-mail as an attempt to use her against her own people, an all-too-common fate for dynamic leaders who must navigate the interests of foreign donors, international NGOs, and their own local constituencies.

In her response, Asioki told Wineland that it was always "good to help women," but before they could collaborate on anything, they would have to address the current conflict in Sukenya. "I'm sure you know that Thompson [*sic*] Safaris bought the land from TBL with conflict. So your company should take full responsibility for settling this conflict."[15] By the time of Wineland's first e-mail to Asioki, Thomson Safaris officials were refusing to meet directly with the entire Soitsambu village government. Instead they chose to work only with a few individuals, including the Soitsambu village chairman and the Sukenya sub-village chairman. "You should understand that the land belongs to three different Maasai tribes living in Soitsambu," Asioki wrote to Wineland. "I understand that you had a meeting with the village chair and other few elders in Sukenya. I suggest that you hold a meeting with the village government which is the legal entity at the village level and express your interests."[16] Asioki reiterated that no one person owned the land in question, not even the village chairman. Reaching out to individual leaders like her was not the right way to resolve the conflict, Asioki told me. Leaders like Asioki continued to rely on the village as the representative body of Maasai interests. This was the only way they believed they could avoid the poisonous politics of individuals competing to be the authentic voice of the people and to represent the interests of Maasai culture.

Asioki went on in the e-mail to outline the legal implications of the Thomson Safaris/TCL land deal, recapping the community stance: "That on the 22nd June 2006 TBL, wrongfully, entered into the 96 years lease agreement with the Thomson Safari[s] on the disputed land. Thus TBL and Thomson Safari[s] acts have caused gross infringement and interference of the Pastoralists right to occupy and use the disputed land."[17] She then offered twelve specific recommendations for Thomson Safaris/TCL to make the situation right, most of it centered on the strong suggestion that the company return the land to the community as quickly as possible.

Asioki told me that Wineland's subsequent response showed that her understanding of community conservation and tourism in Loliondo could not be more different from Asioki's own.[18] Wineland began by apologizing for her delay in answering, saying that she had been busy accepting an award for tour operator of the year from the Tanzanian government, as well as an unspecified humanitarian award for her work. She had also been to New York, where she had met with the U.S. ambassador to Tanzania, the Tanzanian ambassador to the United Nations, and Tanzania's president Kikwete. "It is disconcerting to receive your email," she wrote. "Tourism has continued to be a great source of revenue for Tanzania. We [Thomson Safaris/TCL or Wineland and her husband, Rick Thomson] have continued to believe that in the past local communities do not benefit from tourism. Money goes to the parks, but not to the local communities. So we have made a concerted effort to move our camps outside the parks and to work with local communities to ensure that there is benefit for the people, the land, and ourselves."[19] But as Asioki later wrote to me, "Moving camps is not the same as taking land."[20]

Wineland went on, "Loliondo could be the showcase for this [kind of conservation]. The land has potential to be a wildlife refuge. And if a wildlife refuge, then tourists will come, and if tourists come, then the local community will benefit greatly."[21] Asioki could not contain her anger, telling me, "We don't want tourist money; we want our land."[22] Wineland concluded by making a final appeal to their mutual interests: "I can't imagine why we would be at odds about this piece of land. I truly believe we want the same thing. Or am I being naive? [Rick and I] are good people. We do not oversee a large corporation with thousands of employees. We are dedicated to Tanzania and her future. It has been 30 years since we stepped foot on her soil and from that point on we have continued to be involved with the people of Tanzania."[23]

This was the last direct correspondence between Asioki and Wineland for almost two years. Asioki was worried that Wineland would twist her words and claim that she had negotiated a deal on behalf of the community. Based on later correspondence, it appears Wineland believed that Asioki almost single-handedly directed the opposition against Thomson Safaris/TCL and could not be trusted. Whether Wineland knew as little as she claimed about why the community opposed the Thomson Safaris/TCL project is unclear. If her lack of knowledge is taken at face value, which many of the activists I interviewed did not, Wineland's conviction that turning the land into a private nature refuge would be a boon for local Maasai communities was still far from the vision of Loliondo imagined by Maasai leaders like Asioki.

Blogging the True History of Enashiva: "Get the Facts Here"

When Thomson Safaris/TCL could not enlist the support of leaders such as Asioki, the company embarked on a strategy of questioning the legitimacy of Maasai leaders and organizations that opposed the Enashiva project and of recognizing Maasai from specific ethnic groups as the true owners of the land. The company set up a website that proclaimed, "Thomson Safaris Sets the Record Straight: Thomson replies to online rumors. Get the facts here."[24] The company claimed that opposition to its project was "irrational" and must be based either in personal corruption or ethnic conflict.[25] Posts on the company website and articles by a Thomson Safaris–employed journalist, Jeremy O'Kasick, asserted directly or insinuated that opposition leaders came from the dominant Maasai clans of the Purko and the Loita and that the true members of the community came from the Laitayok ethnic group.[26] Thomson Safaris/TCL directors and staff forged friendships with Laitayok leaders, who were the minority ethnic group in the region overall but the majority in Sukenya subvillage, closest to the Enashiva land. This treatment gave new meaning and value to existing differences among the Maasai (see chapter 2). The majority of Enashiva employees came from the Laitayok ethnic group, and the Laitayok Maasai benefited disproportionately by Thomson Safaris/TCL–supported projects.

According to Thomson Safaris, the underrepresented Laitayok—whom the company called "the people of Sukenya"—supported the Enashiva project:

> The people of Sukenya are the largest population of Maasai around the Enashiva Nature Refuge, and they have lived in the area longer than any other Maasai clan or community. This is, of course, why the farm came to be called Sukenya. The leaders, elders, women's groups, and community at large in Sukenya have given their overwhelming support for Thomson Safaris and the Enashiva Nature Refuge project. That support has gradually spread to other communities. . . .
>
> A highly respected elder, Simat Loong'ung, speaks on behalf of the leaders and communities. . . . Simat has also explained how, throughout greater Loliondo, the people of Sukenya happen to be a political minority and the least educated group. They have not received benefits from tourism. They do not have any NGOs representing them. Their voice is often undermined in local politics.
>
> Thomson recognizes the struggle of the Sukenya people and is honored to work hand-in-hand with them on countless ongoing projects. However, Thomson has also reached out to all communities directly surrounding Enashiva so that they will receive benefits and be instrumental in Thomson's community-based conservation initiatives.[27]

Thomson Safaris' conflation of "the people of Sukenya" with the Laitayok is significant because the company was asserting that land rights are associated with ethnic identity and not village membership. The benefits from the Thomson Safaris investment thus were framed not only as a form of economic development but also as an assertion and recognition of ethnic or Laitayok property rights. Several Laitayok leaders repeated this claim, saying that they have been sidelined in village politics and that Thomson Safaris was addressing historical inequalities and helping to restore Laitayok rights. Such a framing eschews the village as the representative local institution, and therefore the Tanzanian Village Land Act of 1999 (see chapter 3), in favor of ethnically derived rights. The issue is not that Thomson Safaris/TCL was necessarily trying to divide the community. But in the absence of widespread multiethnic support, and in the face of strong opposition from village leaders and residents, the company increasingly aligned its desire to develop the Enashiva property with the latent Laitayok sentiment of being politically marginalized. This connection allowed

Thomson Safaris/TCL to represent opposition to its project as ethnically based jealousy rather than valid criticism.

Describing the conflict over the Thomson Safaris/TCL property as an ethnic conflict that "goes back in time" deploys perhaps the oldest and most enduring cliché to explain Africa's underdevelopment and problems.[28] This tactic used during colonial rule to divide Africans also lets Thomson Safaris/TCL off the hook. As Rick Thomson wrote responding to the critical article, "Tourism Is a Curse to Us," written by journalist Alex Renton (2009) and published in the British newspaper the *Guardian*, "The inter-clan rivalries existed long before Thomson ever came to Enashiva, and to suggest that Thomson is what comes between clans is to grossly oversimplify the culture and history of the Maasai in this area."[29] Suggesting that the opposition to Enashiva is grounded in a history of inter-Maasai ethnic conflict has created confusion and uncertainty for many outside observers, journalists, and international organizations. And when journalists, academics, and community members have pushed Thomson Safaris/ TCL to clarify its arguments that highlight racial and ethnic discrimination, the company has simply responded by appealing to a generic and universal notion of African ethnic difference and antagonism.[30]

Re-ethnicization

One of the legacies of Tanzania's socialist path out of colonialism was the undoing of ethnic-based local authorities established through colonial indirect rule. For Tanzania and its formative president, Julius Nyerere, villages were to be the cornerstone of development, rights, and community (as discussed in chapter 2). The varied effects of villagization have been discussed and debated widely.[31] In the 1960s and 1970s, many intellectuals, politicians, and scholars had hope for Nyerere's vision of development in Africa. Since that time, villagization has been more severely criticized as imposing a singular vision of African modernity and identity on otherwise diverse communities.[32] Whether one supports or vilifies villagization, what is important is that the village has become the de facto marker of community in Tanzania. The state conferred specific powers of local government on villages, and village governments have the responsibility to manage economic and political relationships within their boundaries.[33] Legal authority does not necessarily signify local legitimacy, but in Loliondo, as I have argued, the village has become a meaningful institution representing the interests of local residents as pastoralists.[34]

Few debate that there are inequalities among Maasai ethnic groups in terms of political power and clout. Yet through the struggles over the meaning of tourism investment, those lines of difference, which do not have a natural order, have become increasingly hardened and oppositional. By establishing its legitimacy through an authentic link to "the local community," Thomson Safaris/TCL has contributed to a re-ethnicization of local politics. Safari tourism has become the crucible for generating revenue, legitimating land claims, and redefining the boundaries of ethnic belonging.

In June 2010, a law was passed that divided Soitsambu village into three villages, a process that was in train well before Thomson Safaris purchased the Enashiva land. Nevertheless, Thomson Safaris has described the demarcation of Sukenya village (changed from a subvillage in 2012) in particular as fulfilling the political aspirations of the Laitayok people. And once the boundaries of this newly constituted Sukenya village aligned more closely with the company's existing alliances, Thomson Safaris/TCL was willing to recognize the village as a legitimate institution and partner.[35] The mapping of village boundaries onto ethnic identities was precisely what President Nyerere was trying to avoid when he put Tanzania on its path out of colonialism. Hoping to undo the legacy of indirect rule, in which traditional authorities were empowered though ethnic enclaves, Nyerere created villages with democratically elected leaders to represent the diversity of community interests. In many ways the actions of Thomson Safaris/TCL to defend its investment by linking it with a claim of restorative justice challenges the idea of the village as a possible democratic space in which different ethnic groups live together and hold one another accountable through elected leadership. The indication that the tourism project belonged primarily to one ethnic group over another instead rejuvenated territorial ethnicization. There are no guarantees that grounding Maasai cultural practices in village membership and belonging will lead to positive collective outcomes. However, the alternative of grounding Maasai authority in private-public partnerships is a risky proposition. While the village is not inherently a multiethnic space, there is strong evidence that relying on the interests of foreign investors to help determine the values of the community can easily lead to ethnic division.

Scholars such as anthropologist Peter Geschiere have noted that a predominant effect of economic globalization is the increased reliance on local forms of belonging in order for marginalized groups to claim their stake in the market-driven division of resources.[36] Although this strategic essentialism may offer the best position from which to negotiate with powerful foreign actors, it can also work against connecting multiple overlapping social struggles. Locating each struggle in an isolated context typically framed in terms of authentic and unchanging culture limits the possibilities for translocal collaboration. The perception that the conflict over Sukenya and the Enashiva property was an ethnic struggle reinforced the belief that, left to their own devices, African communities could not effectively organize themselves or overcome historical differences.

Such narratives often lead to a call for an external actor to intervene. In the place of African people's perceived lack of capacity, foreign investors can promote themselves as impartial experts who can educate the locals about development. In this formulation, companies like Thomson Safaris are literally invested with capital, knowledge, and moral authority.

Where Does Maasai Culture Come From?

In December 2008, Lucy Asioki made a crucial connection that would change the course of the fight against Thomson Safaris/TCL. At a Human Rights Defenders workshop in the Netherlands, she gave a presentation about the Sukenya Farm conflict and afterward was approached by Lucy Claridge, head of the Minority Rights Group International (MRG), who wanted to discuss the case in more detail. Based in England and founded over forty years ago, MRG "support[s] minority and indigenous people as they strive to maintain their rights to the land they live on, the languages they speak, to equal opportunities in education, employment, and to full participation in public life."[37] As an international human rights organization, MRG works on education, training, media, and advocacy. MRG is especially known for its use of legal cases to defend land rights. Through its work with the Enderois pastoralists in Kenya, MRG had become knowledgeable about pastoralist dispossession and activism in East Africa.[38] Claridge said that the MRG might be willing to help. Asioki returned to Loliondo and met with Soitsambu village leaders about the offer. The village government and the PWC subsequently requested the MRG's assistance to open a court case against TCL and the Enashiva Nature Refuge.

With some funds from the MRG and the help of the Pastoralists Indigenous Non-governmental Organizations Forum (PINGOS Forum), the largest indigenous rights group in Tanzania, and the PWC, the village hired Eli Furaha Laltaika, a young Maasai lawyer, and Emmanuel Sulle, an independent researcher, as consultants. Sulle visited Loliondo three times, meeting with village government representatives, district councilors, and Thomson Safaris representatives. The first goal of the consultants' report was to investigate the social impact of the Thomson Safaris/TCL plan to determine if the company had "harassed the community or not." The second goal was to examine the "legal merits and remedies of the lease," basically to determine whether the land deal was legal.[39] In August 2009, Laltaika and Sulle finished their report, which determined that there was sufficient cause to open a court case. And in September 2009, after reading the consultants' report, the MRG agreed to help local lawyers and community members pursue such a case.

Rumors of the lawsuit circulated around Loliondo and reached back to

Thomson Safaris/TCL, after which a large painted sign appeared at the road junction that led to the Enashiva property, announcing TCL's intention to change the designated land use of its property from agriculture and pastoralism to conservation and tourism. The hand-painted signboard read further, "If there is anyone who will be affected by such changes, he/she is requested to submit his/her opinion via the office of the District Executive Officer within 30 days from today, the 27th day of October 2009."[40]

It seemed as if TCL was seeking to preempt the court challenge by changing the Enashiva area's land-use status, which was necessary if the site was going to be developed permanently for tourism and conservation. Tanzanian law requires that any such proposed change be announced to the public for comment. One of the legacies of Tanzania's strong local government policies is that local authorities, including the village government, must approve any such land-use change. It was clear to almost everyone I spoke with that to maintain the possibility of returning the land to grazing for both wildlife and livestock, the land-use change had to be stopped before it got started. Other people I spoke with did not consider the change as significant. However, many Maasai believed that the land-use change was a part of the overall approach to turn their land into a new protected area.

Soitsambu village called a meeting of the village government on November 11, 2009. The following are excerpts from the minutes:

> There is a significant conflict between the citizens [of Soitsambu Village] and Tanzania Conservation Ltd (Thomson Safaris) over the Sukenya Farm, and to change the use of the farm from agriculture and pastoralism to conservation and tourism is to plant bad seeds of conflict within the citizens of Soitsambu Village. It is best if the government solve the existing conflict first before taking any other action.
>
> The Sukenya Farm is the property of the people since before and after independence, therefore to dispossess the citizens of their property is to place the citizens into a difficult situation economically and [socially] within their community, which is completely against the promise of CCM [ruling party] of improving the livelihoods of Tanzanians between 2005–2010 [reference to the national poverty-reduction strategy]. How are we to improve our lives, if we are dispossessed of our land?
>
> This farm is used for grazing our livestock; it is very small and does not even satisfy the livestock of the three sub-villages, which are inside the farm. To change the area to conservation is to destroy the economy of the citizens and to leave us poor and destitute instead [of] benefiting within our country by working together, hand in hand to use our resources.

If this farm is changed to conservation it will take away water sources which people and livestock depend on, and water is the source of life for everyone and everything.

Finally, we respectfully request our government and the Tanzania Investment Centre (TIC) to be extremely cautious on the role of investors, they should not be used as a new road to exploit citizens and return us to suffering.[41]

The minutes were signed by twenty-three of twenty-five elected representatives and hand-delivered to the district commissioner, with copies sent to the Ngorongoro District Council; the national land commissioner; the Tanzania Investment Center, which helps investors identify opportunities and see them through completion; and the prime minister. The result was that the village and council were able to halt the land-use change. This did not change the status of the lease but gave local leaders hope that the land would not be irreparably recategorized. Maasai leaders saw stopping this change as critical to the village's court case against TCL.

In January 2010, Soitsambu village employed another lawyer, Samson Rumende, who drafted a complaint on behalf of the village and filed it in the regional High Court of Arusha. He sent a copy to TBL (the official leaseholder) and TCL (the sublessee). Within days of sending the complaint, the Ngorongoro District lawyer, who represented the central government, called a meeting with the Soitsambu village government. At the meeting, he demanded that the village rescind the case immediately, threatening the village leaders by saying that the case was likely to fail and that the village would then be liable for all court fees incurred by TBL and TCL. In Tanzania if a plaintiff loses a legal case, he or she is liable for the legal expenses of the defendant. The village leaders did not back down. The district lawyer then asked who was funding the case, to which the village leaders responded that a legal aid NGO, the Legal and Human Rights Center (LHRC), was helping them. Under Tanzanian law, in a case opened by a village, the village can request an institution like the LHRC to represent it. The LHRC applies for a certificate from the court waiving liability for legal fees in case the village loses, on the basis that the case is in the public interest. Such an arrangement protects the village from liability if its case fails. According to several people at the meeting, the district lawyer told the village representatives to write a letter stating that it was an NGO, and not they themselves, who had opened the case. Grassroots groups like villages depend on the funding, expertise, and connections of a variety of NGOs to assist them in such struggles. Despite this almost ubiquitous relationship, state officials often accuse NGOs of using Tanzanian citizens to pursue their own agendas.

Soitsambu village continued pursuing legal action and opened two separate cases. The first was to stop TCL from developing the Sukenya Farm area as a luxury tented camp. The case called for TCL to stop any construction and to refrain from bringing tourists to the property. It also called for TCL to stop harassing and arresting people for trespassing. The second case, which Eli Furaha, one of the village's attorneys, explained was the more substantial one, challenged the entire lease. In this case the lawyers argued that the land belonged to Soitsambu village and that the court should revoke the title deed and return the land to the village.

Many of the people I spoke with saw these court cases as a last resort. Previous court cases filed by village residents had met with limited success, and village activists have had a hard time finding lawyers who are willing to support their struggle. Nevertheless, one Soitsambu village government member described to me how he hoped that legal challenges might lead to a political solution: "The court case is good for us, if only for the pressure. We are not sure we will win but want the [Thomson Safaris/TCL] owners to come talk to us. They [Thomson Safaris/TCL] have never come to the village to talk. They don't know what people want." He went on to explain his frustration with the land deal: "They are owning the land through papers. That land is our traditional land. They have the right and protection of the government if they believe they own the land through papers. . . . Who to believe, paper or us? They have a legal paper from Dar es Salaam. What about people in this area? This is our ancestors' land."[42]

After Soitsambu village filed the more substantial case challenging the overall TCL lease in February 2010, Thomson Safaris/TCL began to feel increasing pressure and sought to avoid further harm to its reputation. Thomson Safaris/TCL staff complained to the district commissioner that a few people were deceiving the community. The village chairman, Boniface Konjwella, was brought to the police station and interrogated. Among the list of questions, they asked him if he gave women permission to demonstrate. He replied that women in his village would never ask for such permission. The police then asked who was behind the court case, "Was it the village or the NGOs?" Konjwella assured them that the village was behind the case. "If you want more information, then come to the village," he told them.[43]

The case was postponed numerous times, leaving both Soitsambu village and Thomson Safaris/TCL uncertain about the outcome and possibilities. In May 2011, the judge dismissed the case, saying that it was essentially an attempt to reopen a much older case initiated just after the first TBL lease was granted: Civil Case no. 74 of 1987, in which fifteen defendants from Loliondo had challenged the allocation of ten thousand acres to TBL. The judge reasoned that since that case was decided on May 16, 1990, in favor of TBL, there was no reason to hear the new case.

Advocate John Materu, the lawyer representing the village in court, appealed the decision. He argued that the two cases were not the same. First, in 1987 the court case concerned land measuring 10,000 acres. The new case concerned 12,617.15 acres. If the 10,000-acre parcel had been determined to be the property of TBL, then what was the legal origin of the 2003 lease agreement for 12,617.15 acres? Materu also argued that the new case was being brought by the Soitsambu Village Council, the first such land case in Tanzania to take advantage of the 1999 Tanzanian Village Land Act provision enabling a village council to sue a third party. Finally, the defendants in the 2010 case were different from those in 1987. Both the dismissal and the subsequent appeal were based largely on technical legal procedures. In May 2012, the Court of Appeal of Tanzania at Arusha upheld the appeal and returned the case to the lower court for a new hearing by a new judge, ruling that there were many unanswered questions about the circumstances behind TBL obtaining a title deed in 2003 and TCL's lease of the property from TBL in 2006. The Court of Appeal also declared that TCL was responsible for all legal fees associated with the case. This was an important legal victory for the village and its supporters.

In June 2012, lawyers from both sides met with village and company officials to say that while the land was in dispute, both parties could continue to use the land without interruption. Representatives from the MRG then met with village members and advised them to look for ways to negotiate. Village members expressed an interest in Thomson Safaris/TCL returning most of the land and entering into a contractual agreement similar to other joint ventures in the district. According to an MRG official at that meeting, village members approved the following position statement:

> The village members recognize that Thomson Safaris has done investments on some part of the land. The village members agreed that Thomson Safaris could retain exclusive land ownership on 2000 acres around the [area].
>
> The community members are to acquire back the ownership of 10,617 acres of the land and then enter into direct agreement with Thomson Safaris to allow Thomson Safaris to continue to use some of the land for tourism activities.
>
> The process leading to the agreement between the community and the company should be participatory and transparent and stipulate the following:
>
> 1. Recognition of community rights ownership over the 10,617 acres of the land.
> 2. Unrestricted access to water points, foot ways from one sub village to the other, and specified grazing areas for the community.
> 3. Clear rules and procedures for implementation and management of the contract should be put in place.

4. Clarified roles and responsibilities for both parties in terms of security and other relationship resolutions. Items like the length of the contract, the annual land renting fees, the bed fee per nights per person (for tourists entering the community land) and the termination of the contract should be clearly discussed in the contract.

5. The village council will oversee the use of the income generated by the contract for equitable sharing among the three sub villages for their socio-economic development.[44]

Village leaders thought they were poised for a resolution to the conflict.

A Happy Ending at Enashiva?

Within weeks of the court case, Judi Wineland approached Lucy Asioki saying that she wanted a resolution to the issue. The Thomson Safaris and TCL owners remain convinced that their Enashiva project is a good one. When Judi Wineland met with Lucy Asioki in June 2012, she said that she was tired of all the conflict and wanted a peaceful solution. When Asioki explained that the best solution was to return the land and then negotiate with the village, Wineland asked who would repay Thomson Safaris/TCL for the money it had spent. Wineland also reiterated her belief that the Sukenya Farm area was a small piece of land, "less than one percent of Loliondo," and that surely everyone wanted to reduce the number of cattle there.[45] Asioki told her that this land was in fact quite large and significant for the communities that lived next to it and could not easily access "all that other land in Loliondo." She also said that the Maasai did not share Wineland's desire to reduce stock numbers and that taking the Sukenya land out of production would only exacerbate a resource crunch elsewhere.

For years Maasai leaders argued that they were not benefiting from tourism in national parks because revenues were never invested in their communities. By partnering with ecotourism companies to use their lands for tourism, Loliondo communities began to see profits from tourism in the mid-1990s. By incorporating direct tourism revenue into a system of land use and property rights that continued to promote pastoralism and the extensive system of communal grazing, the Loliondo village-based tourism joint ventures became a critical aspect in supporting the backbone of a regional pastoral political economy.

The underlying reason that the Maasai pushed for village-based tourism in Loliondo is that they believed it was one of the few ways for them to sustain their primary livelihood activity: livestock grazing. As discussed in chapter 6, the village joint ventures became a strategic way for communities to leverage their legal standing as villages and to use market mechanisms to earn revenue and make claims to land and natural resources. Despite the company's trying its best to promote the project as community conservation, in the eyes of most Maasai leaders and residents the Thomson Safaris/TCL project was fundamentally different. First, the Thomson Safaris/TCL's ninety-six-year lease was substantially different from the nonbinding five-year village joint-venture contracts. Also, in the Thomson Safaris/TCL case, it is the company determining the dominant land use by telling the community to establish a nature refuge. The meaning of community conservation takes on different value depending on whose interests and values are represented in the project.

At the heart of many of these projects is the idea that local people are partners and that by profiting from conservation they will come to embrace it as a value and an economic activity. As stated in the promotional video about the Enashiva project, Thomson Safaris/TCL "believe[s] that sustainable tourism can continue to empower local people to preserve fragile ecosystems and protect vulnerable wildlife populations." But just as with national parks, which were supposed to cultivate a national appreciation for nature, as well as provide the country with a source of revenue, community conservation would take time. It would need leaders to show local people how to manage such projects. Tourism investors like Thomson Safaris/TCL were indispensable actors in this new model of conservation. As Judi Wineland conveys in the promotional video, "I'm not sure I think it is sustainable right this minute. I think what we are trying to do is make it sustainable. Rick and I ask ourselves, how can we pass the baton carefully over to other people that are there. The Maasai themselves need to be able to control this land and benefit from this land."

Many Loliondo Maasai think that too much land had already been committed to wildlife preservation, and indeed the movement for community conservation was motivated by a search for different models. For Loliondo leaders, village rights to resources became a rallying cry against centralized control over wildlife management and the appropriation of Maasai land in the name of conservation. By grounding discussions of tourism in village governance, the Maasai attempted to shrink the scale of resource management from the national to the village level. Positing local authority as village authority had several effects. One effect was to fuse the meanings of cultural belonging, citizenship, and property rights. Many Maasai I interviewed explained that Maasai cultural practices were separate from the logics of global capitalism. Yet the increased ethnic conflict suggested that the logic of private property bled into the more communal understanding of Maasai culture and changed its form. Future possibilities rested largely on how property rights articulated with cultural categories like ethnicity and citizenship.

The village is by no means a perfect locus of Maasai interests. Rather, placing the village at the center of the political economy of pastoral production necessarily shifts cultural meanings and practices. We can understand the emergence of the village in shaping the meaning of Maasai identity as the process of cultural production. The prevalence of private group ranches among the Maasai in southern Kenya provides a similar grounding for the production of Maasai interests and values in that region, just across the international border that separates northern Tanzania's Maasailand from Southern Kenya's Maasailand. There is no question that villages and investors now play an important role in shaping Maasai culture. The important question is how such institutions will shape the ideas, beliefs, and values that may either bind or divide people and create future political possibilities.

How difference is produced and made meaningful is at the heart of questions in cultural geography. The cultural studies scholar Stuart Hall explains, "'difference' matters because it is essential to meaning; without it, meaning could not exist" (2001a, 328). We use difference to understand the world, construct meaning, and engage in dialogue. But difference is neither natural, nor is it determined completely by one group. Hall writes, "What it means to be 'British' or 'Russian' or 'Jamaican' cannot be entirely controlled by the British, Russians or Jamaicans, but is always up for grabs, always being negotiated, in the dialogue between these national cultures and their 'others'" (2001a, 329). Looking at Maasai culture through this lens, we then see how it is informed by the interests, values, and ideas of others. In this context power can be understood

> not only in terms of economic exploitation and physical coercion, but also in broader cultural or symbolic terms, including the power to represent someone or something in a certain way. . . . Power also seduces, solicits, induces, wins consent. It cannot be thought of in terms of one group having a monopoly of power, simply radiating power downwards on a subordinate group by an exercise of simple domination from above. . . . Power not only constrains and prevents: it is also productive. It produces new discourses, new kinds of knowledge, new objects of knowledge, it shapes new practices and institutions. (2001b, 339)

By positioning ethnic identity and belonging as ahistorical, as a timeless fact, Thomson Safaris/TCL challenges the idea of the village as a legitimate site of community and government. Instead the company relies on naturalized assumptions about ethnicity as the only reliable marker of true Maasai culture. Political scientist Mahmood Mamdani describes such narrative framings as a postcolonial dilemma or contradiction.[46] How, he asks, can Africans be incorporated into modern nation-states as citizens if their status as ethnic subjects is their primary identity? Unlike Mamdani's relatively clear boundaries between citizens and subjects, the Thomson Safaris/TCL case reveals how the relational identities of citizen and subject are constantly being negotiated. If ethnic groups like the Maasai are going to advocate as a marginalized and dispossessed cultural group, while also as part of a larger group of rural peasant and pastoralist citizens throughout Tanzania, then they need to be able to claim both a cultural and a political identity. Thomson Safaris/TCL's tactics, grounding Maasai rights in ethnicity over livelihood-based identity claims, limit the ability of Maasai groups to establish their struggle in concert with other peasant and pastoralist social movements for land and resources rights. By reproducing the commonsense belief that Maasai rights to resources were derived through ethnic belonging, Thomson Safaris/TCL gave support to a historical narrative that limited the possibilities for the Maasai to resist transnational investments such as their own. And unlike Thomson Safaris/TCL, which can benefit from a simplified narrative of ethnic division and conflict, local leaders are forced to navigate the lived experience and contextual meaning of ethnicity, which is embodied only in relation to other categories of belonging and difference.[47]

To be clear, the issue is not one of outside groups questioning the village as a democratic institution. Holding communities accountable to their constituents is an important part of any active democracy. Rather, it seems significant that private investors—in this case, foreign private investors—were able to actively challenge the legitimacy of a locally elected institution because that local institution questioned the investment and the investors' motives and tactics. Not only did Thomson Safaris/TCL raise such questions about local government in Loliondo, but it also influenced how national officials and international observers understood the conflict. All of this worked in part because of a commonsense belief that Maasai culture was stuck in some prehistoric space in which change could only be imposed from the outside.

Private investors come with their own interests, ideas, and values, which are not exclusively based on profit. When their motives or interests are questioned, they can derive power from two commonsense narratives: first, that they are apolitical actors, interested solely in fostering development; and, second, that they are agents of change helping to disrupt the backward-looking African culture and invigorate it with the entrepreneurial vision. Either way, investors have become central producers of knowledge about the meanings of development, conservation, and community in Maasailand.

Conclusion

What can this story tell us about how safari tourism investors in northern Tanzania reshape landscapes, people, and cultural politics? Understanding how companies attempt to gain legitimacy by highlighting certain histories and geographies over others is important in grasping how contemporary landscapes are being remade. The Thomson Safaris/TCL dispute is ongoing, and at the center of the conflict is the question of who should control land and natural resources, and for what purpose. Who determines why land is valuable and how it should be used and managed? The Thomson Safaris/TCL project is not without its supporters. As with any intervention—be it market driven or state sponsored—different people stand to benefit and to lose. One group of Maasai sees the Thomson Safaris/TCL project as a way to solidify its standing in the community and secure its access to resources by maintaining good relationships to the company. A much larger coalition of Maasai leaders and community members has steadfastly resisted the deal. The very fact that eight years after the land deal was consummated and sanctioned by the state it was still in dispute is a remarkable political achievement by those who opposed it. These Maasai have resisted efforts by Thomson Safaris/TCL to fund school classrooms and local women's groups as a way to legitimate its investment locally; they have dealt with evictions, harassment, and violence; and they have listened as government officials declared them ignorant and obstinate.

One of the effects of this regional history of safari tourism in Loliondo is that different groups of Maasai have been reterritorialized as belonging to particular ethnic communities with specific and limited land rights. The discursive and financial power of foreign investment for safari tourism produces new meanings as it creates new value and values. These ideas and practices are linked to discourses about African nature and who is best positioned to care for it. As I describe in the preface, Thomson Safaris has positioned itself as an enlightened investor who is simply attempting to act in the best interests of African nature and in so doing believes it is providing important benefits to Tanzania as a country and to the local Maasai residents. In the process it is representing and translating the meanings of land, identity, and belonging in the greater Serengeti region.

What begins to emerge from this story in northern Tanzania is how transnational interests, through foreign investments, necessarily help reconfigure the relationships between localities, nation-states, and various organizations around the world. These new maps of belonging and rights have the potential to lead to new opportunities for regional solidarity and national recognition of historically marginalized peoples and their interests. But such mapping may also validate more discrete forms of identity and encourage the proliferation of ethnicized identity and authority leading to conflict and violence.

CHAPTER 6

Joint Venture

Investors and Villagers as Allies against the State

In 1987, Dorobo Tours and Safaris (Dorobo Safaris), a relatively small travel company specializing in adventure tourism, including walking safaris in Tanzania, began bringing tourists to Loliondo. Before starting their safari business, the three expatriate Peterson brothers, who all studied ecology in college, had been involved in development projects in Tanzania. The two older brothers, David and Thad, had consulted for the Arusha Planning and Village Development Project in the late 1970s and early 1980s. The youngest brother, Mike, had worked on reforestation projects with the development agency of the Tanzanian Lutheran Diocese. Other than attending college in the United States, the three brothers grew up in Tanzania during the early years of independence (1960s and 1970s). Like many Tanzanians and expatriates during that time, they were taken with President Julius Nyerere and his vision for Ujamaa development based on an ideology of African communalism. Nyerere's message, which resonated with that of the Lutheran Church in which the Petersons were raised, was to uplift all people but especially the poor.

Frustrated with government bureaucracy and the slow pace of the development industry, the brothers believed that they could better help Tanzanians by running a tourism business. They possessed an intimate knowledge of Tanzania's wildlife and ecosystems, having traveled, camped, and hunted extensively with their missionary parents. With two old Land Rovers, they started Dorobo Safaris in 1983, named for the hunter-gatherer people collectively known as the Iltorobo, Ndorobo, or Dorobo. The Dorobo people exhibited a land ethic that appealed to the Petersons' own curiosity about and awe for nature and natural settings in Tanzania. The Dorobo people were at home camping out under the stars and subsisting on tubers, fruits, and occasionally meat. Much as Nyerere saw villages as authentic representations of African culture, the Petersons saw the Dorobo people as embodying a primal, not pejoratively primitive, relationship to nature. "The fact that Dorobo is not one ethnic group but rather many unified by a common lifestyle, a lifestyle characterized by fitting in with and working as part of natural systems, was . . . a compelling reason [for choosing the name]," the Dorobo Safaris newsletter explained. "We hope in some small way [that] our name and philosophy of doing business has or will help some

Dorobo folk to stand with dignity as Dorobo."[1] For the Petersons, Dorobo Safaris was not solely a money-making venture but also an investment in Tanzanian society and ecosystems.

Despite their interest in the Dorobo, the brothers worked largely with Maasai communities in the areas of the Simanjiro plains to the south of Arusha and the Loliondo plateau to the north. In the late 1980s, they worked with the Maasai in southern Maasailand to help them protect their lands from large-scale farming, which was taking hold in the area. The Petersons came to know many Maasai families and had both a scientific and a humanist appreciation for pastoralism and its compatibility with natural systems and wildlife habitat. One reason the brothers worked with the Maasai was because, unlike many hunter-gatherer groups, the Maasai lived in villages, with clearly defined membership, boundaries, and government-conferred land rights. These factors would turn out to be important elements for tourism partnerships. Legally incorporated villages with democratically elected village councils were ideal partners for the company in its mission to promote conservation of wildlife habitat and to sustain pastoralist and hunter-gatherer livelihoods.

In the early 1980s, when the Petersons started Dorobo Safaris, paying communities to protect their landscapes had not yet come into vogue as a conservation strategy.[2] The brothers saw their business as a way to do what they loved, make a living, and get involved in conservation issues on the ground level. At the time, the Petersons also worked with international conservation agencies and rural communities to stop elephant poaching on the border of Tarangire National Park, another major tourist attraction on the "northern tourist circuit" of parks and conservation areas in Tanzania. They worked with an American supporter who provided funding for the project. Such initiatives showed the Petersons that they could draw on their positions as tour operators, their connections with community leaders, and their relationships with wealthy friends and clients to influence policy and ideas.

The founding of Dorobo Safaris in 1983 and its tours to Loliondo in the 1980s coincided with the country's rapid transition from socialism (1964–85) to free-market or neoliberal capitalism (1985–present). The brothers were wary of reforms that called for the privatization of natural resources. They were, however, hopeful that market mechanisms could help recalibrate a national development agenda that in their eyes did little to help indigenous groups like the Maasai and the Dorobo and did not adequately protect nature and natural resources. Dorobo Safaris was part of a vanguard of investors who wanted to use markets to encourage conservation and sustainable land use. As a 1997 Dorobo Safaris newsletter explains, the company wanted to help protect wildlife-rich areas like those in Loliondo by helping to "transform" them into "a 'modern' economic resource option" that could "provide [indigenous people] a bridge allowing a dignified encounter with powerful forces which define today's global culture and economy."[3]

Direct Village Investment

In the early 1990s, the Petersons believed that paying communities to preserve critical rangelands for both livestock and wildlife would influence attitudes, behaviors, and interests in favor of valuing the conservation of wildlife and wildlife habitat. In 1991, Dorobo Safaris formalized arrangements to bring tourists onto Maasai village lands, essentially creating a joint venture between the company and the village governments. After receiving tacit permission from the WD of the MNRT, the Petersons approached three Maasai village governments and proposed to pay the villages for exclusive access to their lands. Dorobo Safaris would pay an annual fee or rent of five thousand dollars and a bed-night fee of ten dollars per person per night to each of the three villages for exclusive use of village land for camping and walking safaris. "The exclusive clause," explained the Petersons, "while controversial, is a critical project component from a marketing perspective. The ability to control tourist activity is essential in being able to guarantee a specific product that could be sold to prospective tourists i.e. an exclusive wilderness experience with an option of walking."[4]

Under the agreement, villagers could continue using the 250-square-kilometer area adjacent to Serengeti National Park for seasonal grazing but promised not to build permanent structures or to allow agriculture in the designated tourism area. They also agreed to prohibit charcoal production, hunting, and live bird capture. These restrictions were primarily to deter external threats, as the Maasai did not typically engage in these activities. Dorobo Safaris would not build permanent structures or develop any infrastructure either, "other than access tracks and campsites." The company would use temporary tent camps "that left little trace after each tour group finished." Addressing a common concern among the Maasai that investors wanted to control their land in order to exploit other resources, like gemstones, the company clarified that its activities were "limited solely to those related to tourism and natural resource conservation."[5] The contract with each village was for five years, at which point the two parties would decide whether to renew, renegotiate, or cancel their agreement.

As foreign investors, the Petersons depended on the Tanzanian state for business licenses as well as residency permits for themselves and their families. Experimenting with new political economic arrangements carried risks. The Petersons had to find a way to pursue their interests while maintaining good relations with a variety of state and nonstate actors. As they wrote in their project summary paper, to succeed the company needed the WD's approval together with the central government's recognition of village property rights: "The official and legal basis for establishment of the projects was dependent on two primary conditions being met—approval and support from the Wildlife Division and the procurement by the concerned villages of legal title deeds for 99 years to their respective traditional areas."[6]

Villages in Loliondo obtained title deeds in 1990 after a several-year-long project funded by the Arusha Catholic Diocese Development Office and the Serengeti Regional Conservation Strategy. Prior to this effort, village property rights were established under the national program of villagization. Notwithstanding the state resources spent on demarcating and establishing villages in the 1970s and 1980s, very few villages had official title deeds. In the 1980s, several development and conservation organizations believed that stronger and legally recognized titles could help the Maasai protect their land from external pressures, including large-scale agricultural schemes and settler immigration by peasant farmers. Elected district officials also hoped that the title deeds would mitigate border disputes with the neighboring agricultural Batemi people.

As of 1991, the Maasai had yet to apply their new legal standing to a real political context. As with all rights, their meaning and usefulness would not be known until tested. The Dorobo Safaris proposal to sign legal contracts with village governments rested largely on the villages being legal rights-bearing "owners" of village land. Having the titles reassured the village governments that the Maasai would retain all rights to land when they signed a tourism contract. Without acknowledging as much at the time, the Dorobo Safaris agreements effectively leased village land for tourism. This was a radical departure from how the Maasai had previously understood and related to their territory.

Skeptical observers might conclude that Dorobo Safaris took advantage of village leaders to gain access to a lucrative area for tourism. However, gaining the trust of village leaders and defending its approach to work directly with village governments to national government officials was not a simple affair. It took both creativity and risk. First, the company had to get permission from the WD. As discussed in chapter 3, at the time of the Dorobo Safaris agreements the WD had only recently taken control of trophy hunting throughout the country. It was reluctant to cede its authority over wildlife to nonhunting tourism. Nevertheless, WD officials were under pressure from foreign donors, specifically the USAID and the WWF, to pursue policies that incorporated rural people into conservation management.[7] On April 30, 1991, the WD's director of wildlife finally replied to Dorobo Safaris' multiple contact attempts about its "proposal to establish village wildlife wilderness areas adjacent to the Tarangire and Serengeti National Parks." The letter indicated support for the tour operator's projects:

The venture you are about to engage in is in keeping with departmental policy objectives, i.e. enhancing the value of wildlife to the immediate local community through fees paid to the village councils. In due course the beneficiaries will appreciate the value of wildlife to them and therefore be responsive to and responsible for its conservation. Over time the villagers will engage in anti-poaching patrols and stop harassment of the game. Secondly, the country stands to gain through this expanded utilization of the environment and its teaming wildlife. . . . Please be informed that your intended operation has the support of the Department of Wildlife.[8]

The letter came just as national leaders and officials overseeing wildlife in Tanzania were beginning to address community participation in conservation (see chapter 3). The letter indicates that WD officials hoped that private-sector investment such as the Dorobo Safaris project would not only expand markets for wildlife but also acculturate local people to conservation, a process that served their own interests in promoting conservation as a Tanzanian value.

Even with the support of the WD, Dorobo Safaris still had to convince village leaders that the company's business model had the interests of villagers in mind. The company needed to demonstrate that it was not allied with either international conservation organizations that were responsible for the creation and enforcement of Serengeti National Park and the NCA, nor was it the typical investor who made "deals" in the capital city of Dar es Salaam or in district headquarters.[9] Approaching the villages as primary partners and recognizing village rights to resources went a long way in convincing Maasai leaders that Dorobo Safaris was a trustworthy partner.

The Maasai have entered into plenty of alliances in the past.[10] Many Maasai leaders are well aware of the competing interests and agendas within such relationships. In 2003, I asked Thomas Lekuton, a Maasai political leader from Loliondo, about such partnerships. He told me that history mattered, pointing to the FZS as an example.[11] This international NGO was intimately involved in funding and supporting the management of Serengeti National Park, and like many influential conservation organizations, the FZS was beginning to promote CBC projects. Lekuton said, "Frankfurt [FZS] took Serengeti from us. They moved us to the NCA. They give millions to national parks for cars and enforcement." He explained that to work with the FZS now "just because they say they are interested in the community does not seem right." History says that the FZS should not be trusted: "All work relies on faith. If people trust you or not will determine the outcome of the work," Lekuton told me. "People might refuse our work simply because Frankfurt is involved." He ended with a familiar metaphor: "If a lion enters a livestock pen, even if it has lost its teeth, cows will run." In contrast to groups like the FZS, Lekuton said, "these tourism investors [like Dorobo Safaris] share many of our concerns." Among these he listed preserving rangelands, generating income for local people, and defending Maasai land rights. Although the promise of the village tourism contracts and joint ventures were yet to be fully realized, Lekuton expressed his belief that they protected Maasai interests. This was significant in soliciting local support by many Maasai leaders for the village tourism projects and in creating the understanding of the village contracts as a useful political tactic.

The Loliondo Maasai have a history of challenging investment schemes and of skepticism toward investors who have aligned themselves with the state to exploit Maasai land and culture.[12] But for many leaders in Loliondo, working directly with foreign investors of a different type, whom they perceive as partially unmoored from state interests and imperatives, presents interesting possibilities. Maasai leaders and activists in Loliondo have come to understand neoliberalism—specifically, their ability to negotiate directly with foreign investors—as an attractive option to overcoming long-standing and habitual resource appropriation by state institutions. Maasai leaders in Loliondo recognize the inherent contradictions of market-driven relationships with foreign investors. On one hand, they provide the possibility of recognition for Maasai land rights; on the other hand, they present a threat of enclosure and resource appropriation. Perhaps due to their limited room for maneuver, or maybe their genuine enthusiasm for these new joint ventures, a large number of Maasai leaders and citizens have embraced village-based tourism contracts despite such agreements' uncertain and unfulfilled promises.

These village-based joint ventures are best explored in the context of CBC and the idea of the green economy in general as they have developed over the past three decades in Tanzania. In that milieu, the Maasai, investors, and the state are remaking spaces for safari tourism and conservation. This new spatiality of conservation in Loliondo rests on an articulation of the village as a rights-bearing entity (with clear geographic boundaries and legal standing), grounded in historical, culturally based territorial rights. Through this new understanding, the village has become a meaningful social and spatial unit of rights and belonging. Market tools and ideologies have generated new value and profit while also being used to defend land rights. The process has created new meanings of both market and society. The Maasai have come to understand the potential of the market and the possible benefits of their alliances with investors as a way to remake their social and political relationships with state institutions. This new discursive framing of market-led land-rights claims has come to centrally inform Maasai land struggles in Loliondo today.

The Green Economy Comes to Tanzania

Perhaps the biggest trend in global environmentalism in the 1990s, embraced by the public and private sectors alike, was the widespread belief that the best way to protect nature was to make it a more tangible commodity by more explicitly identifying its monetary value. Economists argued that people did not protect or sustainably manage their environment because they did not monetarily benefit from such practices. The answer to this problem was to use capitalist markets to create new values, or to more efficiently capture existing values, and to make them evident as part of a new global accounting of natural resources. The market approach was embraced by many quarters, including the private sector, international financial and development institutions, and the nonprofit sector. The idea that nature should be valued as a commodity that provides specific environmental goods and services has become a hegemonic idea in global conservation thinking and practice.[13]

Many important environmental institutions have adopted some form of market-based environmental policy. For example, the IUCN has encouraged using market incentives by promoting "payment for environmental services" programs. As economist Lucy Emerton, head of the IUCN's Global Economics and the Environment Programme, describes it, "Payments for environmental services are something which we are increasingly using in conservation to give normal people incentives to save the environment."[14]

Other market-based conservation approaches include initiatives such as the European Union sponsored Economics of Ecosystems and Biodiversity and the United Nations research initiative Towards a Green Economy.[15] It is worth noting that the idea of using markets to promote conservation and sustainable resource management is not exclusive to the past few decades. Many scholars studying the history of conservation have shown how the protection of nature has been integral to the expansion of capitalism.[16] Still, the market-oriented reforms applied in the late 1980s were a direct reaction to what was widely regarded as overbearing and inefficient state involvement in conservation planning and management. Critics of state-led development attacked government bureaucracies for disrupting market forces, creating perverse incentives, promoting bad policies, misallocating funds, and allowing environmental harms to go unchecked. The solution, these critics said, was to more closely link environmental conservation initiatives with market mechanisms to determine the appropriate value of nature and how to most effectively allocate these goods and services. This included many elements, but one central tenet was to clarify property rights over nature in order to better understand who owned what aspect of nature. Neoliberalization had delegitimated the state as a credible owner. By identifying owners, policy makers could create specific incentives and encourage the values and practices desired in a new global balance sheet for nature. "Neoliberal conservation, then," writes Bram Büscher, "is the contemporary push to make environmental conservation not only compatible with capitalism but also a source for economic growth."[17]

Making Wildlife a Commodity

In Tanzania, wildlife is the property of the state. Wherever wild animals roam, including on village lands, the central government is responsible for their management and for determining the most appropriate use of this "national-natural resource." Both the colonial government and the independent Tanzanian state worked hard to transform wildlife from a common resource with important local-use values to a private commodity with an internationally recognized exchange value. Capturing the value of wildlife became essential for generating the all-important foreign exchange. Tanzania's first president, Julius Nyerere, famously summarized Tanzania's interest in protecting wildlife: "I personally am not very interested in animals. I do not want to spend my holidays watching crocodiles. Nevertheless, I am entirely in favor of their survival. I believe that after diamonds and sisal, wild animals will provide Tanganyika [Tanzania] with its greatest source of income. Thousands of Americans and Europeans have the strange urge to see these animals."[18]

No matter the various political and economic ideas and systems in place (imperialism, colonialism, national socialism, neoliberalism), controlling wildlife in Tanzania has remained central to accumulating state wealth and maintaining authority. Neoliberal reforms starting in the late 1980s took hold in a context also shaped by concerns about the coercive history of centralized conservation.[19] Policy makers, international donors and organizations, and a number of interested experts began searching for new approaches to conservation that combined poverty reduction, social justice concerns, and new ideas for the sustainable management of biodiversity.

This new approach includes actively incorporating local people into conservation, and it gained influence and legitimacy in the early 1990s. Schemes that embraced these goals went by various names, including integrated conservation and development projects, CBC, and community-based natural resource management (CBNRM). Successful practitioners of such projects sought to "make nature and natural products meaningful to rural communities."[20] And the main methodology for cultivating meaningful relationships between people and nature was "through markets." The major goal behind these initiatives was to develop markets to deliver more benefits to more "stakeholders."[21] Project planners saw the concerns of social justice and livelihood security as following naturally from this profit-motive orientation. The belief that CBC was a way for communities to "regain control over natural resources for livelihood security and conservation" quickly became a lesser focus of most projects, which could more easily promote the benefits of a new source of income.[22] In Tanzania, this meant leveraging safari tourism to fund CBC and CBNRM projects. Increasing overall tourism revenue, in part by creating new markets for community-based tourism, was central to fulfilling the promise of these efforts in Tanzania.

The emergence of CBC in the early 1990s in Tanzania occurred simultaneously with widespread support for and interest in market-led conservation. Funders like the USAID, international conservation organizations like the AWF and the WWF, and smaller NGOs like the SCF played important roles in fostering market-led approaches to conservation on community lands in Tanzania. While these groups needed to convince government agencies and leaders that devolving authority to local communities was ultimately in the best interests of the state, they also needed investors and communities to get on board with the idea that direct investment projects were the future of conservation in Tanzania. By the early 1990s, the USAID-funded CAMPFIRE project in Zimbabwe provided the primary model for CBC in African rural areas.[23] CAMPFIRE encouraged government wildlife officials, many of them white Zimbabweans, to switch from centralized control of wildlife management and hunting to decentralized oversight in which communities participated in management decisions and benefited directly from hunting revenues. CAMPFIRE was praised as a way to overcome the legacies of colonial development by returning local rights and authority over land and natural resources. Project backers believed that local attitudes toward wildlife would change if communities themselves became stakeholders in wildlife management. This would in turn lead to the development of new institutions and to practices promoting conservation of communal land.

CAMPFIRE devolved partial authority over wildlife management to newly created district councils. In Zimbabwe, district councils were the most local unit of government. With new powers to direct wildlife use, district councils coordinated with "producer communities" regarding both the management of and the distribution of benefits from wildlife use. As discussed in chapter 2, the smallest unit of local government in Tanzania was the village, not the district. Devolving "appropriate authority" to villages involved a greater commitment to decentralized management. Eventually the question of scale would become central to all CBC stakeholders in Tanzania. For Dorobo Safaris, working directly with villages made the most sense, because as legal entities, villages held property rights and governmental authority. Villages could also enter into direct contracts with investors like Dorobo Safaris.

Critics of neoliberal conservation say that using markets to "free nature" does not protect ecosystems, livelihoods, or other collective benefits that might be difficult to monetize or that might not attract investment. Rather, markets primarily make nature available for capital accumulation and exploitation with scant regard for questions of equity, sustainability, or accountability. While they may be good at making new resources available for investment, they do not effectively value "many aspects of environmental transformation and degradation, particularly those that impact mainly the poor or the non-human."[24] Nature is intimately entangled with social life, and critics of neoliberal conservation fear that market discourses will dominate other values and interests. But when markets are used to free nature for capital, other forces can be set in motion too. In Tanzania, the hopes of many groups like the Maasai include attaching their own social and cultural agendas to the "freeing forces" of neoliberal globalization. In addition to investors and powerful elites, more marginalized social groups also hope that they might harness neoliberal forces to express their own agendas.[25]

Social groups like the Maasai may not share the same goals as some of their partners, either of saving nature for its own sake or for maximizing profit from nature. Perhaps, as some Maasai believe, their best chance to secure land rights for pastoralism will be achieved as an unintended consequence of the problematic quest for total market integration. David Harvey sees the ever-expanding logic of capital as part of a "spatial fix" through which "capitalism solves its contradictions merely by bringing them to higher levels and scales, or displacing them geographically and/or temporally."[26] The Maasai in Loliondo have tried to upend the logic of the spatial fix, displacing the diverse efforts to universalize the meaning of nature, and instead use the forces of capital to help reveal how nature is an unambiguously locally produced commodity. By demonstrating the central role of pastoralism in creating Tanzanian nature, the Maasai hope to support their rights both to use and to benefit from it.

The Maasai in Loliondo are likely to challenge the conclusions of scholars like James McCarthy, who argues that "reliance on market logics and mechanisms in a context of severe economic inequality guarantees [that] environmental inequities and injustices undermine the very categories of public goods and collective rights."[27] McCarthy's overall argument is one that many political ecologists would agree with. Markets are not "inherently good or the (only) realistic option for policy making."[28] However, this academic position fails to account for the ways that market ideologies inform contemporary understandings about collective rights. In their efforts to "free nature" from state control, the Maasai are attempting to remake their landscapes. In the end, McCarthy's warnings may yet come to pass. Questions of how the Maasai might achieve equity and justice by engaging directly with markets remain speculative.

Creating Aspirational Spaces within the Green Economy

The Petersons are clear that their safari business is not a philanthropic opera-tion. They are passionate about what they believe is the inherent value of wil-derness and see adventure travel as one of the best ways to introduce tourists to the beauty of Tanzania's natural landscapes and to the complex relationship that people like the Dorobo and the Maasai have with their land. The brothers offer walking and camping safaris, and they arrange cultural encounters that introduce tourists to the ways that indigenous people interact with their land. In neighboring Kenya, a tourist can independently visit the parks and conserva-tion areas by renting a vehicle or using the elaborate public transportation net-work. In contrast, when Dorobo Safaris began operating in the early 1980s, Tan-zania presented many challenges to the independent traveler. There was little infrastructure for travelers. The roads were largely in disrepair or nonexistent, and there was limited public transport outside large cities and towns. Travelers who wanted to visit Tanzania off the main tourist circuit had very few options. A few tour operators began to fill a niche that the Tanzanian tourism sector was sorely missing. And Dorobo Safaris quickly developed a reputation as one of the leading adventure and ecotourism companies specializing in tourism outside core parks and protected areas in Tanzania.

The company was well aware that the area it favored for tourism over-lapped with the Loliondo hunting blocks controlled by the WD. From the mid-1980s, Dorobo Safaris operated tours in the area without formal agreements with either local villages or central government authorities such as the WD; the company directors believed that they could conduct their walking and camping activities without interfering with trophy hunting. At that time, the government-managed TAWICO still controlled the hunting rights in Loliondo and concentrated its activities in locations to the north and the south of the area preferred by Dorobo Safaris. By concentrating their activities in these seldom-used areas, the Petersons believed they could help maximize the value of Loliondo's landscape for both consumptive and nonconsumptive tourism. With private- and public-sector actors embracing the basic idea of CBC, the Petersons felt empowered to develop new tourism enterprises that generated revenue for local communities and, in their estimation, created real incentives for the Maasai in Loliondo to embrace conservation.

Despite the new room for maneuver created by the emergent discourse of CBC, Dorobo Safaris' directors also understood that their efforts might ruffle some feathers in the central government, especially in the WD, which had ex-clusive control of all wildlife-related activities throughout the country. In part, Dorobo Safaris approached village governments directly because it was initially unable to gain official permission from the WD to conduct tourism on community lands. Only after Dorobo Safaris began its village joint ventures did the WD indicate some support for its efforts. The Petersons believed that the Maasai were better stewards of the environment than the state agencies entrusted with their management. With their in-depth understanding of pastoralism and range ecology, they were able to grasp a more nuanced view of nature, one that was produced in relation to Maasai livelihoods. They drew on former president Nyerere's original vision for Ujamaa socialism, which considered the village the building block of Tanzanian society. They were also buoyed by a growing global consensus that indigenous people should be given more rights to land and natural resources. Principle 22 of the 1992 Rio Declaration on Environment and Development states, "Indigenous people and their communities and other local communities have a vital role in environmental management and development because of their knowledge and traditional practices. States should recognize and duly support their identity, culture and interests and enable their effective participation in the achievement of sustainable development."[29]

For the Petersons, the village was the logical site of the community in Tanzania. The Local Government Act of 1982 had enabled village governments "to manage village lands and to determine the uses and users therein."[30] The Petersons decided that contracts between Dorobo Safaris and village governments would link the international discourse of CBC and indigenous rights to a legitimate and state-recognized institution in Tanzania.

The village contracts gave exclusive use of a specified area to Dorobo Safaris and stipulated a number of land-use restrictions, including a ban on permanent settlements and agriculture and limitations on cattle grazing. Although these land-use restrictions echoed well-worn and controversial strategies of fashioning pastoral landscapes to conform to a specific conservation aesthetic, Maasai village leaders saw the village-based tourism contracts as a new way to mark their landscape as simultaneously valuable for tourism and pastoralism. In the tour operators' eyes, recognition of Maasai land rights in accordance with international principles lent legitimacy to the village-based joint ventures. For the communities, the contracts represented recognition from relatively powerful transnational actors and became one tactic in a new arsenal to assert Maasai land rights.

Off the Beaten Path: Adventure Tourism in Loliondo

Dorobo Safaris specialized in organizing tourist safaris off the beaten path, primarily to southern and northern Maasailand. In Loliondo, the company was drawn to Soit Orgoss, an area of mixed savannah *Acacia* woodland dotted with mammoth rock kopjes. The kopjes provided a picturesque backdrop for campsites nestled between the massive rock formations. Close to the border with Serengeti National Park, the Soit Orgoss area teems with wildlife for much of the year. The Maasai use the region for grazing during dry seasons and times of prolonged droughts, but due to wildlife disease vectors, risks of predation, and cattle theft, they had few permanent settlements in the area.

In exchange for access to the Soit Orgoss area, Dorobo Safaris offered financial assistance to the three villages that shared rights to the area. Initially, in the late 1980s and early 1990s, the company helped pay to maintain village infrastructure including maintenance costs for village vehicles as well as providing scholarships for Maasai children in each village. Clients offered to help too, and the company directed some of this money into a fund for school fees and other village needs. After a few years of hosting camping and walking safaris in Loliondo, the Peterson brothers wanted to find a way to "make the benefits of tourism visible to everyone in the community."[31] They approached villages they had been doing tourism in about the possibility of formalizing the arrangement with the village council.[32] Munkakillerai, the company's financial administrator, and a Maasai man from Loliondo helped facilitate these agreements. The council agreed to let the company set up campsites on village land, and Dorobo Safaris hired young men from the village to accompany their tours.

In 1994, CBC advocates asked Dorobo Safaris to present its model of tourism at a CBC workshop in Arusha, Tanzania. There the Peterson brothers explained that subsistence pastoral economies were vulnerable to threats, including land loss and population increase. They argued that pastoralists would be increasingly pushed into agriculture or forced to migrate for work. The brothers did not believe that subsistence farming was viable in the drought-prone semiarid environment, and they also argued that widespread agriculture would limit future possibilities for pastoralism, as well as for wildlife habitat. The Dorobo Safaris project set out to create incentives for pastoralists to maintain their landscapes for grazing and to resist the short-term temptation of increasing agricultural production.[33] The resource crunch presented the Maasai with limited options: intensify pastoralism or embrace more agriculture, which would place further limits on pastoral production. The Petersons and other CBC advocates in Tanzania posed ecotourism as a third way. The Petersons saw their brand of safari tourism as a way to create added value to subsidize pastoralism and help sustain it as a long-term livelihood strategy in the region.

Before signing the contracts with villages in 1991, Dorobo Safaris received approval from the WD to "initiate community-based conservation projects in areas adjacent to Serengeti National Park." The company directors hoped that this initial endorsement would lead to more substantial support. "For the projects to succeed," the Petersons wrote, "it would be necessary for the Wildlife Division to excise these areas from the hunting concessions as the non-consumptive type of tourism we were proposing directly conflicted with hunting. Because the proposed areas were small in relation to the entire hunting concessions, it was expected that the revenues generated from tourist hunting would not be significantly reduced."[34]

Throughout most of the 1990s, the WD left the village-based joint ventures alone, as the agency worked on developing a national policy to integrate local communities into conservation and wildlife management on village lands. During that time, other tour companies followed Dorobo Safaris' lead and negotiated directly with village governments in Loliondo. By 2000, seven Maasai villages had signed contracts with private tourism companies. Each village government had leased access to its titled land to at least one ecotourism company. By this time, it was becoming clear that the WD would no longer sanction the projects or embrace Dorobo Safaris' vision for using portions of hunting blocks for high-value nonconsumptive tourism. With state support for this alternative model looking less and less likely, the tour operators opted to stay the course and try to demonstrate the effectiveness of their approach of village-based joint ventures.

Coordinating their efforts for the greatest impact, the tour operators founded their own umbrella organization, the Loliondo Tour Operators Forum (LTOF). Although small in size and influence compared to either the Tanzania Association of Tour Operators or the Tanzania Hunting Operators Association, the LTOF was able to advocate for the village-based joint-venture model at the national level. The group laid out the following agenda:

> The Loliondo Operators Forum is a private sector initiative made up of nine companies in Loliondo that have agreements with villages bringing in over 100 million Tanzanian shillings of revenue to villages. It is a forum to exchange ideas and set where to go. We are worried in Loliondo, that after we have worked for 4 or 5 years with villages, that others will come in and move us out. Also, we are concerned with how to maintain wildlife. The objectives of the group include:
>
> 1) To control input into photographic tourism in Loliondo;
> 2) To prevent someone from putting up a hotel, which would destroy the nine companies' market. We want visual experience, no main roads, no construction of large buildings or phone lines; and
> 3) We want some official license from the government.

Forming the LTOF was an explicit attempt to manage nonconsumptive tourism in Loliondo. If the government would not recognize the tour operators' projects, the companies wanted to regulate themselves in ways that would most effectively allow them to achieve their goals. As new national policies for CBC emerged in the late 1990s and early 2000s, the village-based joint ventures were increasingly marginalized. Policy makers saw the existing model as hostile to the conservation and tourism policy direction in the country. The tour operators hoped that the LTOF could assist in legitimizing their approach of working directly with villages as partners. The safari companies also needed to attract tourists to this brand of tourism and to show them the value added of their particular approach. To that end, rather than focusing on their relationships with specific villages, the tour companies concentrated marketing efforts on representing Loliondo as a specific and unique CBC destination.

Loliondo: A Park with Pastoralists?

A British tourism consultant promoting high-end wilderness travel to Africa describes the appeal of Loliondo to potential travelers:

> Loliondo could perhaps be described as the Serengeti with fewer rules, offering as it does excellent walking safaris, night drives and for much of the year rewarding game viewing. Spanning the entire eastern edge of the Serengeti National Park, it's a critical part of the whole ecosystem—yet visited by remarkably few tourists. Loliondo is actually a huge Maasai community area but in our opinion is worth treating as a separate park because the range of safari activities on offer here is significantly greater than those within the Serengeti National Park boundaries.[35]

Loliondo's value as a tourist destination rests largely on its representation as an alternative to Serengeti National Park. A tour company can tell its clients that they will view the same wildlife as they would in the park—including four of Tanzania's famous "big five": lion, leopard, buffalo, elephant, and rhino—but without the crowds of people and vehicles.[36] Safari customers are promised a more authentic wilderness experience, with "fewer rules" than if they traveled solely through the famous northern circuit of national parks.[37]

Part of the allure of a place like Loliondo is that it satisfies the demand for travel experiences that combine leisure with a sense of adventure or even "risk" while also appearing to contribute to sustainability. This budding market is well illustrated in a consultant's report commissioned by the FZS on how best to promote high-end tourism in the Serengeti region. The report specifically targets high-net-worth individuals, of whom the authors estimate there were close to ten million worldwide in 2006.[38] These people, defined as having more than one million dollars in liquid assets, represent a vital consumer base for high-end tourism. Specifically the report declares that these individuals desire tourism experiences that "uphold the three principles of environmental, social and economic sustainability—the 'triple bottom line.'" The report continues,

"If governments, investors, and developers wish to cater to the needs of HNWIS [high-net-worth individuals], they must incorporate the values of this demographic group into the production of their products. Increasingly, these values are oriented towards sustainability of the 'triple bottom line.'"[39] Though the report specifically addresses tourism experiences within Serengeti Park, a close reading indicates that a place like Loliondo can also offer experiences that meet this idea of the elusive triple bottom line.

Tourism investors in Loliondo understand the scarcity of Loliondo's qualities as an adventure safari destination. Perhaps better than the hoteliers and companies investing within national parks, they understand the stakes outlined in the report: "Successfully creating products that meet this triple bottom line will dictate the winners and losers in the increasingly competitive high end market."[40] Along with an outstanding vacation experience, investors can make a case to their clients that tourism on community lands in Loliondo provides benefits to local people. While most tourists traveling to Loliondo do not understand the complex history of conservation or the details of community tourism arrangements, they are made aware that their ability to enjoy African nature in a place like Loliondo is supported by local people and that a portion of their payment goes to the community rather than the park authorities.[41]

The companies attracted to working in Loliondo specialize in small, private, relatively low-environmental-impact adventure camping and walking safaris. All these companies also use the national park system extensively, but they have cultivated a niche for trips outside of Tanzania's main system of government-managed protected areas. While not all tourists want an off-the-beaten path experience or can afford it, for those with the longing and the means, many tour operators see Loliondo as a safari tourism Mecca. As described by one tour operator,

> The Alamana Reserve [in Loliondo] is undoubtedly one of the few sanctuaries left in northern Tanzania where our guests can discover the true essence of safari-exclusivity, remoteness and a true reflection on just how good the wilderness can be. Because the Alamana Reserve is an exclusive use area under our own management, we have complete freedom to Game Drive by day and by night and also to outfit Game Walks and overnight Non-Traditional Fly Camps across over 300 square kilometers of true wilderness.[42]

Although a small sector of the overall tourism industry in Tanzania, the handful of companies that organize such trips provide an important outlet for the growing international market for ecotourism. Not only are these companies helping to create and promote new forms of tourism in Tanzania; most believe that their business models can contribute to conservation and sustainable livelihoods by promoting CBC. These often high-end safari companies attract tourists who are willing to pay extra for an exclusive experience that they believe has a positive impact on the environment and the local communities.

As CBC policies became more widespread, communal areas like Loliondo are valuable spaces in the overall conservation landscape in Tanzania. For many conservationists, these areas are critical because they are not under the protection and management of government conservation authorities. For safari companies hoping to influence conservation policy through their business practices, communal lands are appealing sites for intervention. These companies create market incentives, hoping to secure their own access and business success and to promote conservation values and attitudes among local people. From their position within the business and conservation communities, these companies have become an important constituency for the emerging coalition of organizations in Tanzania promoting market-led CBC.

Seen through the lens of these companies' marketing materials, the Loliondo landscape is a contiguous area of natural wonder and cultural heritage. But as the history and geography of Loliondo shows, presenting Loliondo as a place where pastoralism and tourism could coexist depended on it having been spatially divided into separate villages, each with its own boundaries and property rights. Without these locally and nationally recognized property rights, tour companies would have no foundation for their contracts and access. The very ability to present Loliondo as an unfragmented natural African landscape rests on the activist history of Maasai villages in the region.

Placing Nature within Village Boundaries

Where is nature located? What is the relationship between nature and geographical, cultural, and political boundaries? These are important questions in trying to understand the changing relationships between the meaning and value of nature and natural resources, social relations, and political economic power. One important lesson from the joint ventures in Loliondo is that the village-based contracts were seen by tourism companies and the Maasai as a way to free nature from national control and to situate it within locally meaningful boundaries, namely, within the village.

As discussed in chapter 3, the Maasai had few ways to benefit from tourism on their lands. All of Loliondo was a designated game controlled area, enabling the WD to lease the area as a hunting concession. After the national hunting corporation (TAWICO) stopped using the area in 1987, the government subleased the hunting rights to two foreign-owned companies. The hunting companies rarely interacted with the Maasai residents. When they did run into each other, the hunters acted as if they "owned the place."[43] Although a few Maasai leaders were invited to the hunting camps and were provided "benefits," like crates of beer or diesel fuel, most of the Maasai I spoke with resented the hunting companies. Many Maasai associated the hunters with the larger conservation bureaucracy, which they saw as a direct threat to Maasai land rights and sovereignty in Loliondo.

As expatriates and conservationists, the Petersons appeared to have more in common with the foreign hunting companies and the rest of the conservation bureaucracy than with the Maasai. However, they presented themselves and their ideas differently. Rather than working through a central government agency or with an influential conservation NGO, Dorobo Safaris went directly to the village governments with its idea. It continued to try to convince central government officials to support its project but faced significant resistance at every turn. The Petersons' personal connections and relationship of trust built over the years made direct negotiations with the villages both appealing and possible. The Tanzanian wildlife management structure made no space for adventure-oriented ecotourism on village lands. Dorobo Safaris hoped to show how this kind of tourism could create local incentives for conservation and be a win-win situation for villages and the state. It was convinced that helping to make tourism more valuable for villages would ultimately lead to more collective interest in conservation, as well as increased revenue for local and national institutions.

The Petersons believed in the idea of villagization, even if they were suspicious of much of its implementation. Conservationists and development agencies had previously collaborated in Loliondo to register villages for title deeds (see chapter 3). In October 1990, nine villages in Loliondo gained legal certificates of occupancy valid for ninety-nine years, the first pastoralist villages in Tanzania to gain such certificates. The 1990 demarcation and village certification process reinforced village boundaries as discrete territories following the initial villagization process in the mid-1970s. It was the first formal program allowing local residents to participate in describing and defining their village boundaries. Supporters of the village-titling effort believed that the clearly demarcated boundaries would help Loliondo villages protect their land from outside interests.

The village titles showed the area of Soit Orgoss spanning the three villages of Losoito/Maaloni, Olorien/Magaiduru, and Oloipiri. While Dorobo Safaris had started its relationship with only one village, Losoito/Maaloni, the company decided to work with all three villages. It wanted exclusive access to the entire Soit Orgoss area and wanted to encourage conservation among all the villages with rights over the land. Not only did the village title deeds make clear which villages contained the coveted Soit Orgoss area; they also made clear who the beneficiaries of the Dorobo Safaris project would be. The company would pay village governments, which would distribute the benefits of tourism to all village residents. A seemingly simple business decision turned out to produce a new configuration of Maasai community. Linking village boundaries with village membership to tourism revenue was a novel way of formulating the social and spatial relationships that constituted resource rights and cultural belonging in Loliondo.

Neoliberal Villagization

Tanzanian villages are modern institutions, developed as part of a strategy to combat the impoverishing forces of colonialism and its methods for incorporating peripheral agrarian societies like Tanzania into the global commodity trade. Based on the dominant development theory of the day, comparative advantage, the Tanzanian village was to be the center of rebuilding an independent agrarian nation and the engine that connected rural production with national development. Critics have charged that villagization was an example of an overly zealous interpretation of state planning and power forcing an ideology ill suited to the realities of rural agrarian life. The implementation of villagization was uneven, and the national program had different effects depending on local social and ecological conditions as well as the resources and attitudes of regional officials. Despite its mixed results, villagization was a deliberate tactic to overcome Tanzania's disadvantage as a peasant society within the structure of the emerging postcolonial global economy (see chapter 2 for a more thorough discussion of villagization). This policy did end up remaking Tanzanian society, if not in the ways originally imagined by its planners.

As an instrument of state power, the village in Maasailand was in many cases rather inept at promoting collective forms of labor or consciousness in the manner envisioned by national leaders and international consultants. However, early resistance to the Maasai village as a representation of a meaningful Maasai community was turned on its head in the 1990s. When Maasai communities in Loliondo entered into contractual agreements with ecotourism companies, the history of the village as a marginally functional site of community articulated with an emerging idea of the Maasai as members of a transnational indigenous community.[44] Through the land struggles over tourism and conservation, the Loliondo Maasai came to see the village as a legitimate form of local-state authority. Within the neoliberal rules of engagement, the village was a legible form of community that just might guarantee local rights and access to resources. In this way the village-state vied for authority with the nation-state in Loliondo.

By drawing on the material and symbolic legacies of the village as an idealized African community under socialism, the Maasai turned the village into their own idealized Maasai community.

Village-based tourism in Loliondo posed several challenges to dominant ideas about how foreign investment for tourism should be organized in Tanzania. Centralized ownership of resources was one of the main targets of structural adjustment policies and neoliberal reforms. Yet the pressure from international institutions and Tanzanian civil-society organizations to decentralize ownership and oversight of economic activities constantly rubbed against state institutions and bureaucracies that were often founded on the very notion of centralized management of wildlife and other natural resources.

In the late 1990s, villages in Loliondo for the first time became a significant factor in shaping Maasai social relations and territoriality. In large part because villages were legally recognized by the state as rights-bearing communities, the Loliondo Maasai used villages as sites for organizing Maasai political claims. By asserting the primacy of villages for representing Maasai interests, the Loliondo Maasai were able to negotiate directly with investors, to resist the government's proposed WMA and to force all investors, regardless of their influence with national elites, to deal directly with Maasai village leaders on questions of tourism on village land. By using the village to represent their Maasai interests in resisting national and international projects from transforming rangelands into farms, parks, and buffer zones, the Maasai transformed the village from a site of state-led development and encompassment to a local territorial claim to land and belonging.[45]

The village-based joint ventures were based on the idea that the village was a legitimate political-economic entity that also represented culturally accepted Maasai values, institutions, and practices. Authenticating the village empowered the Maasai to participate in the new struggle over tourism. As the actions of the Loliondo Maasai show, however, building a village representative of Maasai social and economic relations was not an easy undertaking. Turning the village from an externally imposed idea into a locally meaningful community took a series of political acts in which the village became an instrument to advocate for Maasai land and cultural rights.

The desire of investors to gain access to land adjacent to national parks for wildlife viewing and the ability of Maasai communities to at least partially regulate access to those lands rested on the belief of village sovereignty over land use, if not completely over wildlife management. From the mid-1990s into the twenty-first century, the Loliondo Maasai resisted land alienation under neoliberal economic policies by commodifying their land and culture through the joint-venture agreements with ecotourism companies. The durability of these joint ventures turned on the discursive production of the village as a legitimate site of belonging in the eyes of local, national, and international groups. The village was a source of rights for the Maasai and a means to gain access to desirable tourism sites for relatively small tourism investors. The parties were drawn together by their mutual conviction that the state would not otherwise recognize either groups right to "use" wildlife—the main resource in question—on village lands.

If the nation-state would not recognize the right of villagers or ecotourism investors to access wildlife outside national parks and game reserves, then the two groups believed that their mutual relationship was an effective way to stake their respective claims to nonconsumptive wildlife viewing. Ultimately, one of the ways that ecotourism investors were able to exploit wildlife on village lands was by physically going where few state officials ever did: the village itself.

Initially, the Maasai were able to use their village land rights to defend local rangelands from external interests, such as state and private agricultural schemes, the spread of peasant farmers, and the implementation of conservation buffer zones. However, under neoliberal economic conditions in the 1990s, defending pastoralist village land claims increasingly hinged on the ability of Maasai to attract, not repel, investors. To assure investors of their access to local resources, village leaders had to demonstrate local sovereignty or authority over their village territories. Clearly recognized village boundaries were important for investors, who not only hoped to gain national recognition for their business ventures but also needed to defend their exclusive rights to use an area against competing companies. Without fences or any clear markers dividing one village from the next, it was largely through local knowledge and regulation that village boundaries were made meaningful and enforceable.

Neoliberal Natures and Maasai Knowledge Production

As disenchantment with the socialist project was mounting in the early 1980s, Maasai leaders such as Lazaro Parkipuny reiterated their claim that the Serengeti and its surrounding areas had been taken illegally by the state. In the process, they advanced an argument that Maasai landscapes were distinct territories within the boundaries of the nation-state.[46] For Dorobo Safaris and other ecotourism investors, the belief in indigenous landscapes and the role that cultural and ecotourism could play in supporting sustainable land use and conservation was integral to their personal and business philosophies. By working directly with village leaders, the assemblage of ecotourism operators symbolically embraced the locality over the nation-state as the site of legitimate property rights to nature.[47] The village tourism contracts were an essential part of constructing a narrative about local rights to resources based on historical land-use patterns and Maasai ethnic belonging.

In June 1991, Parkipuny published the article "Pastoralism, Conservation and Development in the Greater Serengeti Region." In it he summarized how conventional wildlife protection policies were used to evict people to create parks and protected areas. With this as his starting point, he evaluated how local communities benefited from wildlife throughout the region. He pointed to several projects in neighboring Kenya, which weren't ideal but which granted the Maasai both monetary benefits from wildlife and important concessions for access to grazing lands in times of drought. Despite its "progressive image," Parkipuny argued, the Tanzanian state had "persistently toed the old conservation line" and "refused to concede recognition of even the most fundamental grievances of local communities."[48] Conservation had been used to dominate the Maasai and their landscapes: "Local communities . . . have been forced by the authorities to perceive wildlife enclaves as exotic entities, imposed against their will and at their expense."[49] Just as market reforms were taking hold in Tanzania, with his writings and speeches Parkipuny helped lay the ideological foundation for turning CBC into a struggle for Maasai liberation. He illustrated how national wildlife management policies and practices were attacks on Maasai citizenship, a people who "have persistently been denied their rights."[50] He cited the government's monopoly on tourism revenue as an affront to the Maasai people, who have been "denied the opportunity to participate in the decision making processes on issues located in their homelands."[51]

Neoliberal reforms took hold during a time when marginalized social groups like the Maasai were expressing their aspirations for political and economic change. The emergence of community conservation in the 1990s was a decidedly market-oriented development strategy. And yet this policy that embraced free-market ideas and ideologies also resonated with Maasai ambitions to be recognized as environmental stewards and to share in the management of and revenue from tourism and conservation. CBC provided tourism investors and Maasai communities an opportunity to remake conservation in ways that both groups, for different reasons, had been calling for.

Demand for ecotourism on Maasai village lands presented new possibilities to reimagine and remake landscapes that would generate revenue for local communities. By appealing to the transnational discourse that positioned indigenous people as close to nature and politically marginalized, village-based tourism contracts provided an alternative to national regulation as the only means of gaining access to wildlife. Articulating their claims to land as indigenous people with the recognition provided by joint ventures with international ecotourism investors, the Loliondo Maasai attached their ongoing land claims to market ideas and ideologies. The historical struggles between the Maasai and the state produced the landscapes of the current struggle over conservation and tourism, which in turn shape the meanings of identity and rule in Tanzanian Maasailand. The struggle over the meaning of nature and its relationship to property rights turned on the ability of the Maasai to claim wildlife as a village commodity over and against its status as a national commodity. From an initial relationship of convenience and mutual dependence, the joint ventures came to represent a new way to understand property rights and brought the potential for greater local control of resources.

As the Maasai continued to struggle to control tourism revenues on their lands, the time and energy invested in the village-based joint ventures informed their tactics. As discussed in chapters 4 and 5, the Maasai in Loliondo fought against several state-led and state-supported efforts to commodify their land for hunting and ecotourism. Time and again, Maasai leaders refused to accept policies and projects that they believed limited their opportunities to use the idea of the market to support their interests. The Maasai eschewed conservation efforts that separated economic from political benefits. The village-based joint ventures gave hope to the Maasai that market-based relationships could provide both revenue and rights.

Regulating the Market, Controlling Space

As the central government repeatedly failed to gain the support of Loliondo leaders, it took direct action to influence the ecotourism investors. The Non-consumptive Tourism Regulations released in 2007 effectively forced tourism companies using village lands to pay fees directly to the central government. The government began to formally regulate all tourism activities on village lands by establishing a fee schedule for different activities, including a wildlife activity fee of ten dollars per adult; a camping fee of twenty dollars per adult; vehicle entry fees ranging from five to thirty dollars per night; and miscellaneous fees for, among other things, night drives, fly camps, filming, and sport fishing. On top of these charges, each company operating in a game controlled area was now required to pay the WD an annual concession fee of twenty-five thousand dollars. These rules were the latest in a series of attempts to reassert national control over wildlife and tourism outside protected areas. Earlier attempts to regulate tourism on village lands had been difficult to enforce, and the Maasai had strongly resisted. These new regulations claimed national territorial control and circumvented local Maasai authority by forcing ecotourism companies to pay significant fees directly to the central government. This undermined village property rights and the village role in authorizing tourism on Maasai land. As one elected village leader explained to me,

> For a while up until the government crackdown in 2008, companies with contracts [with villages] were not paying the government. You could go to the Serengeti without going into the park and paying park fees. You could get everything in Loliondo that you would get in the park; you could even get animals like wild dogs that you don't see in the park. Now [after a new policy cracking down on such cogovernance arrangements] the money has to pass through the government treasury. It is hard to resist. Companies are nervous and afraid of the government.[52]

He went on to explain that companies that had "their own land" or that had managed to obtain a direct lease or title were in a better position than companies that had chosen to work directly with villages. Companies working with villages were now being "asked" to pay twice, whereas companies that "had land" did not have to pay the new government fee. As another resident of this leader's village explained, "These companies [that had land] were already paying rents on the land [to the government]," whereas the village-based tourism projects were paying rents directly to the communities.

The Loliondo Tour Operators Forum, which included all the companies with village-based contracts, tried to organize against the new directive. The coalition arranged a meeting with the minister of tourism and natural resources in Dar es Salaam. According to one of the tour operators present, the minister gave them five minutes, telling them, "I don't understand what you are worried about. This will be much simpler for you. You won't have to meet or negotiate with the community." Since the government's enforcement of this new policy, ecotourism companies have responded differently. Some companies now pay the state exclusively; some pay the state and the village, although less; and some companies continue to honor their original contracts. Loliondo Maasai leaders and ecotourism companies have had ongoing discussions about possible alternatives, but the regulatory reforms and the government's commitment to enforcing them have dealt a major blow to the ability of village-based joint ventures to challenge state territoriality. At the same time, the experience and history of the joint ventures have left a lasting impression on Maasai leaders in Loliondo. Just as Parkipuny and other Maasai leaders had earlier tried to remake socialism to fit the needs of pastoralists, they are now engaged in trying to refashion neoliberalism to address their interests. Their new experience and knowledge of what markets look and feel like informs their ideas and practices. The market remains a contingent site of engagement. As one of the Oloipiri village leaders told me, our *lengo* (goal) is to "lease our land for tourism to save it for pastoralism." The village is not a tool easily wielded, but in an era of market-driven development, in which property ownership is central to the idea of a rights-bearing subject, it is one of the few institutions the Maasai have to work with.

Conclusion

In this chapter I have argued that ecotourism joint ventures have refashioned the village into a site for regulating people's claims on and access to resources, as well as a meaningful representation of Maasai communities. Through their joint ventures with ecotourism operators, the Maasai in Loliondo have re-presented the meaning of their landscapes as a place for both pastoralist production and wildlife conservation. In the process, commodifying their land and identity has changed how the Maasai understand their land and themselves. The Maasai in Loliondo have relied on their partnerships with foreign tourism investors to demonstrate that they are capable of governing nature. By framing nature as a local commodity, the Maasai themselves are helping to position market-derived property rights at the center of Maasai identity in Loliondo.

The Loliondo Maasai have challenged state sovereignty by negotiating directly with investors. This process was contingent on a number of factors, including the status of some ecotourism investors, who were situated outside the state-NGO-conservation complex and were themselves dependent on the village partnerships to secure access to desirable areas for ecotourism safaris. For these ecotourism investors, Maasai villages represented a legible indigenous community recognized by the state as a property-owning community with which they could form quasi-legal partnerships. The legitimacy of these arrangements depended on the ability of village and regional Maasai leaders to represent the village as concurrently a local and transnational place. The ability to create new political openings, although often fleeting, has emboldened the communities in Loliondo to collectively organize within and across villages to resist government efforts to centralize control over Maasai landscapes. As the village became more important to defining claims of indigenous belonging and rights over natural resources, the communities in Loliondo increasingly depended on village institutions as sites to advocate for their rights.

CHAPTER 7

Conclusions

Neoliberal Land Rights?

This book is an account of tourism, land rights, and development in northern Tanzania. The economic policies put in place in the late 1980s and early 1990s reorganized the meanings of Tanzanian villages into new forms of international commodities. To focus simply on whether tourism is good or bad obscures the ways that tourism shapes the meanings of property, citizenship, and community. From my first visit in 1991 until the completion of this book in 2014, these issues have remained salient and enduring, despite the ebbs and flows of the story. I have shown how the development of different forms of safari tourism under neoliberal conditions in northern Tanzania remade the meaning of Maasai identity and landscapes. These political and economic forces structure not only individual choices but also collective ideas, values, and practices.

Much like the Serengeti itself, the Tanzanian village is both a place and an idea. My main argument is that liberalization policies introduced in the late 1980s changed the context in which foreign investors and Maasai residents imagined Maasai communities as rights-bearing villages. Although the village was initially seen as a state imposition, Loliondo Maasai turned it into a legitimate political entity capable of representing the interests of its citizens, a space of belonging for the Maasai, and finally a site for foreign investment where travel companies could gain access to land for safari tourism.

For many groups including travelers, tourists, hunters, philanthropic organizations, development agencies, students, researchers, and Tanzanian officials themselves, the village often transmitted a nostalgic quality. It was the embodiment of authentic African life, communal, bounded, and rooted in place. This understanding resembled Julius Nyerere's own nostalgia for building a modern African nation in the image he had of precolonial African communalism. For state officials, the village was the most tangible example of Tanzanians' path toward modernity with clear boundaries, elected representatives, and democratic norms for its citizens to participate in social, economic, and political life within the nation state. For Maasai residents the village was largely an externally imposed idea, one that tried to remake Maasai social relations by transplanting kinship with village government as the primary locus of access to grazing land for livestock. This change was part of a larger reform effort to replace ethnicity and lineage with modern state institutions. For many Maasai, the village was a flawed experiment that failed to increase their land security or citizenship status. The creation of Maasai villages in the 1970s did, however, have lasting effects. I argue that neoliberalization created a context for new meanings of the village, community, and land rights to emerge.

This book is neither a tragic nor a triumphant tale of safari tourism in Tanzania. Rather, it has tried to illustrate how globalization is unfolding in a specific place, Loliondo, and the broader implications of neoliberal development on Maasai landscapes. Safari tourism investment on village lands bordering Serengeti National Park is valuable for conservation, economic development, and community livelihoods. This book has tried to answer the question: what happens when foreign investment becomes a driving discourse for conservation and development? I have specifically examined the changing meaning of Maasai villages after the deregulation of the safari tourism industry. In the following discussion, I outline the three primary ways that the political economy of tourism in Tanzania has reshaped the cultural landscape.

Land and Property

Market-led globalization has intensified the importance of delineated property rights. In order for investors to participate in economic projects, they require clear property regimes. In places like northern Tanzania, where property rights have remained somewhat flexible, as well as contested, neoliberalization encouraged efforts to clarify and codify property relationships. This new policy context created openings to appropriate land with ambiguous tenure regimes, leaving Tanzanians with uncertain land rights vulnerable to market-based dispossession. In one example of how neoliberalization encourages the state to claim land and resources in the name of efficient and productive investment, the government established the Tanzanian land bank to allocate "unused or underutilized land" to foreign investors. In order to retain access to land and critical natural resources, groups lacking clearly defined land rights needed to respond. One way Tanzanian citizens have done so is by codifying their property rights, making them more visible and legitimate to investors. In Loliondo, villages, as territorially bound units of production and belonging, became important sites for the Maasai to organize their cultural and economic claims to land and natural resources. As a legible symbol of community, the village became the material representation of Maasai society through which the Maasai could interact with national and international groups. If not an equal player, the Maasai village resident or village representative had a recognizable seat at the table. For good or for bad, property claims have become the language of activism under neoliberal globalization. Despite the dangers associated with privatizing communal lands, this study has shown how the Maasai have used the new discourse of CBC and village-based tourism to organize community interests. One of the primary ways that the shifting paradigm of private property has influenced cultural formations in northern Tanzania is the propensity for property disputes to encourage ethnic conflict and differentiation. As property lines become the legitimate and legible symbol of community, other, more fluid social relationships are subsumed by their logic.

Development experts, donors, and some conservation groups proposed CBC as the best way to address the problematic divide between people and nature. CBC meant different things to different groups, but at its core it meant devolving management authority over and redistributing benefits from wildlife living on or near communal and privately held land. As experts and bureaucrats embarked on a decade-long search for a policy approach to CBC in Tanzania, rural communities like those in Loliondo and private safari tourism operators searched for their own approaches. Maasai villages in Loliondo signed contracts with tourism investors for exclusive access to their village lands in exchange for a share of the tourism revenue. This was a novel way to earn money and to assert village land rights. Notwithstanding the relatively small size and influence of these tourism investors compared to other foreign investors, including hunting companies that competed for access to the area, the contracts between the ecotourism investors and villages symbolized the transnational recognition of Maasai land rights. Although property rights have long been the bedrock of capitalist social and economic relationships, they have historically been grounded in state recognition and enforcement. What was different about the approach in Loliondo was that the Maasai drew primarily on international recognition to try to leverage the state to enforce their rights.

Maasai leaders in Loliondo came to see the "contracts" between villages and ecotourism companies, which grant access to local resources, as a way to remake their social relationships with the state. Drawing on their understanding, Maasai leaders distinguished such access to resources from ownership of those resources. Many of the leaders and residents I interviewed contrasted contracts, which they said depended on the legitimacy of community ownership and rights, with state granted "titles" or "leases" through which the state intended to grant and guarantee secure long-term property rights. As one male elder from Ololosokwan village told me, the agreement between the village and a tourism investor "is not a title; it is a contract. The company doesn't need or want a title; they want a strong contract. Now [it] is on the village to prove we own the land." Ultimately, such proof involved a long and complicated struggle between villages and state agencies. If investors could enter into direct partnerships with communities, Maasai leaders believed that they could exploit the qualities of ecotourism for both private profit and community gain. Yet state agencies used similar tactics by partnering with tourism investors to solidify their own claims. In this case, state officials promoted certain investors and forms of tourism that enhanced their own territorial claims. Thus the state legitimated the OBC hunting lease and the Thomson Safaris/TCL nature refuge while it marginalized the village joint ventures.

Re-ethnicization

The need to draw on neoliberal discourse and emphasize private property rights to secure their own economic interests meant that the Maasai helped to remake the meaning of their landscapes in a form more legible to capitalist markets and understandings. As land with clear boundaries and definitive owners became the necessary means to capture tourism revenue, questions of precisely which Maasai ethnic groups belonged to what territory become consequential in new ways. Village tourism contracts became one important instrument that the Maasai used to demonstrate their property rights to Tanzanian state officials, foreign investors, and transnational organizations. The contracts produced new property regimes that imbued village boundaries with greater regulatory significance, changing the very meaning of territory that increasingly divided the community along ethnic lines. Smaller Maasai ethnic groups like the Laitayok Maasai felt that they were being squeezed by more-powerful groups and feared long-term exclusion from essential rangelands. Whereas these groups had faced discrimination in the past, reciprocal social arrangements helped maintain regional access to pastures for all Maasai ethnic groups in Loliondo. With village boundaries mapping directly onto tourism revenue streams, the economic logic of rigid boundaries began to override the cultural logic of flexible boundaries. This situation led some Maasai groups to see the village tourism contracts as a direct threat to their livelihoods. This partly explains why some members of the Laitayok Maasai ethnic group viewed the Thomson Safaris/TCL investment as possible protection for their access to land and resources. As one Laitayok man told me, "If the Purko have their investors, then we need our own investors."[1]

In 2006, Sanna Ojalammi published an excellent study of the history of land conflicts in Loliondo. In her dissertation, Ojalammi writes, "Today sectional boundaries inevitably cut across present-day administrative and even national boundaries. Thus, their importance has diminished as a result of State territoriality."[2] This book makes a different argument. My research shows that ethnic territorial affiliations have become more, not less, significant over the past two decades.[3] Rather than eroding ethnic territorial identifications, neoliberalization has encouraged ethnic identification as a source for territorial claims. Whereas past violence was often perpetuated based on the claim that "you stole our cattle," current violence is being carried out based on claims that "your cattle are on our land." I argue that ethnic territoriality has taken on greater significance under neoliberal imperatives to commoditize land.

The Political Ecology of Tourism

A political ecological approach to nature-society relationships starts with the premise that the environment is as social and political as it is ecological. The meanings and values of nature are not simply products but recursively constitute the environment itself. Describing these "constitutive spatial politics" regarding resettlement schemes in Zimbabwe's eastern highlands, anthropologist Donald Moore argues that "livelihood practices have a spatial dimension, while they are also constitutive of popular understandings of the significance of the relationship between locality and identity (Pred 1986). An emphasis on the cultural politics of place underscores the simultaneity of symbolic and material struggles over territory. These struggles are highly localized, laying claim to specific terrain, yet are never simply local, sealed off from an outside beyond" (1998b, 347). A political ecology approach to the production of place demands that we situate the Serengeti and the Maasai villages in Loliondo in a larger political economic context.

Safari tourism is one of the key sites through which local meanings and value are produced. Scholarly literature on tourism often revolves around the tourist gaze and the role of tourist desires and nostalgia in shaping the meaning and value of far-from-home landscapes. Such a framing places the power to transform tourism in the hands of the tourists and tour companies. Complying with a checklist like the one created by Thomson Safaris for sustainable or green tourism often simplifies the effect of tourism on local places to a series of moral or ethical decisions in the hands of privileged travelers. Rarely do such checklists illustrate the historical and geographical formation of regional landscapes; rather, they reproduce a Western idea of African nature that contributes to the discursive justifications that dispossess Africans of agency in conserving or managing that nature. Such understandings help frame tourism as a passive practice of consuming the visual representations of the landscape, in this case symbolized best by the well-known African big five game animals: lion, elephant, buffalo, leopard, and rhino. Reproducing Loliondo as a tourist landscape that extends the "Serengeti experience" runs the risk of writing the Maasai and pastoral livelihoods completely out of the story of the Serengeti, rendering them almost unimaginable, except perhaps as tourist curiosities themselves.

Relying on these dominant understandings of African nature that reproduce the "myth of wild Africa," conservationists have been able to defend their practices in the name of global interests or as Bernhard Grzimek put it in the film "Serengeti Shall Not Die," the interests of humankind. Knowingly or not, tourists participate in a political economy that privilege specific ideas and values of what African nature is and who it is for. The room for alternative representations of African nature that incorporate the agency of African people like the Maasai is quite limited. For example, framing Enashiva as a place that needs to be conserved gave the owners of Thomson Safaris/TCL credibility in the eyes of the state and international groups, as well as their safari clients. Such a discursive framing of conservation as an ethical practice supports the commonsense narrative that establishing a nature refuge in the middle of Maasai villages is a sensible way to preserve nature, educate local people, and provide them with tangible benefits. There is little room in such a narrative for alternative understandings of the land as providing essential pasture for both livestock and wildlife. The irony of course is that prior to Thomson Safaris/TCL's purchase of the land in 2006, the Maasai had managed it for decades precisely in this way. The apparent "need" to conserve this land was established upon Thomson Safaris' arrival, not before it. Prior to the Thomson Safaris purchase in 2006, the government was willing to lease the land for a multiplicity of land uses, including agriculture, which would have destroyed the area not only for livestock but also for wildlife. This contingent history was quickly erased by Thomson Safaris' efforts to document the authentic origin story of the area as a nature reserve.

So what does this all mean for the politics of tourism under neoliberal globalization? The Maasai in Loliondo are not against tourism or even conservation. To the contrary, they have been actively participating in tourism and conservation for decades. Their primary goal, however, is often different from that of the tourism companies. For most Maasai I have worked with and interviewed in Loliondo, the primary benefit of tourism is not revenue but rights. Maasai want tourism to add value to their land so that they can continue to use it for pastoralism. The village-based joint ventures provided the clearest model of this multipurpose land-use strategy. The Enashiva nature refuge and the government's attempt to excise the Loliondo hunting blocks represent a radically different course. Maasai communities want to profit from tourism, but monetary benefits alone cannot compete with the value of the land for supporting local livelihoods.

The Neoliberalization of Conservation

The rapid transition from socialism to neoliberal capitalism in Tanzania was associated with profound changes in a number of policies. In Tanzania, as in many other African nations, neoliberal reforms to privatize state functions, decentralize management and planning, and encourage foreign investment were fully in place by the late 1980s. Foreign investors, whom the Nyerere government kept at arm's length, were to be welcomed as the vanguard of a new era. Because international experts deemed the bureaucratic state the problem, they felt that unleashing market forces would be the solution to create new value and harness latent opportunities. The economic reforms were accompanied by a number of political reforms aimed at facilitating the growth of civil-society institutions to fill the gap left by structural adjustment's "rolling back" of the state.[4] Although many Tanzanians were skeptical of market-led reforms, the promise of a more powerful civil society offered intriguing possibilities for social and economic justice never fulfilled by national development plans. This shift did not mean a simple retreat of the state. As I have described throughout this book, state actors and institutions adapted to these new conditions to reinvigorate the role and authority of the state itself. Tanzanian officials and agencies are not driven by a neoliberal ideology as much as they are responding to the constraints and openings created by neoliberalization. For all the public and scholarly criticism of neoliberalization, many marginalized groups in Tanzania and around the world saw the reforms of the late 1980s and early 1990s as new opportunities to fulfill long-held aspirations for development and social justice.

Global economic policies like structural adjustment are most often understood as macro-level interventions. Yet these policies and reforms take shape in local contexts. One of the sectors most transformed by neoliberalism in Tanzania is conservation. Much has been written about the history of conservation in northern Tanzania and the close relationship between conservation and state power.[5] The mid-1980s was a period of crisis in Tanzania not only for the overall economy but also for the conservation community. The lack of state resources to manage the vast network of protected areas, recognizing that ecosystem boundaries did not neatly correspond with park boundaries, and well-organized transnational social movements against fortress conservation models led to a rethinking of the relationships among the state, communities, and international conservation groups and interests. Conservationists and state officials began to realize and accept that large state-funded parks and reserves were not a sustainable model in highly indebted and underdeveloped countries like Tanzania. Although tourism was a vital part of Tanzania's economy, it did not pay for the costs of the necessary conservation bureaucracy and infrastructure. Not only would it be necessary to privatize lodges and hunting concessions; it would also require rethinking the role of communities living adjacent to conservation areas.

Beginning in the early 1990s, two distinct approaches to safari tourism development emerged in northern Tanzania. One involved private ecotourism operators signing contracts with village governments to carry out walking and camping safaris on village land. This approach involved multiple tourism companies and six different villages, each with its own contracts and relationships. Maasai residents living in Loliondo drew on these projects collectively, highlighting the central role played by village governments in overseeing and benefiting from tourism activities. The other dominant approach to tourism in Loliondo over the past two decades took the form of state-facilitated tourism investment. The two best-known examples of this were the granting of a hunting concession, which overlapped with Maasai village land, to OBC, and the long-term lease of communal pastoral grazing land to the U.S. travel company Thomson Safaris/TCL for use as a private nature refuge. Loliondo residents came to associate these two projects with a state-supported effort to dispossess the Maasai of their territory and to assert national economic and political power over Maasai land and interests.

For years, the Maasai commodified their culture in order to earn minimal income on the margins of a political economic system in which they were but a sideshow on Tanzania's famous wildlife safaris.[6] For the most part, the appealing landscapes in which tourists snapped photos of the Maasai were controlled by national agencies.[7] Encounters between tourists and Maasai people in Loliondo certainly share affinities with cultural encounters in more-staged settings, such as official cultural *bomas* located just off the well-traveled tourist route.

One thing that distinguished tourism in Loliondo, as opposed to cultural tourism en route to Serengeti National Park for instance, was that tourists encountered not only the Maasai people and their homesteads as cultural sites but also how Maasai pastoralism functioned on village land, with fewer restrictions than within nationally managed protected areas. Despite being able to read in park brochures and pamphlets that the history of the NCA and Serengeti National Park was shaped by Maasai herding practices, signboards, gates, and of course park entrance fees were clear signals that these protected-area spaces were Tanzanian and not Maasai. When tourists turn off the main road leading to Serengeti National Park and make the dusty journey north to Loliondo, they are often surprised that the land resembles that within the park boundaries. The lack of fences is an awe-inspiring and somewhat confusing sight for many tourists. The excitement of experiencing such a natural landscape and the absence of gates, guards, and entrance fees mark this landscape as more authentic and wild than those of the NCA or Serengeti National Park. The growing desire of tourists and tour companies to experience such rare landscapes shifted the relationships between tourists and the Maasai, from one of simple objectification to more-complex relations of production, consumption, and subjectification.

Safari Tourism, Imperialism, and the Idea of Development in Africa

In February 1970, President Nyerere asked the students at the University College, Dar es Salaam (now the University of Dar es Salaam), to debate all aspects of socialist development in Tanzania.[8] A group of students who were also members of the Tanganyika African National Union Youth League (TYL) presented a paper for public debate. In their letter, the students discussed the merits and limits of pursuing tourism as a strategy for socialist economic development. The "Tourism Debate," as it was widely known, played itself out in the *Standard* newspaper for four months, from May to August 1970. The students largely criticized tourism for reinforcing colonial relationships that did little to achieve the goals of development, self-reliance, and freedom on which the country's socialist path was built. They were critical of the arguments that tourism would bring in much-needed foreign exchange earnings and create promising employment. They rightly pointed out that given the high standards of tourist facilities, the import substitution effect and taxation on locally produced goods would be minimal for some time. If tourism did spur industrial production, they argued it would not benefit the average Tanzanian: "If our industrial policy is geared towards producing tourist goods, it will mean that we shall not be able to satisfy the needs of our people."[9] They went on to say, "Whether it is a designed tapestry for the hotel room, a fan, water-heater, or a whisky, the tourists' requirements are those of a developed consumer society as opposed to our developing investment oriented rural society."[10]

The TYL was skeptical that tourism would stimulate secondary industries that could substantially develop the national economy. In its view the development of "small-scale" or "cottage" industries such as producing crafts and souvenirs would never stimulate a vibrant industrial economy. "The most that tourism would encourage is fruit and poultry 'gardens'—not farms—probably tended by the wives of the bureaucrats and politicians in town during their leisure time. Tourism may stimulate some taxi business and of course the 'oldest profession on earth'—prostitution. We tender that no person with his full sense will argue that that is economic development."[11] As good young socialists, the authors of the TYL letter state that benefits from tourism will not accrue to all social classes. Rather, they will mainly benefit the elites or the "international bourgeoisie."

The group was critical of the idea that tourism would promote local culture by developing "indigenous folklore" and promoting intercultural exchange and understanding. Rather, they argued that tourism made it "all the more difficult for [them] to destroy the colonialist inherited bourgeois outlook for [their] cities."[12] The class consciousness of the letter is an important reminder of Tanzania's history. Whether Tanzania's socialist experiment was deemed a success or a failure, the debate surrounding tourism in the 1970s set the tone for Tanzanian politics in that era. Such socialist analysis still has meaning in Tanzanian public life today and is perhaps more popular in retrospect than during its heyday.

Issa Shivji, law professor and leading public intellectual, edited a book in 1973 that was dedicated to publishing the debate for a wider audience. Shivji largely shared the critique of tourism laid out by the TYL. He reiterates the degrading effects of tourism, especially for a society struggling to emerge from the legacies of colonialism. Invoking the conclusions of Ngugi wa Thiong'o in his famous essay "Decolonizing the Mind," Shivji writes that tourism only serves to reinforce the biased cultural hierarchy put in place during colonial rule.

> Tourism . . . with the extremely humiliating subservient "memsahib" and "sir" attitudes and, above all, the unavoidable dampening of vigilance and militancy that accompanies the necessity to create a hospitable climate for tourists—is a major component in this "cultural imperialism." One has only to go to some of our palatious beach hotels (only the outside of which a Tanzanian fisherman will ever see) and watch the waiters and waitresses in their immaculate uniforms, moving up and down the corridors like disciplined school children . . . to understand what an outrageous, alien structure we are harbouring in the midst of our policy of ujamaa. (Shivji 1973, ix)

By the 1990s, the TYL no longer existed, but the University of Dar es Salaam continued to be a place where critical debates about development took place. Shivji, still a law professor at the university, headed the president's Commission on Land Reform. One of his main recommendations was that land should not be sold outright so that peasants and pastoralists could continue to afford their rural livelihoods. This recommendation, along with many others, was rejected. Shivji started the Land Rights Research Institute to advocate on behalf of groups that he felt were particularly vulnerable to the exploits of unfettered capitalist development. Pastoralists and hunter-gatherers were chief among these groups.

The "Tourism Debate" notwithstanding, Tanzania like many other developing nations in Africa and Latin America has embraced tourism as one path to economic prosperity. Critics rarely blamed tourism for contributing to the failure of development or the debt crisis in the 1980s. Rather, they remained convinced that a robust tourism sector with the proper management and investment was still one of Tanzania's best options for development. The 1990s saw a resurgence of the idea that tourism could help revitalize stagnant economies like Tanzania's, in sharp contrast to the TYL argument decades earlier. Tourism dovetailed nicely with the dominant ideas of neoliberal development and sustainability. Development experts believed that private-sector investment together with increased global demand for foreign travel would be a boon for Tanzania. Although cultural imperialism remained a valid critique, there was a limited audience either within the country or outside it for such arguments. The idea that people could spend significant money on travel and at the same time contribute to the economic development of a country became an integral selling point of Tanzania's tourism economy during the 1990s. Tourists could see their safari to an African country not only as a once-in-a-lifetime vacation experience but also as a way to help poor African people. In particular, ecotourism emerged as way for wealthy Westerners to simultaneously enjoy nature and promote conservation and sustainable development.

Tourism may be part of a strategy of economic development for rural areas, but I am concerned that we are asking the wrong questions. How tourism can contribute to development is typically cast in terms of straightforward economic benefits. How many jobs does it provide? Does it create new markets for local crafts and agricultural goods? What revenue does it bring to households and communities? Embedded in these questions is a simple cultural assumption. If people benefit financially from tourism, they will value tourism. For many conservationists, this is the critical link between tourism and building a broad constituency for nature preservation. One of the guiding principles of community conservation is that people will value conservation if they profit from it. It is this seemingly simple, rational economic logic that has led so many conservation organizations to embrace or at least experiment with community conservation projects. Much of the research on community conservation has tried to assess this connection between the economic value of conservation and community values and interests.[13]

What most of these studies fail to examine is the political economy of resource access, use, and control with which questions of conservation and tourism are intimately entwined. In the case of Loliondo, economic benefits, be they cash payments to village governments, the funding of a health clinic, the building of school classrooms, or the sponsoring of local children's school fees, cannot easily be separated from long-term control and authority over land and natural resources. As many Maasai see it, these benefits are used as self-legitimizing tools to justify the good intentions and philanthropy of tourism investors. Throughout this book, I have argued that economic benefits alone will not tell us much about changing ideas, values, and attitudes of communities toward conservation and tourism. Rather, we need to understand how tourism and conservation projects articulate with political economic questions about resource access and control. I have explored how different types of consumptive and nonconsumptive safari tourism reinforce or challenge dominant development discourses and how they influence ongoing efforts to remake landscapes.

Ecotourism epitomizes a contemporary return to the ideas of the mid-1980s and the Brundtland Commission's report that economic growth would have to be sustainable in order to contribute to consistent and reproducible development.[14] To many observers, safari hunting tourism may appear to do the opposite. But despite the efforts of many international conservation and animal-rights organizations, the preference for hunters or hikers may be decided not by the morality of taking pictures or animal trophies but rather by how these forms of safari tourism articulate with competing claims for territorial control.

The Cultural Politics of Land and Tourism

In a meeting in Dar es Salaam in 2004, a United Nations Development Program official asked me if I was "against markets." We were discussing the prospects of the country's land law for safeguarding local land rights in light of the current policy environment to promote private investment by setting up a national land bank for foreign investors. The request that I declare whether I was "for them" or "against them" seemed quite strange given that we were talking about a variety of forces influencing the new law's implications for rural livelihoods and development. This question was problematic not only for the false choice that it posed but also for presenting a development narrative in which that choice was even imaginable. For many Africans, rejecting all markets is neither plausible nor desirable, any more than blindly embracing widespread and deepening market relations as a solution for poverty, insecurity, and rights. In this book, I have shown why the discourse of neoliberalism, despite its troubled history and uncertain promises, appeals to the Maasai and other groups in Africa. Rather than a simple embrace or refusal of "the market," this study demonstrates how development practices make markets meaningful, opening up new possibilities, as well as limiting choices of civil-society groups and their constituencies.

Market forces have restructured property relations, thereby enabling novel political tactics. Embracing ecotourism companies as allies against the national government did reshape the meanings of conservation. However, as Loliondo leaders consistently point out, the new conservation paradigm is less a solution to land insecurity and more an ongoing and contingent site of struggle. It would be easy to criticize the village-based model as counter to the very ideals that pastoralists claim they are fighting for: their ability to determine their own path to development, which depends largely on flexible property rights and broadly based cultural-political alliances. However, village-based conservation was less a strategic attempt to determine future land use and more one of the few viable options to claim resources in an environment where market-driven relationships were remaking the Tanzanian landscape. The freedom that the communities associated with their joint ventures offered no guarantees of long-term rights and continued to expose them to significant risk. While Loliondo communities have made significant gains by linking tourism to a political economic understanding of pastoral land rights, investors like the OBC and Thomson Safaries/TCL working more directly through state institutions have been able to use current policies to push for more exclusionary understandings of property and benefits.

The development and growth of the village-based joint ventures played a significant role in shaping the regional understanding of a Maasai landscape and land rights in Loliondo. They allowed the Maasai to draw on these geographic understandings both to defend their model of tourism and to challenge competing forms of tourism investment. The recent history of ecotourism in the region has fashioned new relationships among pastoralists, the market, and their land. In seeing landscapes as dynamic and relational productions rather than as fixed containers, we can better understand the effects of conservation and development projects and show how green narratives of environmental sustainability promoted by investors, international organizations, and the state may or may not articulate with local agendas and practices.[15]

This book tells a specific story about Loliondo Maasai and Maasai land-scapes. But it is also an illustration of how the connections that link rural land struggles and market-driven conservation structure the terrain of cultural politics in sites where tourism, private land accumulation, and historically tense state-society relationships are deeply entangled. By comparing the relationship between the Maasai people, landscapes, national development policies and experts, and tourism investors, I show that so-called global processes are always simultaneously local and translocal. Understanding how territory, politics, and identity are spatially constituted in Maasai landscapes sheds important light on the relationship between global development, indigenous struggles, and nature in a site, the Serengeti, with important implications for conservation, development, and cultural rights the world over.

The Politics of the Present

In late September 2013, the prime minister of Tanzania, Mizengo Pinda, announced that the government would halt its plan to excise fifteen hundred square kilometers, nearly 40 percent of Maasai village land, to create a national protected area and hunting reserve bordering Serengeti National Park. The declaration was the clearest sense of victory for Maasai villagers and activists who had been fighting the plan since it was first leaked in July 2010 and then formally announced in April 2013. Maasai leaders had been bracing for a state-led scheme to expand the boundaries of Serengeti National Park and the NCA since they were first created in 1959. The political tactics of Maasai leaders over the past three years built on a longer history of Maasai politics in which leaders creatively advocated for pastoralism as a modern and sustainable livelihood practice and culture. In the 1970s and 1980s, the Maasai largely tried to create space for pastoralists within the national-socialist developmental state. But by the 1990s, many Maasai were disillusioned with nationalism and sought new arenas in which to advocate for their cultural, economic, and political rights. As I have shown in this book, the Maasai creatively engaged with market-driven development discourse, specifically with their identities as property-owning villagers, to challenge the state's and foreign investors' claims over land and natural resources.

Pressuring the state to back off its plan to permanently divide the Maasai and their cattle from large segments of their village land, which also supported large wildlife populations, was no small feat. The Maasai organized themselves to protest the government-led eviction. Twenty thousand Maasai, close to half of the region's total population, turned out to protest the action. Three thousand Maasai women from across Loliondo assembled for nine days in the village of Magaiduru, where they met with traditional leaders as well as elected district councilors. These meetings prompted the regional security officer to warn government officials that "something crazy [was] happening in Loliondo." The Maasai from Loliondo contacted elected representatives, traditional leaders, and NGOs from the five districts with large Maasai populations. Representing close to two hundred thousand citizens, this group collectively threatened to abandon the ruling party, Chama Cha Mapinduzi/Party of the Revolution, and join the opposition party Chama cha Demokrasia na Maendelea/Party for Democracy and Progress.

In July and August 2013, a delegation of eighty-nine Maasai, including six women from each Loliondo village, went to the capital city of Dodoma. Sitting near the entrance to the parliament building, they demanded an explanation and a reversal of the government action to dispossess them of their land. Over ninety University of Dar es Salaam students joined them, demonstrating diverse societal support for the Loliondo Maasai land struggle. To their surprise, the prime minister agreed to meet with the Maasai delegation, welcoming them to a meal where he slaughtered a cow on their behalf. After several hours of discussion, the prime minister asked the delegation to return home to Loliondo, assuring them that he would address their concerns.

Organizing mass protests and forming regional alliances cutting across class, age, ethnicity, and urban-rural differences were impressive undertakings. Unlike past efforts in which the Maasai protested largely as indigenous people, marginalized because of their ethnic and cultural status, this movement was largely based on the idea that the Tanzanian state was unfairly persecuting Tanzanian citizens, specifically Tanzanian villagers who happened to be Maasai. During the previous two decades, the Maasai had used their status as villagers to connect their fight for land rights to a broader discourse of globalization in which the state and capital conspired to dispossesses peasants and pastoralists of their land and citizenship rights. It is hard to say for certain what led to the Tanzanian government's reversal of its plan, but it seems clear that the political activism, based on Maasai collective claims as villagers, was an important approach. State authorities did not concede their control over land in Loliondo for international trophy hunting or their sovereign power to negotiate with foreign investors. However, it does seem that local activists have found important ways to organize the interests of the Maasai and other Tanzanians across Loliondo and the country. Such collective action is an essential component of any effort that hopes to hold government actors, as well as foreign investors, accountable. As of the final editing of this book, the conflict over land in Loliondo remains as contested as ever, and the government's interest in making of Loliondo a national conservation area appears very strong. In November 2014 the Tanzanian government apparently reversed its position and planned to go ahead with the evictions and create a wildlife corridor for safari hunting, dispossessing the Maasai of over one-third of their land. They have offered six hundred thousand dollars as compensation. Immediately, Maasai leaders and organizations directly challenged this effort, working with their international partners and allies to once again raise transnational awareness about the issue. Journalists reported widely on the latest attempt to create a hunting reserve on the edge of Serengeti Park. Avaaz renewed its campaign and in the short term seemed to have once again slowed the enclosure of Maasai land in Loliondo. This story may never have a clear ending. What remains salient to this book is the relentless efforts by Maasai communities to actively resist these forms of conservation by organizing their interests and communities and working both locally and transnationally to shape their landscape and their power to participate in making their future.[16]

The Enashiva Nature Refuge remains the property of Thomson Safaris/TCL. Community leaders have managed to fight back against the company and its efforts to divide the community along ethnic lines and to limit its use of its traditional grazing land. The biggest challenge to the Enashiva project is the ability of the Maasai community to work together and present a united front to the company. Without a clear community faction supporting the project, it has become more difficult for Thomson Safaris/TCL to prevent the Maasai from using the area for grazing. By consistently challenging the aims and intentions of the nature refuge tourism project and working across ethnic lines, Maasai leaders

from the Purko and the Loita ethnic groups have been able to join together with
the Laitayok Maasai to challenge the investors claims to the land. Although
there remains some political and ethnic division among the Maasai, the vast
majority of residents and leaders now see the project as threatening Maasai
land security for all Maasai ethnic groups. The idea that one ethnic group would
gain land rights at the expense of others has been largely discredited through
continued meetings with traditional and elected leaders, as well as NGOs. From
the beginning of 2013, the directors of the Enashiva Nature Refuge have allowed
the Maasai to graze on their land with minimal interference. Although Maasai
leaders expect a renewed effort by Thomson Safaris/TCL to assert their rights
in the future, their efforts to unite the community and demonstrate collective
Maasai land rights grounded in a multiethnic and multivillage strategy appears
to be paying dividends.

Major Wildlife and Land Legislation

The following data were compiled from Madulu et al. 2007 and Augustino et al. 2013.

The Wildlife Act of 1974

The act created three layers of authority in the management of wildlife resources: the president, the minister (of the Ministry of Natural Resources and Tourism), and the director of wildlife. The president is given powers to appoint the director of wildlife (S.3) the power to establish game reserves (S.5); powers to modify any restrictions in game reserves, game controlled areas, and partial game reserves, and powers to declare any category of persons unfit for the grant of a game license (S. 22).

The WCA provided the basic framework for wildlife management in Tanzania and the allocation of existing rights and authority. It concerned itself primarily with the creation of and provisions for certain protected areas (game reserves, game controlled areas, partial game reserves), and the regulation of wildlife uses throughout mainland Tanzania.

Land Act (1999) and Village Land Act (1999)

Wildlife is dependent on what happens to their habitats, and there is a strong link between land and wildlife legislation. In 1999 the Land Ordinance of 1923, which had been the principal governing statute regarding land tenure and management in Tanzania, was repealed and replaced by two pieces of legislation, the Land Act No. 4 of 1999 and Village Land Act No. 5 of 1999, which came into force on May 1, 2001.

The Land Act establishes three categories of land: general land, reserved land, and village land. The Village Land Act deals with the management of the latter category of land, while the Land Act deals primarily with the management of reserved land and general land in line with the sectoral pieces of legislation under which the reserved lands are established.

The Wildlife Conservation (Tourist Hunting) Regulations, 2000—GN. No. 306/2000 (revised edition, 2002)

The regulations establish procedures for the allocation of hunting blocks to tourist hunting companies and to attach conditions to each hunting company while performing its hunting activities. It imposes fines and the possible cancellation of a hunting block license for any company or person that conducts activities contrary to it. Regulation 16(5) of GN. 306 states: "No person shall conduct tourist hunting, game viewing, photographic safari, walking safari or any wildlife based tourist safari within a hunting block or within any wildlife protected area outside Ngorongoro Conservation Area, and National park, except by and in accordance with the written authority of the Director of Wildlife previously sought and obtained. This regulation includes not only photographic tourism activities but also game viewing and walking safari as activities prohibited in hunting blocks."

Wildlife Conservation (WMA) Regulations of 2002

The WMA Regulations (subsidiary legislation under section 84 of the WCA of 1974) provide for the creation of WMAs on village lands and implementation of the Wildlife Policy's objectives. The regulations allow communities to become corporate entities and participate in and benefit from wildlife utilization in WMAs. However, in order to use any other natural resource products like fish, forests, or bees, one needs to consult sectoral policies, laws, and regulations regulating that particular resource. The regulations describe the process that the communities must follow in order to qualify for receiving wildlife user rights.

The Wildlife Policy of Tanzania of 2007

The Wildlife Policy of Tanzania of 2007 provides direction for wildlife subsector in sustainable conservation of wildlife and wetland resources.

The Wildlife Conservation Act of 2009

The objective of the Wildlife Conservation Act (WCA) of 2009 was to enhance the protection and conservation of wildlife resources and its habitats in game reserves and game controlled areas, wildlife management areas, dispersal areas, migratory route corridors, and buffer zones and of all animals found in areas adjacent to these areas by putting in place appropriate infrastructure and sufficient personnel and equipment. The WCA applies to all establishments in the central government, local government, public authorities, and agencies. Also, it applies to private and local communities that deal with wildlife issues.

The Wildlife Conservation (Tourist Hunting) Regulations of 2010

The wildlife conservation tourist hunting regulations of 2010 provide day-to-day guidelines of all activities related to tourist hunting. The Wildlife Conservation (Tourist Hunting) Regulations of 2010 require the Wildlife Division to conduct an in-depth analysis or evaluation of the performance of all hunting companies in the third year of the hunting term. This analysis is used to determine if the company is eligible for the renewal of the hunting offer the following hunting term.

NOTES

1. See Hall 1992; Neumann 1998; Adams and McShane 1992.

2. Hall draws on the work of Said (1978) and Foucault (1972, 1980) to develop his arguments about discourse, history, and power.

3. Unless otherwise noted, "dollars"/"$" refers to U.S. currency.

4. To situate Grzimek and the film in a historical context, see Lekan 2011; Shetler 2007; and Neumann 1998.

5. For early writings on the Washington consensus, see Williamson 1993 and Gore 2000.

6. For important critiques of neoliberal development, see Stiglitz 2003 and Davis 2006.

7. See Harvey 2005; McCarthy 2006; Brenner and Theodore 2002; Wolford 2007; Ferguson 2010; Castree 2006, 2010.

8. Hodgson 2001, 2010, 2011; Igoe 2000, 2003, 2006; Igoe and Brockington 1999.

9. For examples that do situate local social relations within a global context, see Schroeder 2012 and Ferguson 2006.

10. In the past few years a proposed road through the heart of the area and Serengeti National Park has become a controversial issue.

11. John ole Monte is a pseudonym. I use pseudonyms throughout the book unless I have received permission to use real names. This practice does not apply to some individuals who are public figures or who have used their identity to intervene in the public domain.

12. For more on this history, see Neumann 1998; Shivji 1998; Shetler 2007; and Monbiot 1994.

13. See Packer et al. 2011; Århem 1985b; Homewood and Rodgers 1991; Spear and Waller 1993.

14. Juma, Nkwame, and Ndaskoi 2008; *Arusha Times* 2006.

15. For more information about pastoral range management and wildlife interaction, see Ellis and Swift 1988; Homewood, Kristjanson, and Trench 2009; Parkipuny 1991; and Parkipuny and Berger 1993.

CHAPTER ONE. INTRODUCTION

1. "Stop the Serengeti Sell-Off," <http://www.avaaz.org/en/save_the_maasai/?fp> accessed December 11, 2012.

2. For media reports about the OBC, see C. Alexander 1993; Mbaria 2002a, 2007; *East African* 2009; *Guardian* 2009, 2012; Renton 2009; Ihucha 2010.

3. I am specifically referring to the six villages in Loliondo division where the hunting concession and Maasai villages overlap. These are from north to south Ololosokwan, Soitsambu, Oloipiri, Olorien/Magaiduru, Losoito Maaloni, and Arash. The deal was controversial because the government granted the OBC a hunting lease after the official allocation period had ended. It also initially granted the OBC a ten-year contract when all other hunting leases were for a five-year period. Eventually the OBC's lease was reduced to five years, and it has maintained control of the area through all subsequent allocation including the most recent allocation from 2013 to 2018. See Loefler 2004; Mbaria and Mgamba 2003; Mbaria 2002a; C. Tomlinson 2002; C. Alexander 1993.

4. Mbattiany 2009.

5. Mbaria 2002a; Ihucha 2010.

6. This story is widely reported in the media and used to exemplify Tanzanians' concerns that foreign investment leads to foreign control over resources and sovereignty. See Renton 2009; FEMACT 23 September 2009b; Mbaria 2007.

7. Mbaria 2007; Ihucha 2010.

8. Village and district leaders were told to vacate the area prior to the arrival of the OBC. Local leaders explicitly denied the request, considering it outside the boundaries of state authority.

9. For a history of the separation of people and nature in Tanzania, see Lekan 2011; Neumann 1992, 1997, 1998; and Shetler 2007.

10. Århem 1985b, 1985c; Shivji and Kapinga 1998.

11. For a discussion of neoliberalism, see G. Hart 2002b and Harvey 2005.

12. Schroeder and Neumann 2006; Brockington 2002, 2008; Brockington and Igoe 2006.

13. Baldus and Cauldwell 2004.

14. Ellis and Swift 1988; Coppock, Ellis, and Swift 1986; Warren 1995.

15. The area where Thomson Safaris established its "nature refuge" was formerly known as "The Breweries" or "Sukenya," the name of the subvillage area within Soitsambu village where the land was located.

16. Philanthropic tourism or travel describes the desire by many participants in the travel industry to design tourism in ways that "further the well-being of local communities." The Center for Responsible Travel describes philanthropic tourism as an "emerging movement [that] is helping to support and empower local and indigenous communities by providing jobs, skills, and lasting improvements in health care, education, and environmental stewardship." http://www.travelersphilanthropy.org/what-is-travelers/definition.shtml, accessed November 30, 2012.

17. http://www.thomsonsafaris.com/socially-responsible-travel, accessed August 13, 2013.

18. Tour companies apply to be considered for this award. Leaders from the travel industry and nongovernmental organizations rate each company in five key areas: poverty

alleviation, cultural and/or environmental preservation, education, wildlife conservation, and health.

19. Pastoralism refers both to a system of economic production in which livestock are central to livelihoods and property rights and also to a political position from which Maasai assert their right to a different cultural system. Maasai struggles have consistently been entangled with the discursive framing of pastoralism as an inefficient, destructive, and outdated mode of production. Much like the concept of indigeneity, the meaning of pastoralism is both an identity claim and a historical site of struggle.

20. Mike Saningo is a pseudonym.

21. *Arusha Times* 2006.

22. Thomson Safaris 2009a.

23. Thomson Safaris and Tanzania Conservation Limited are two separate business entities under common ownership as divisions of Wineland-Thomson Adventures Inc. For the purposes of this book, I refer to the two companies as one entity using the abbreviation Thomson Safaris/TCL. Although TCL is the legal entity on the lease agreement, the owners and directors regularly invoke Thomson Safaris when discussing TCL. For example, when the land deal was criticized in the media, Thomson Safaris set up a blog, "Thomson Safaris' Outlook. Thomson responds to online rumors. Get the facts here."

24. Thomson Safaris 2009a.

25. Thomson Safaris took several measures to rebrand the land, including producing a film about the area that reinforced the narrative that this land is a timeless piece of nature and Thomson's efforts are simply to protect and preserve it for future generations. See Thomson Safaris, 2012.

26. In 1993 South African Breweries (SAB) bought a 50 percent share in Tanzania Breweries Limited. In 2002 SAB bought Miller Brewing Company from Philip Morris Companies, forming the second largest beer company in the world.

27. The forged minutes were submitted as part of legal action taken by the village.

28. Thomson Safaris 2009a, 2009b; Thomson Safaris 2010a, 2010b.

29. Ihucha 2009, 2010; FEMACT 2009b; Ubwania 2011; *Guardian* 2010a, 2010b; Mwalongo 2010a, 2010b; Juma 2010; Peter 2010.

30. Nkwame 2008.

31. Thomson Safaris 2010a, 2010b.

32. http://www.tnrf.org/about, accessed 13 December 2012.

33. Loliondo is located within the greater Serengeti ecosystem, and wildlife from Serengeti National Park, including the world famous wildebeest migration of over one million wildebeests, utilize village lands adjacent to the park for wet-season grazing and calving from late January to early March.

34. Dowie 2009; Brockington and Igoe 2006; Peluso 1993.

35. Neumann 1998.

36. TALA, FEMACT, NGONET, and PINGOS Forum 2012.

37. Kamndaya and Mkinga 2008.

38. Christopher Tipat is a pseudonym.

39. See Hodgson 1996, 1999a, 1999b, 2000b, 2000c, 2001.

40. Maasai man in his forties from Soitsambu village, interview with the author, June 24, 2010.

41. See Li 1999, 2000; Watts 2004.

42. Hodgson 2002a, 2002b, 2010, 2011; Igoe 2000, 2006.

43. See B. Anderson 2006; Moore 1993, 1998b; Massey 1991; Swyngedouw 1989.

44. Foucault 2003; Hall 2001.

45. See also Castree 2010.

46. Ferguson 2010.

47. Cliffe 1970; Hyden 1980; Kjekshus 1976.

48. Nyerere 1966.

49. Coulson 1979; Scott 1998; Parkipuny 1979; Schneider 2004, 2006a.

50. See Hodgson and McCurdy 1996; Hodgson 1996, 2000a, 2000b, 2000c; Schneider 2006a, 2006b; Parkipuny 1979.

51. Halimoja 1985.

52. Neumann 1997, 1998.

53. Lazaro Parkipuny, interview with the author, August 20, 2004.

54. Schneider 2006b.

55. Chachage and Cassam 2010; see also Schroeder (2012) for a discussion of the culture of Tanzanian nationalism.

56. Parkipuny 1979, 157.

57. For a discussion of "rights talk," see Mamdani (2000) and Hunter (2010).

58. Ferguson 2010, 170.

59. Maasai woman in her thirties, Ololosokwan village, interview with the author, July 29, 2010.

60. Cronon 1983; Parkipuny 1989b.

61. Parkipuny 1991.

62. Parkipuny 1989a.

63. G. Hart 2002a, 2006.

64. Maasai man in his forties from Soitsambu village, interview with the author, July 12, 2010.

65. David Methau is a pseudonym.

66. P. Meitaya 2008.

67. Hall 1985, 1996a, 1996b.

68. Ferguson 2010, 173.

69. For foundational work in political ecology, see Moore 1993; McCarthy 2005; Neumann 1992, 1995; Watts 2001; and Schroeder 1999, 2008. Critical development studies include Ferguson 1990, 2006; Hart 2002a, 2002b; and Watts 1994. For ethnographies of neoliberalism, see Comaroff and Comaroff 2009; Gregory 2007; and Postero 2007. For shifting paradigms of conservation, see Neumann 1998; Igoe and Brockington 1999, 2007; and West 2006.

70. Peck and Tickell 2002; G. Hart 2002a, 2006; Harvey 2006.

71. Namanyere 2011; Zoomers 2010; Schutter 2009.

72. Deininger 2011; Arezki, Deininger, and Selod 2012; Deininger and Byerlee 2012.

73. Ferguson 1990, 2006; Ferguson and Gupta 2002; Geschiere 1982; Geschiere and Jackson 2006.

74. Smith 1992, 2008; Massey 1994, 2009.

75. McCarthy 2005; Smith 1992; Liverman 2004; Brenner 1999.

76. I use historical, textual, and ethnographic methodologies in the form of extensive participant observation, interviews, oral histories, and document analysis to analyze the context of these developments. I have conducted (along with a research assistant) more than one hundred interviews in either Swahili or English. Because oral histories can yield only contemporary views of historical processes, this project also depends on extensive archival research. I also examined the communications between tourism companies and their clients including letters, informal campfire conversations, and promotional materials, situating this discourse as a critical site of knowledge production about tourism, identity, and history.

CHAPTER TWO. LOLIONDO

1. For anthropological accounts of Maasai history and culture, see Berntsen 1976, 1979; Spear and Waller 1993; Rigby 1983, 1992; Hodgson 2001; Århem 1985b; and Jacobs 1980.

2. KIPOC 1992.

3. The Barabaig are a pastoralist group living in central Tanzania.

4. See Lane and Pretty 1991.

5. Charles Tano is a pseudonym

6. Lane 1996.

7. The group would eventually found another NGO, the PINGOS Forum, to coordinate lobbying and advocacy efforts of pastoralist and hunter-gatherer groups throughout Tanzania.

8. See Hodgson 2001, 2011; Igoe 2000, 2006.

9. Fratkin and Wu 1997; KIPOC 1992.

10. Based on author interviews and conversations in 1997, 2002, 2003, and 2004.

11. See Blaikie and Brookfield 1987; Blaikie 1985; Hecht and Cockburn 1989; Watts 1983.

12. Many Maasai in Loliondo cultivated maize and beans, but there were few large-scale farms fragmenting the area's rangelands. See O'Malley 2000.

13. Århem 1985a, 1985b; Parkipuny 1991.

14. See F. Nelson et al. 2009; Gardner 2012; D. Meitaya and Ndoinyo 2002; Ngoitiko et al. 2010.

15. Igoe 2000.

16. Shivji and Kapinga 1998.

17. See also Goldman 2003; Rogers 2002.

18. Nyerere 1968a; Neumann 1996, 1997, 1998; Hodgson and Schroeder 2002; Århem 1985b.

19. Parkipuny 1979; Neumann 1998; Rogers 2002.

20. See Århem 1985b, 1985c; Neumann 1998; Shetler 2007; Shivji and Kapinga 1998.

21. Lions are one of the few species that Maasai hunt and kill. They do not hunt wild animals for food as they observe a strict cultural taboo against killing and eating wild animals, which is seen as a desperate measure by a poor pastoralist who cannot adequately keep livestock.

22. Kjekshus 1996; Nelson, Nshala, and Rodgers 2007.

23. Nelson, Nshala, and Rodgers 2007.

24. Koponen 1986, 1989.

25. Shivji 1998.

26. KIPOC, June 1, 1993. Donor/NGO workshop on pastoralism and development, organization factsheet, document in author's possession.

27. Shivji and Kapinga 1998.

28. Århem 1985c; Neumann 1998; Parkipuny 1989b; Shivji and Kapinga 1998; Nelson, Nshala, and Rodgers 2007.

29. The Maasai did not hunt large game as part of their diet and livelihood strategy. Occasionally Maasai would hunt small animals like dik dik, hare, or quail. However, killing lion was an important aspect of the Maasai coming of age ritual, and restrictions on hunting lion were seen as a major challenge to Maasai culture. Bans on burning, which Maasai used as a pasture-management tool, were much more threatening to their livelihood system.

30. O'Malley 2000.

31. Neumann 1998; Rogers 2002; Shivji and Kapinga 1998.

32. Most of the Maasai leaders present had gained standing and official administrative roles under the indirect-rule system established by the British. The leaders maintained status and authority largely through their relation to the colonial state. How this factored into the agreement is not clear, but many Maasai today see the negotiations as deceptive and unjust.

33. Monbiot 1994; Dowie 2009.

34. Shivji and Kapinga 1998.

35. Århem 1985b.

36. Shivji and Kapinga 1998.

37. Brandon and Wells 1992; Western 2001; Hulme and Murphree 2001.

38. Fallon 1963.

39. Fallon 1963, cited in Seidman 1975.

40. Fallon 1963, cited in Forstater 2002.

41. Common pool management describes a system in which communal access to all resources is available to all people. Critics believed that common pool management would inevitably lead to environmental degradation and resource collapse. In its place they argued for private-property rights in order to regulate both access to resources and the behavior of authorized users. Contrary to this perception, the Maasai did regulate access to resources and the behavior of land users through kinship and other forms of association.

42. Parkipuny 1979.

43. Ibid.; Hodgson 2001.

44. Hoben 1976.

45. Parkipuny 1979.

46. Hoben 1976.

47. Parkipuny 1979.

48. Ibid.

49. Nyererẹ 1968b.

50. For more on villagization, see Ingle 1972; Freyhold 1979; Pratt and Yeager 1976; Schneider 2004; and Kjekshus 1977.

51. Nyerere 1968b.

52. Ibid.

53. Ibid.

54. Ibid.

55. Ibid.

56. Ibid.

57. Ibid.

58. Coulson 1979; Cliffe 1970.

59. Mamdani 1996; Shivji 1999.

60. Kjekshus 1977; Kikula 1997; Scott 1998.

61. Ndagala 1982; Hoben 1976; Parkipuny 1979.

62. Ndagala 1982.

63. Parkipuny 1979.

64. Hodgson and Schroeder 2002; Ndagala 1982.

CHAPTER THREE. COMMUNITY CONSERVATION

1. African Wildlife Foundation 1991.

2. Letter from Raphael Long'oi (Arash Ward Councilor) to Ngorongoro District Executive Director, January 18, 2001, re: Stopping the effort to measure and demarcate a WMA in Arash Ward.

3. Shivji 1998; 1999; Sundet 2005.

4. All previous village land titles or certificates were made obsolete by the new acts, requiring that villages go through a sanctioned process of demarcation and boundary conflict resolution. This process has been driven largely by the desire of village members to secure village title in light of the possibilities for lands deemed underutilized to be moved from village land to general land.

5. Brockington 2008, 131. See also Neumann 1998; Brockington 2002; Nelson and Makko 2005; Sachedina 2008; Schroeder 2008; Nelson et al. 2009; Dressler et al. 2010; Lele et al. 2010.

6. See Nelson and Agrawal 2008; Dressler et al. 2010; Goldman 2003.

7. Benjaminsen and Svarstad 2010.

8. Brockington 2002; Bergin 2001; Sachedina 2008.

9. Baldus and Siege 2001; Baldus 1991, 2001.

10. Baldus and Cauldwell 2004.

11. Ibid.

12. Caro and Scholte 2007; Baldus and Siege 2001.

13. Baldus, Kibonde, and Siege 2003. For a critical perspective see Neumann 1996, 1997, 2001.

14. Norton-Griffiths and Southey 1995.

15. Western and Gichohi 1993; Western 2001.

16. O'Malley 2000; Ojalammi 2006.

17. Baldus, Kaggi, and Ngoti 2004; J. S. Adams and McShane 1992; W. M. Adams and Hulme 2001; Brockington 2004; West, Igoe, and Brockington 2006; Chapin 2004.

18. Brandon and Wells 1992; Dressler et al. 2010; Barrow et al. 2001; Hulme and Murphree 2001; Western, Strum, and Wright 1994; Anderson and Grove 1987.

19. Igoe and Croucher 2007; Brockington 2002; Lele et al. 2010.

20. Unless otherwise noted all information in this section is based on participant observation and interviews at the meeting and in Loliondo.

21. Kallonga, Nelson, and Stolla 2003; Sulle, Lekaita, and Nelson 2011; TNRF 2008.

22. Wildlife Division 2003.

23. Sulle, Lekaita, and Nelson 2011; Nelson, Nshala, and Rodgers 2007; Nelson 2007.

24. Wildlife Division 2003, 24.

25. Ibid.

26. Sulle, Lekaita, and Nelson 2011.

27. All quotations are from author interviews or field notes. Original quotes were either in English or translated by the author from Swahili.

28. Nelson, Nshala, and Rodgers 2007.

29. Ministry of Natural Resources and Tourism, United Republic of Tanzania 2000.

30. World Bank Group/Multilateral Investment Guarantee Agency (MIGA) 2002.

31. Ministry of Natural Resources and Tourism 2010, 2011.

32. Mkumbukwa 2008; Formo 2010.

33. Shetler 2007; Lekan 2011.

34. Neumann 1998; Nelson, Nshala, and Rodgers 2007.

35. SRCS 1986.

36. Ibid.

37. Ibid.

38. Ibid. Working Group 3 consisted of, among others, D. S. Babu, director of TANAPA; M. Borner, representative of the Frankfurt Zoological Society; F. M. R. Lwezaula, director of the WD; B. Maregesi, chief park warden for Serengeti National Park; and M. A. Ndolanga, general manager of the Tanzania Wildlife Corporation.

39. SRCS 1986.

40. Bergin 1995.

41. See O'Malley 2000; Hodgson and Schroeder 2002.

42. African Wildlife Foundation 1991.

43. Ibid.

44. Cited in Nelson, Nshala, and Rodgers 2007.

45. Cited in Nelson, Nshala, and Rodgers 2007.

46. Leader-Williams, Baldus, and Smith 2009.

47. Ministry of Natural Resources and Tourism, United Republic of Tanzania 2000.

48. For an excellent analysis of the role of conservation NGOs in northern Tanzania, see Sachedina 2008, 2010.

49. http://www.tnrf.org/about, accessed December 13, 2012.

50. Ministry of Natural Resources and Tourism, United Republic of Tanzania 2002b.

51. Sulle, Lekaita, and Nelson 2011.

52. For a thorough discussion of the implications of Tanzanian land law, see Wily 1998 and Sundet 1997.

53. For a good discussion of land reform in Tanzania, see Shivji 1998.

54. For more background on this topic, see Nelson 2005.

CHAPTER FOUR. "THE LION IS IN THE BOMA"

1. Various reports place the number of evicted people at 500–800 and the number of displaced livestock at 35,000–60,000 head.

2. For media and journalist reports of the evictions, see Ihucha 2009; *Guardian* 2010a; Survival International, "Maasai Evicted and Imprisoned to Make Way for Safari Hunting Concession," *Survival International*, http://www.survivalinternational.org/news/4884, accessed December 11, 2012; Norwegian People's Aid 2009; FemAct 2009a, 2009b; "8 Maasai Villages Unlawfully Burnt" 2009; Mbattiany 2009; *East African* 2009; Renton 2009; *Guardian* 2009.

3. Maasai man in his thirties, interview with the author, June 18, 2010.

4. They also claim, however, that international conservation NGOs play a central role in promoting and sponsoring conservation around the world.

5. Kamndaya and Mkinga 2008.

6. Letter from Ngorongoro District Executive Director to Ngorongoro District Councilors, May 20, 2009, (ref. no. NGOR/DC/M, 1/94), copy in author's possession.

7. FemAct 2009b; Juma 2010; Philemon 2010; Peter 2010; Agola 2010.

8. "8 Maasai Villages Unlawfully Burnt" 2009. This interview was assembled together with other media coverage by Maasai activists and leaders and circulated on the Internet. See http://www.youtube.com/watch?v=iqP2MRuJ4Ac and http://www.youtube.com/watch?v=i-FP2gRvziw.

9. "8 Maasai Villages Unlawfully Burnt" 2009.

10. Ibid.

11. Kipobota 2010; Ngorongoro NGO Network 2009.

12. FemAct 2009b.

13. Ortello Business Corporation 1992.

14. Author interviews in 2003.

15. Translated from Swahili to English by author.

16. All but Arash village were misspelled in the contract.

17. For more on the political economy of hunting and community conservation efforts by hunting companies in Tanzania, see Schroeder 2008.

18. See Neumann 1997; Adams and McShane 1992.

19. Price Waterhouse 1996.

20. Barnett and Patterson 2006; Baldus and Cauldwell 2004; TAHOA 1998; Nshala 1999.

21. Baldus and Cauldwell 2004.

22. Cited in Lekan 2011.

23. Parkipuny 1989b, emphasis in the original.

24. Baldus and Cauldwell 2004.

25. Author interviews 2003 and 2004.

26. Ibid.

27. Maasai man in his early thirties, Soitsambu village, interview with the author, December 15, 2003.

28. Maasai man in his late twenties, Soitsambu village, interview with the author, August 1, 2010.

29. Maasai man in his twenties, Soitsambu village, interview with the author, May 18, 2004.

30. Maasai man in his forties, Soitsambu village, interview with author, May 18, 2004.

31. There is a 40 percent minimum utilization criteria per annum. See Thirgood et al. 2008.

32. Ihucha 2010.

33. Department of Wildlife, Planning and Assessment for Wildlife Management (PAWM) 1996.

34. Ministry of Natural Resources and Tourism 2002a.

35. According to the chairman of the Tanzanian Hunting Operators Associations (TAHOA), private outfitters typically pay for the maintenance of roads, as well as for antipoaching activities within their hunting blocks.

36. Department of Wildlife, Planning and Assessment for Wildlife Management (PAWM) 1996.

37. Nshala 1999; Nelson, Nshala, and Rodgers 2007.

38. Based on meeting minutes, December 18, 2007, and author interviews in July 2010.

39. Based on meeting minutes, December 18, 2007.

40. Maasai man in his forties from Losoito/Maaloney village, interview with the author, July 20, 2010.

41. Leu 2000; Mbaria 2002a, 2002b; Meitaya and Ndoinyo 2002; C. Alexander 1993.

42. Mbaria 2002a.

43. Shivji 1993a, 1993b.

44. *East African* 2009.

45. See Sachedina 2008; Garland 2006.

46. Ferguson and Gupta 2002, 989.

47. These included the six original villages and three additional villages that had access to or claims over the area used for hunting.

48. Nkolimwa 2010.

49. Ibid.

50. Such meetings are an important part of Maasai advocacy and politics and symbolize one type of intervention enabled by neoliberal reforms. See Hodgson 2002a, 2002b; Cameron 2001; Igoe 2000, 2003.

51. Quotations here and in the following paragraphs recorded by the author at the meeting, August 11, 2010, Karatu, Tanzania.

52. This two-page publication was a response to an article titled "Game 'Carnage' in Tanzania Alarms Kenya," published in the *East African* newspaper in February 2002. See Mbaria 2002a.

53. Ministry of Natural Resources and Tourism, United Republic of Tanzania 2002a.

54. For an excellent discussion of the importance of *ujamaa* and Tanzanian nationalism to the ideas and practices of Tanzanian conservation professionals, see Garland 2006.

CHAPTER FIVE. NATURE REFUGE

1. In this chapter I refer to the two entities that operate under the same ownership and with the same interests as Thomson Safaris/TCL when appropriate.

2. Thomson Safaris 2009a.

3. Ibid.

4. Thomson Safaris 2012. Transcript of Thomson Safaris promotional video about Enashiva Nature Refuge.

5. Thomson Safaris 2009a, 2009b.

6. Ngoitiko 2008.

7. See Hodgson 2002a, 2002b.

8. Persepo Mathew, interview with the author, July 2, 2010.

9. Ibid.

10. *Arusha Times* 2006.

11. Several villagers remembered the district solicitor's words this way. Unless otherwise noted, quotations from villagers about this meeting are from my interviews conducted in June and July 2010.

12. John ole Perseti (pseudonym), interview with the author, July 15, 2010.

13. Paulo Silas (pseudonym), interview with the author, July 18, 2010.

14. Lucy Asioki, e-mail to Judi Wineland, August 2007.

15. Lucy Asioki, e-mail to Judi Wineland, September 14, 2007.

16. Ibid.

17. Ibid.

18. Lucy Asioki, interview with the author, December 1, 2007.

19. Judi Wineland, e-mail to Lucy Asioki, November 13, 2007.

20. Lucy Asioki, e-mail to the author, November 21, 2007.

21. Judi Wineland, e-mail to Lucy Asioki, November 13, 2007.

22. Lucy Asioki, interview with the author, June 20, 2010.

23. Judi Wineland, e-mail to Lucy Asioki, November 13, 2007.

24. Thomson Safaris 2010b.

25. Thomson Safaris 2009b, 2009c.

26. Examples include the following excerpts from Thomson's blog: "As with countless other issues, the people of Sukenya have had their voice of support for Enashiva Nature Refuge undermined and ignored due to their status as a political minority"(Thomson Safaris 2010d); "For decades, the people of Sukenya have lamented how their rights have been trampled upon and their civic voice undermined due to clan tensions and their marginalized status in the Soit Sambu Village Council. . . . The people of Sukenya are the largest population of Maasai around the Enashiva Nature Refuge, and they have lived in the area longer than any other Maasai clan or community"(Thomson Safaris 2010c); "The inter-clan rivalries existed long before Thomson ever came to Enashiva, and to suggest that Thomson is what comes between clans is to grossly oversimplify the culture and history of the Maasai in this area. . . . The media has given a megaphone to the few who oppose us and who have the political savvy to contact journalists. The vast majority of people are those whose names do not appear in local papers and who do not stand to gain anything by inviting attention and making accusations. There are also those who are not even aware of the controversy. This majority have been utterly ignored by the media and by our detractors" (Thomson Safaris 2009d).

27. Thomson Safaris 2010a.

28. Quotation from Thomson Safaris 2009d. For more on the representations of ethnic conflict in Africa, see Mamdani 2002, 2011; Geschiere 2009; Ranger 1983; and Geschiere and Jackson 2006.

29. Thomson Safaris 2009c.

30. See Hall 1992, 1997.

31. For a discussion of villagization and its legacies, see Ergas 1980; Århem 1985a, 1985b; Ndagala 1982; Parkipuny 1979; Coulson 1979; Kjekshus 1976; and Schneider 2004.

32. Scott 1998; Schneider 2004, 2007.

33. Local Government Act of 1982.

34. Gardner 2007; Nelson et al. 2009.

35. Thomson Safaris 2010c.

36. For a discussion of the resurgence of ethnic identification and autochthony, see Geschiere and Nyamnjoh 2000; Geschiere and Meyer 2002; Crang, Dwyer, and Jackson 2003; Ceuppens and Geschiere 2005; Geschiere and Jackson 2006; and Geschiere 2009.

37. Minority Rights Group International, http://www.minorityrights.org.

38. Claridge 2010.

39. Laltaika and Sulle 2009.

40. Letter from Tanzania Investment Center to Commissioner of Lands, Change of Land Use over Farm 373 Sukenya Soitsambu Village Ngorongoro District, December 11, 2008, ref. no. TIC/B.10/17/32, copy in author's possession.

41. Minutes of the Soitsambu village government meeting, November 11, 2009, doc. KUMB. NA. KJ/402/vol.11/25, copy in author's possession.

42. Soitsambu village government member, interview with author, July 21, 2010.

43. Boniface Konjwella, interview with the author, June 19, 2010.

44. Batundi 2012.

45. Interview with Lucy Asioki, August 21, 2013.

46. Mamdani 1996.

47. I am suggesting that the narrative of ethnic conflict helps serve Thomson Safaris/ TCL interests. One of the companies' consistent challenges to foreign and national journalists has been that they lack the knowledge and expertise to understand the ethnic conflict and therefore cannot really understand it. In explaining that ethnic conflict is so complex and historically entrenched, they imply that no outsider could ever understand and therefore is not sufficiently informed to intervene. This is a problematic position in which culture is framed as an internally logical system that cannot be understood or influenced by external forces. What Thomson Safaris/TCL seems unaware of is how the meaning of the contested property is one of the specific struggles through which the meaning of culture is produced. Although the companies may not be directly responsible for manipulating ethnic identity, they must take responsibility for promoting an untenable position that they are only innocent bystanders.

CHAPTER SIX. JOINT VENTURE

1. Peterson, Peterson, and Peterson 1998.

2. Direct payments for conservation became an increasingly common strategy among conservation groups from the 1990s.

3. Peterson, Peterson, and Peterson 1997.

4. Peterson, Peterson, and Peterson 1998.

5. Ibid.

6. Ibid.

7. Baldus, Kaggi, and Ngoti 2004; Baldus and Cauldwell 2004; Baldus and Siege 2001.

8. Letter from C. Mlay, Director of Wildlife, for the Principle Secretary, Ministry of Lands, Natural Resources and Tourism, to David Peterson and Paul Oliver, ref. no. PA/ GWC/177, copy in author's possession. This letter was also addressed to another tour operator interested in working in Maasailand, Oliver's Camp.

9. It is important to note that the ecotourism investors were unable to use central state channels to access resources open to larger and more influential companies such as the OBC.

10. For more on Maasai political and cultural history, see Hodgson 1999b, 2000a, 2000c, 2001, 2011; Parkipuny 1979; Spear and Waller 1993; Waller 1976; Berntsen 1979; Rigby 1992; and Jacobs 1980.

11. Thomas Lekuton (pseudonym), a Maasai man in his thirties from Ololosokwan village, interview with the author, October 20, 2003.

12. Parkipuny 1979, 1991; Gardner 2007.

13. For literature on neoliberalism and nature, see McAfee 1999; Robertson 2006; Bakker 2010; Castree 2010; Heynen and Robbins 2005; Heynen et al. 2007; and Schroeder 2010.

14. Interview with Lucy Emerton, *Global Economics & the Environment Programme*, IUCN, https://www.youtube.com/watch?v=L31ZIf1w_U0, uploaded April 5, 2008, accessed January 23, 2015.

15. MacDonald and Corson 2012.

16. Büscher and Arsel 2012; Büscher 2010; Brockington and Duffy 2010; Igoe and Brockington 2007.

17. Büscher and Arsel 2012.

18. Nyerere quoted in Nash 1982, 342.

19. Brockington 2002; Peluso 1993; Dressler et al. 2010.

20. Dressler et al. 2010.

21. Much of the project design and evaluation was carried out according to economic theories and methodologies. The language of stakeholders was commonly employed when describing CBC projects.

22. Western, Strum, and Wright 1994, cited in Dressler et al. 2010.

23. J. Alexander and McGregor 2000; Murphree and Metcalfe 1997.

24. McCarthy 2012.

25. Polanyi 1944, 1957; Hart 2002a, 2006.

26. Harvey 1982; Büscher and Arsel 2012.

27. McCarthy 2012, 192.

28. Büscher and Arsel 2012.

29. The Rio Declaration on Environment and Development was drafted at the United Nations Conference on Environment and Development in Rio de Janeiro, June 3–14, 1992. The declaration was an attempt to affirm and extend the declaration from the conference focused on the same issues that took place twenty years earlier on June 16, 1972, in Stockholm, Sweden.

30. Nshala 1999.

31. David Peterson, Thad Peterson, and Mike Peterson, interview with the author, July 21, 1997.

32. Charles Tomal is a pseudonym.

33. Dorobo Tours and Safaris Directors 1994.

34. Ibid.

35. http://www.naturalhighsafaris.com/explore/tanzania/serengeti-loliondo, accessed December 11, 2012.

36. The fifth animal of the iconic group, the rhinoceros, is not found in Loliondo.

37. Most tours that visit Loliondo and other community tourism sites combine their trips with visits to national parks and other well-known destinations. Tour companies like Dorobo Safaris often have a hard time persuading visitors to spend most of their time in community tourism areas, as visitors come with high expectations of seeing Ngorongoro Crater and Serengeti National Park.

38. Economic Research Associates 2007.

39. Ibid.

40. Ibid.

41. Based on the author's interviews and discussions with tour operators and tourists in 2000, 2003, and 2004.

42. http://www.naturalhighsafaris.com/explore/tanzania/the_serengeti/nduara -loliondo, accessed December 11, 2012.

43. Maasai man in his sixties, Ololosokwan village, interview with the author, July 21, 1997.

44. See Hodgson 2002a, 2002b, 2010, 2011; and Igoe 2000, 2006.

45. Winichakul 1997; Vandergeest and Peluso 1995.

46. Parkipuny 1991.

47. A number of reasons contributed to the ecotourism operators seeking local support to conduct tourism activities in the area. These include the lack of a regulatory structure for photographic tourism outside national parks, the small scale of investment compared with hunting in the eyes of the central government, and a lack of permanent buildings or roads.

48. Parkipuny 1991, 20.

49. Ibid, 21.

50. Ibid.

51. Ibid.

52. Maasai man in his early thirties, interview with the author, June 22, 2010.

CHAPTER SEVEN. CONCLUSIONS

1. Joseph Paulo (pseudonym), a Maasai man in his forties from Sukenya, interview with the author, July 21, 2010.

2. Ojalammi 2006, 75.

3. Geschiere 2009; Geschiere and Nyamnjoh 2000; Moore 1998a, 1999; Mamdani 1996, 2000.

4. Peck and Tickell 2002.

5. Brockington and Duffy 2010; Brockington 2002, 2004; Nelson, Nshala, and Rodgers 2010; Neumann 1997; Schroeder 2008; Goldman 2011.

6. Bruner and Kirshenblatt-Gimblett 1994; Bruner 2001.

7. Neumann 1998; Shetler 2007.

8. The following section refers to Shivji (1973) unless otherwise noted.

9. Shivji 1973, 3.

10. Ibid., 3–4 .

11. Ibid., 7.

12. Ibid., 10–11. The TYL then cites colonial critic Franz Fanon at length to support its argument. I include an abridged version of the quote: "The national bourgeoisie will be greatly helped on its way toward decadence by the Western bourgeoisies, who come to it as tourists avid for the exotic, for big game hunting and for casinos. The national bourgeoisie organises centres of rest and relaxation and pleasure resorts to meet the wishes of the Western bourgeoisie. Such activity is given the name tourism, and for the occasion will be built up as a national industry. . . . The national middle class will have

nothing better to do than to take on the role of manager for western enterprise, and it will in practice set up its country as the brothel of Europe" (ibid., 11).

13. Agrawal and Gibson 1999; Dressler et al. 2010; Büscher and Dressler 2012; Büscher et al. 2012.

14. Brundtland 1987.

15. Moore 1993, 1998b; Li 1996, 2002, 2003; Castree 2008.

16. D. Smith 2014; Gayle 2014.

BIBLIOGRAPHY

Adams, J. S., and T. O. McShane. 1992. *The Myth of Wild Africa: Conservation without Illusion.* New York: Norton.

Adams, W. M., and D. Hulme. 2001. "If Community Conservation Is the Answer in Africa, What Is the Question?" *Oryx* 35 (3): 193–200.

African Wildlife Foundation. 1991. *Community Benefits through Wildlife Resources: A Community-Based Conservation and Development Project in Loliondo Division, Ngorongoro District and Kiteto District, Northern Tanzania.* A project amendment paper submitted to the Royal Netherlands embassy. Dar es Salaam: African Wildlife Foundation.

Agola, E. 2010. "Call to Act against Loliondo Human Rights Culprits." *Guardian* January 16. http://www.ippmedia.com/frontend/functions/print_article.php?l=12516.

Agrawal, A., and C. Gibson. 1999. "Community in Conservation: Beyond Enchantment and Disenchantment." *World Development* 27 (4): 629–49.

Alexander, C. 1993. "The Brigadier's Shooting Party." *New York Times,* November 13. http://www.nytimes.com/1993/11/13/opinion/the-brigadier-s-shooting-party.html?src=pm.

Alexander, J., and J. McGregor. 2000. "Wildlife and Politics: CAMPFIRE in Zimbabwe." *Development and Change* 31: 605–27.

Anderson, B. 2006. *Imagined Communities: Reflections on the Origin and Spread of Nationalism.* London: Verso.

Anderson, D., and R. H. Grove. 1987. *Conservation in Africa: Peoples, Policies and Practice.* Cambridge: Cambridge University Press.

Arezki, R. K. Deininger, and H. Selod. 2013. "What Drives the Global 'Land Rush'?" *World Bank Economic Review,* 1–27.

Århem, K. 1985a. *The Maasai and the State: The Impact of Rural Development Policies on a Pastoral People in Tanzania.* IWGIA (International Working Group for Indigenous Affairs) Document no. 52.

———. 1985b. *Pastoral Man in the Garden of Eden: The Maasai of the Ngorongoro Conservation Area, Tanzania.* Uppsala: University of Uppsala, Department of Cultural Anthropology, in cooperation with the Scandinavian Institute of African Studies.

———. 1985c. "Two Sides of Development: Maasai Pastoralism and Wildlife Conservation in Ngorongoro, Tanzania." *Ethnos* 49 (3): 186–210.

Arusha Times. 2006. "TBL, Villagers Locked in Dispute over Barley Farm." February 1. http://www.arushatimes.co.tz/2006/7/front_page_1.htm.

Augustino, E., et al. 2013. *A Performance Audit Report on the Management of Wildlife in Game Reserves and Game Controlled Areas.* MNRT, URT.

Bakker, K. 2010. "The Limits of 'Neoliberal Natures': Debating Green Neoliberalism. *Progress in Human Geography* 34 (6): 715–35.

Baldus, R. D. 1991. *Community Wildlife Management around the Selous Game Reserve.* Wildlife Division and SCP Discussion Paper no. 12. Dar es Salaam: Wildlife Division, Selous Conservation Programme, Deutsche Gesellschaft für Technische Zusammenarbeit.

———. 2001. Wildlife Conservation in Tanganyika under German Colonial Rule. *Internationales Afrikaforum* 37 (1): 73–78.

Baldus, R. D., and A. E. Cauldwell. 2004. "Tourist Hunting and Its Role in Development of Wildlife Management Areas in Tanzania." Paper presented at *Sixth International Game Ranching Symposium—Paris July 6th to 9th, 2004,* sponsored by Gesellschaft für Technische Zusammenarbeit.

Baldus, R. D., D. T. Kaggi, and P. M. Ngoti. 2004. Community Based Conservation (CBC): Where Are We Now? Where Are We Going? *Miombo* 27: 3–7.

Baldus, R. D., B. Kibonde, and L. Siege. 2003. "Seeking Conservation Partnerships in the Selous Game Reserve, Tanzania." *Parks* 13 (1): 50–80.

Baldus, R. D., and L. Siege. 2001. *Experiences with Community Based Wildlife Conservation in Tanzania* (Dar es Salaam: Deutsche Gesellschaft für Technische Zusammenarbeit, Wildlife Division).

Barnett, R., and C. Patterson. 2006. *Sport Hunting in the SADC Region: An Overview.* TRAFFIC East/Southern Africa, USAID, The Ruffor Foundation.

Barrow, E., H. Gichohi, M. Infield, D. Hulme, and M. Murphree. 2001. "The Evolution of Community Conservation Policy & Practice in East Africa." In Hulme and Murphree 2001, 59–73.

Batundi, F. 2012. "Tanzania: Maasai Land Dispute with Safari Tourism Group." *Minority Rights Group, Minority Voices Newsroom,* September 4.

Benjaminsen, T. A., and H. Svarstad. 2010. "The Death of an Elephant: Conservation Discourses versus Practices in Africa." *Forum for Development Studies* 37 (3): 385–408.

Bergin, P. 1995. "Conservation and Development: The Institutionalisation of Community Conservation in Tanzania National Parks." PhD diss., University of East Anglia.

———. 2001. "Accommodating New Narratives in a Conservation Bureaucracy: TANAPA and Community Conservation. In *African Wildlife and Livelihoods: The Promise and Performance of Community Conservation,* edited by D. Hulme and M. Murphree, 88–105. Cape Town: D. Philip; Portsmouth, N.H.: Heinemann.

Berntsen, J. L. 1976. "The Maasai and Their Neighbors: Variables of Interaction." *African Economic History* 2: 1–11.

———. 1979. "Maasai Age-Sets and Prophetic Leadership: 1850–1910." *Africa* 49 (2): 134–46.

Blaikie, P. 1985. *The Political Economy of Soil Erosion in Developing Countries.* New York: Longman.

Blaikie, P., and H. Brookfield. 1987. *Land Degradation and Society*. New York: Methuen.

Brandon, K. E., and M. Wells. 1992. "Planning for People and Parks: Design Dilemmas. *World Development* 20 (4): 557–70.

Brenner, N. 1999. "Beyond State-Centrism? Space, Territoriality, and Geographical Scale in Globalization Studies." *Theory and Society* 28 (1): 39–78.

Brenner, N., and N. Theodore. 2002. "Cities and the Geographies of 'Actually Existing Neoliberalism.'" *Antipode* 34 (3): 349–79.

Brockington, D. 2002. *Fortress Conservation: The Preservation of the Mkomazi Game Reserve, Tanzania*. London: James Curry.

———. 2004. "Community Conservation, Inequality and Injustice: Myths of Power in Protected Area Management." *Conservation and Society* 2 (2): 411.

———. 2008. "Preserving the New Tanzania: Conservation and Land Use Change." *International Journal of African Historical Studies* 41 (3): 557–79.

Brockington, D., and R. Duffy. 2010. "Capitalism and Conservation: The Production and Reproduction of Biodiversity Conservation." *Antipode* 42 (3): 469–84.

Brockington, D., and J. Igoe. 2006. "Eviction for Conservation: A Global Overview." *Conservation and Society* 4 (3): 424–70.

Brundtland, G. H. 1987. *Our Common Future, from One Earth to One World: An Overview by the World Commission on Environment and Development*. Oxford: Oxford University Press.

Bruner, E. M. 2001. "The Maasai and the Lion King: Authenticity, Nationalism, and Globalization in African Tourism." *American Ethnologist* 28 (4): 881–908.

Bruner, E. M., and B. Kirshenblatt-Gimblett. 1994. "Maasai on the Lawn: Tourist Realism in East Africa." *Cultural Anthropology* 9 (4): 435–70.

Büscher, B. 2010. "Derivative Nature: Interrogating the Value of Conservation in 'Boundless Southern Africa.'" *Third World Quarterly* 31 (2): 259–76.

Büscher, B., and M. Arsel. 2012. "Introduction: Neoliberal Conservation, Uneven geographical Development and the Dynamics of Contemporary Capitalism." *Tijdschrift voor Economische en Sociale Geografie* 103 (2): 129–35.

Büscher, B., and W. Dressler. 2012. "Commodity Conservation: The Restructuring of Community Conservation in South Africa and the Philippines." *Geoforum* 43 (3): 367–76.

Büscher, B., S. Sullivan, K. Neves, J. Igoe, and D. Brockington. 2012. "Towards a Synthesized Critique of Neoliberal Biodiversity Conservation." *Capitalism Nature Socialism* 23 (2): 4–30.

Cameron, G. 2001. "Taking Stock of Pastoralist NGOs in Tanzania." *Review of African Political Economy* 28 (87): 55–72.

Caro, T., and P. Scholte. 2007. "When Protection Falters." *African Journal of Ecology* 45 (3): 233–35.

Castree, N. 2006. "From Neoliberalism to Neoliberalisation: Consolations, Confusions, and Necessary Illusions." *Environment and Planning A* 38 (1): 1.

———. 2008. "Neoliberalising Nature: The Logics of Deregulation and Reregulation." *Environment and Planning A* 40 (1): 131.

———. 2010. "Neoliberalism and the Biophysical Environment: A Synthesis and Evaluation of the Research." *Environment and Society: Advances in Research* 1 (1): 5–45.

Ceuppens, B., and P. Geschiere. 2005. "Autochthony: Local or Global? New Modes in the Struggle over Citizenship and Belonging in Africa and Europe." *Annual Review of Anthropology* 34: 385–407.

Chachage, C., and A. Cassam. 2010. *Africa's Liberation: The Legacy of Nyerere.* Cape Town: Pambazuka Press.

Chapin, M. 2004. "A Challenge to Conservationists." *World Watch Magazine* 17 (6) (November/December), 16–31.

Claridge, L. 2010. "Landmark Ruling Provides Major Victory to Kenya's Indigenous Endorois." Centre for Minority Rights Development & Minority Rights Group International (MRG) on Behalf of the Endorois Community v The Republic of Kenya." Briefing. Minority Rights Group International. Minority Rights Group International. http://www.minorityrights.org/10226/briefing-papers/landmark-ruling -provides-major-victory-to-kenyas-indigenous-endorois.html.

Cliffe, L. 1970. *The Policy of Ujamaa Vijijini & the Class Struggle in Tanzania.* Dar es Salaam: University of Dar es Salaam.

Comaroff, J. L., and J. Comaroff. 2009. *Ethnicity, Inc.* Chicago: University of Chicago Press.

Coppock, D. L., J. E. Ellis, and D. M. Swift. 1986. "Livestock Feeding Ecology and Resource Utilization in a Nomadic Pastoral Ecosystem." *Journal of Applied Ecology* 23 (2): 573–83.

Cosgrove, D. E. 1984. *Social Formation and Symbolic Landscape.* London: Croom Helm.

Coulson, A. 1979. *African Socialism in Practice: The Tanzanian Experience.* Nottingham, England: Spokesman.

Crang, P., C. Dwyer, and P. Jackson. 2003. "Transnationalism and the Spaces of Commodity Culture." *Progress in Human Geography* 27 (4): 438.

Cronon, W. 1983. *Changes in the Land: Indians, Colonists, and the Ecology of New England.* New York: Hill & Wang.

Davis, M. 2006. *Planet of Slums.* London: Verso.

Deininger, K. 2011. "Challenges Posed by the New Wave of Farmland Investment." *Journal of Peasant Studies* 38 (2): 217–47.

Deininger, K., and D. Byerlee. 2012. "The Rise of Large Farms in Land Abundant Countries: Do They Have a Future?" *World Development* 40, no. 4: 701–14.

Department of Wildlife, Planning and Assessment for Wildlife Management (PAWM). 1996. "Potential Benefits from Tourist Hunting Available for Local Communities in Tanzania." In Leader-Williams, Kayera, and Overton 1996, 97–101.

Dorobo Tours and Safaris Directors. 1994. "Community Centered Conservation: A Potential Model for Pastoral Communities Adjacent to Protected Areas in Northern Tanzania." Paper presented to the Tanzania Community Conservation Workshop, February 8–11.

Dowie, M. 2009. *Conservation Refugees: The Hundred-Year Conflict between Global Conservation and Native Peoples.* Cambridge, Mass.: MIT Press.

Dressler, W., B. Büscher, M. Schoon, D. Brockington, T. Hayes, C. A. Kull, J. McCarthy, and K. Shrestha. 2010. "From Hope to Crisis and Back Again? A Critical History of the Global CBNRM Narrative." *Environmental Conservation* 37 (01): 5–15.

East African. 2009. "Loliondo Residents Must Come First." Editorial, September 14. http://www.theeastafrican.co.ke/OpEd/editorial/-/434752/657210/-/121dewoz /-/index.html.

Economic Research Associates, Hart Howerton, A. R. E. Sinclair, and HKLM. 2007. *Maximizing the Economy of the Serengeti National Park through Conservation: The Republic of Tanzania.* Project report prepared for Frankfurt Zoological Society. San Francisco: Economic Research Associates (www.econres.com).

"8 Maasai Villages Unlawfully Burnt in Loliondo, Tanzania: Two Part Video Documentary." 2009. *Indigenous Peoples Issues and Resources* (September 14). http:// indigenouspeoplesissues.com/index.php?option=com_content&view=article&id =1928:8-maasai-villages-unlawfully-burnt-in-loliondo-tanzania-two-part-video -documentary&catid=68:videos-and-movies&Itemid=96.

Ellis, J. E., and D. M. Swift. 1988. "Stability of African Pastoral Eco-Systems: Alternate Paradigms and Implications for Development." *Journal of Range Management* 41 (6): 450–59.

Emerton, L. 2012. *Rethinking Economics, Markets and Incentives Using Economic Tools at the Landscape Level.* Gland, Switzerland: IUCN.

Ergas, Z. 1980. "Why Did the Ujamaa Village Policy Fail? Towards a Global Analysis." *Journal of Modern African Studies* 18 (3): 387–410.

Evans-Pritchard, E. E. 1940. *The Nuer.* Oxford: Clarendon.

———. 1951. *Kinship and Marriage among the Nuer.* Oxford: Clarendon.

———. 1956. *Nuer Religion.* Oxford: Oxford University Press.

Fallon, L. 1963. *Development of the Range Resources.* Dar es Salaam: USAID Mission to Tanganyika.

FemAct (Feminist Activist Coalition). 2009a. "Gross Violations of Human and Citizenship Rights in Tanzania." *Pambazuka News*, September 2. http://www.pambazuka .org/en/category/advocacy/58422.

———. 2009b. "Tanzania: Loliondo Report of Findings." *Pambazuka News*, September 23. http://www.pambazuka.org/en/category/advocacy/58956/print.

Ferguson, J. 1990. *The Anti-politics Machine: "Development," Depoliticization, and Bureaucratic Power in Lesotho.* Cambridge: Cambridge University Press.

———. 2006. *Global Shadows: Africa in the Neoliberal World Order.* Durham, N.C.: Duke University Press.

———. 2010. "The Uses of Neoliberalism." *Antipode* 41: 166–84.

Ferguson, J., and A. Gupta. 2002. "Spatializing States: Toward an Ethnography of Neoliberal Governmentality." *American Ethnologist* 29 (4): 981–1002.

Formo, R. K. 2010. "Power and Subjectivation: The Political Ecology of Tanzania's Wildlife Management Areas." Master's thesis, Norwegian University of Life Sciences.

Forstater, M. 2002. "Bones for Sale: 'Development,' Environment and Food Security in East Africa." *Review of Political Economy* 14 (1): 47–67.

Foucault, M. 1972. *The Archeology of Knowledge.* London: Tavistock.

———. 1980. *Power/Knowledge.* Brighton, England: Harvester.

———. 2003. *Society Must Be Defended: Lectures at the Collège de France, 1975–1976.* New York: Picador.

Fratkin, E., and T. S. M. Wu. 1997. "Maasai and Barabaig Herders Struggle for Land Rights in Kenya and Tanzania." *Cultural Survival Quarterly* 21: 55–61.

Freyhold, M. von. 1979. *Ujamaa Villages in Tanzania: Analysis of a Social Experiment.* New York: Monthly Review Press.

Gardner, B. 2007. "Producing Pastoral Power: Territory, Identity and Rule in Tanzanian Maasailand." PhD diss., University of California Berkeley.

———. 2012. "Tourism and the Politics of the Global Land Grab in Tanzania: Markets, Appropriation and Recognition." *Journal of Peasant Studies* 39 (2): 377–402.

Garland, E. 2006. "State of Nature: Colonial Power, Neoliberal Capital and Wildlife Management in Tanzania." PhD diss., University of Chicago.

Gayle, D. 2014. "Tanzania Orders 40,000 Maasai Tribesmen to Leave Their Homeland after Going Back on Their Promise Not to Turn Their Land into a Hunting Ground for Dubai Royal Family." DailyMail.com, November 17.

Geschiere, Peter. 1982. *Village Communities and the State: Changing Relations among the Maka of South-Eastern Cameroon since the Colonial Conquest.* Boston: Kegan Paul International.

———. 2009. *The Perils of Belonging: Autochthony, Citizenship, and Exclusion in Africa and Europe.* Chicago: University Of Chicago Press.

Geschiere, P., and S. Jackson. 2006. "Autochthony and the Crisis of Citizenship: Democratization, Decentralization, and the Politics of Belonging." *African Studies Review* 49 (2): 1–7.

Geschiere, P., and B. Meyer. 2002. "Globalization and Identity: Dialectics of Flow and Closure; Introduction." *Development and Change* 29 (4): 601–15.

Geschiere, P., and F. Nyamnjoh. 2000. "Capitalism and Autochthony: The Seesaw of Mobility and Belonging." *Public Culture* 12 (2): 423.

Goldman, M. 2003. "Partitioned Nature, Privileged Knowledge: Community-Based Conservation in Tanzania." *Development and Change* 34 (5): 833–62.

———. 2011. "Strangers in Their Own Land: Maasai and Wildlife Conservation in Northern Tanzania." *Conservation and Society* 9 (1): 65.

Gore, C. 2000. "The Rise and Fall of the Washington Consensus as a Paradigm for Developing Countries." *World Development* 28 (5): 789–804.

Gregory, S. 2007. *The Devil behind the Mirror: Globalization and Politics in the Dominican Republic.* Berkeley: University of California Press.

Guardian. 2009. "Launch Independent Probe into Loliondo Land Wrangles." Editorial, September 15. http://www.ippmedia.com/frontend/functions/print_article.php?l=7341.

———. 2010a. "Ngorongoro Land Row: Government Forsakes Small Beleaguered

Community for Revenue!" April 15. http://www.ippmedia.com/frontend/functions/print_article.php?l=15628.

——. 2010b. "Make Loliondo 'Abuses' Report Public—Activists." April 27. http://www.ippmedia.com/frontend/functions/print_article.php?l=16035.

——. 2012. "Hunting Firm Denies Plan to Evict Loliondo Maasai." September 8. http://www.ippmedia.com/frontend/functions/print_article.php?l=45593.*Guardian*.

Halimoja, Y. 1985. *Sokoine: Mtu Wa Watu* [Sokoine: Man of the people]. Dar es Salaam: Tanzania Publications.

Hall, S. 1985. "Signification, Representation, Ideology: Althusser and the Post-Structuralist Debates." *Critical Studies in Media Communication* 2 (2): 91–114.

——. 1992. "The West and the Rest: Discourse and Power, 276–331. In S. Hall and B. Gieben, *Formations of Modernity*, 276–331. Oxford: Polity Press.

——. 1996a. "Gramsci's Relevance for the Study of Race and Ethnicity." In *Stuart Hall: Critical Dialogues in Cultural Studies*, 411–40. London: Routledge.

——. 1996b. "The Problem of Ideology." In *Stuart Hall: Critical Dialogues in Cultural Studies*, 24–45. London: Routledge.

——. 1997. "The Local and the Global: Globalization and Ethnicity." In *Culture, Globalization and the World System*, edited by A. D. King, 19–39. Minneapolis: University of Minnesota Press.

——. 2001a. "Foucault: Power, Knowledge and Discourse." In *Discourse Theory and Practice: A Reader*, edited by M. Wetherell, S. Taylor, and S. J. Yates, 72–81. London: Sage.

——. 2001b. "The Spectacle of the Other." In *Discourse Theory and Practice: A Reader*, edited by M. Wetherell, S. Taylor, and S. J. Yates, 324–44. London: Sage.

Hardin, G. 1968. "The Tragedy of the Commons." *Science* 162 (3859): 1243–48.

Hart, G. P. 2002a. *Disabling Globalization: Places of Power in Post-Apartheid South Africa*. Berkeley: University of California Press.

——. 2002b. "Geography and Development: Development/s beyond Neoliberalism? Power, Culture, Political Economy." *Progress in Human Geography* 26 (6): 812.

——. 2006. "Denaturalizing Dispossession: Critical Ethnography in the Age of Resurgent Imperialism." *Antipode* 38 (5): 977–1004.

Harvey, D. 1982. *The Limits to Capital*. Chicago: University of Chicago Press.

——. 2005. *A Brief History of Neoliberalism*. Oxford: Oxford University Press.

——. 2006. *Spaces of Global Capitalism: Towards a Theory of Uneven Geographical Development*. New York: Verso.

Hecht, S. B., and A. Cockburn. 1989. *The Fate of the Forest: Developers, Destroyers, and Defenders of the Amazon*. Chicago: University of Chicago Press.

Heynen, N., J. McCarthy, W. S. Prudham, and P. Robbins. 2007. *Neoliberal Environments: False Promises and Unnatural Consequences*. New York: Routledge.

Heynen, N., and P. Robbins. 2005. "The Neoliberalization of Nature: Governance, Privatization, Enclosure and Valuation." *Capitalism Nature Socialism* 16 (1): 5–8.

Hoben, A. 1976. *Social Soundness of the Masai Livestock and Range Management Project*. USAID Mission to Tanzania. N.p.: USAID.

Hodgson, D. L. 1996. "'My Daughter. . . Belongs to the Government Now': Marriage, Maasai, and the Tanzanian State." *Canadian Journal of African Studies* 30 (1): 106–23.

———. 1999a. "Images and Interventions: The Problems of Pastoralist Development." In *The Poor Are Not Us: Poverty and Pastoralism in Eastern Africa*, edited by D. M. Anderson and V. Broch-Due, 221–39. Oxford: J. Curry; Nairobi: EAEP; Athens: Ohio University Press.

———. 1999b. "Pastoralism, Patriarchy and History: Changing Gender Relations among Maasai in Tanganyika, 1890–1940." *Journal of African History* 40 (01): 41–65.

———. 2000a. "Gender, Culture & the Myth of the Patriarchal Pastoralist." In Hodgson 2000b, 1–28.

———. 2000b. *Rethinking Pastoralism in Africa: Gender, Culture & the Myth of the Patriarchal Pastoralist*. Oxford: James Curry; Kampala: Fountain: Nairobi: East African Educational Publishing; Athens: Ohio University Press.

———. 2000c. "Taking Stock: State Control, Ethnic Identity and Pastoralist Development in Tanganyika, 1948–1958." *Journal of African History* 41 (01): 55–78.

———. 2001. *Once Intrepid Warriors: Gender, Ethnicity, and the Cultural Politics of Maasai Development*. Bloomington: Indiana University Press.

———. 2002a. "Introduction: Comparative Perspectives on the Indigenous Rights Movement in Africa and the Americas." *American Anthropologist*, n.s., 104 (4): 1037–49.

———. 2002b. "Precarious Alliances: The Cultural Politics and Structural Predicaments of the Indigenous Rights Movement in Tanzania." *American Anthropologist*, n.s., 104 (4): 1086–97.

———. 2010. "Becoming Indigenous in Africa." *African Studies Review* 52 (3): 1–32.

———. 2011. *Being Maasai, Becoming Indigenous: Postcolonial Politics in a Neoliberal World*. Bloomington: Indiana University Press.

Hodgson, D. L., and S. McCurdy. 1996. "Wayward Wives, Misfit Mothers, and Disobedient daughters: 'Wicked' Women and the Reconfiguration of Gender in Africa." *Canadian Journal of African Studies* 30 (1): 1–9.

Hodgson, D. L., and R. A. Schroeder. 2002. "Dilemmas of Counter-Mapping Community Resources in Tanzania." *Development and Change* 33 (1): 79–100.

Homewood, K., P. Kristjanson, and C. Trench. 2009. *Staying Maasai? Livelihoods, Conservation and Development in East African Rangelands*. New York: Springer.

Homewood, K. M., and W. A. Rodgers. 1991. *Maasailand Ecology: Pastoralist Development and Wildlife Conservation in Ngorongoro, Tanzania*. Cambridge: Cambridge University Press.

Hulme, D., and M. W. Murphree. 2001. *African Wildlife and Livelihoods: The Promise and Performance of Community Conservation*. Oxford: James Curry.

Hunter, M. 2010. *Love in the Time of AIDS: Inequality, Gender, and Rights in South Africa*. Bloomington: Indiana University Press.

Hyden, G. 1980. *Beyond Ujamaa in Tanzania: Underdevelopment and an Uncaptured Peasantry*. Berkeley: University of California Press.

Igoe, J. 2000. "Ethnicity, Civil Society, and the Tanzanian Pastoral NGO Movement." PhD diss., Boston University.

———. 2003. "Scaling Up Civil Society: Donor Money, NGOs and the Pastoralist Land Rights Movement in Tanzania." *Development and Change* 34 (5): 863–85.

———. 2006. "Becoming Indigenous Peoples: Difference, Inequality, and the Globalization of East African Identity Politics." *African Affairs* 105 (420): 399.

Igoe, J., and D. Brockington. 1999. *Pastoral Land Tenure and Community Conservation: A Case Study from North-East Tanzania*. London: IIED, 1999.

———. 2007. "Neoliberal Conservation: A Brief Introduction." *Conservation and Society* 5 (4): 432.

Igoe, J., and B. Croucher. 2007. "Conservation, Commerce, and Communities: The Story of Community-Based Wildlife Management Areas in Tanzania's Northern Tourist Circuit." *Conservation and Society* 5 (4): 534.

Ihucha, A. 2009. "Arusha Regional Government Blamed for Human Rights 'Abuses.'" *Guardian*, August 8.

———. 2010. "United Front to Fight Renewal of Emirates Hunting Contract." *East African*, August 16. http://www.theeastafrican.co.ke/news/United-front-to-fight -renewal-of-Emirates-hunting-contract/-/2558/976818/-/view/printVersion /-/d83pfrz/-/index.html.

Ingle, C. 1972. *From Village to State in Tanzania: The Politics of Rural Development*. Ithaca, N.Y.: Cornell University Press.

"Inside the Wildlife Division (WD)." N.d. "Inside the Wildlife Division (WD)." Power Point presentation shared with the author.

Jacobs, A. H. 1980. "Pastoral Development in Tanzanian Maasailand." *Rural Africana* 7 (1): 1–14.

Juma, M. 2010. "LHRC Files Petition on Eviction." *Citizen* (Dar es Salaam), December 3. http://www.thecitizen.co.tz/news/4-national-news/6077-lhrc-files-petition-on -eviction.html.

Juma, M., V. M. Nkwame, and N. Ndaskoi. 2008. "Former TBL Farm Brews New Crisis." *Arusha Times*, August 9. http://www.arushatimes.co.tz/2008/31/front_page_ 1.htm.

Kallonga, E., F. Nelson, and F. Stolla. 2003. "WMA's and Beyond: Options and Opportunities for Community-Based Natural Resource Management in Tanzania." In *Report on a Workshop Held in Arusha, Tanzania, May, 6–7*. Copy in author's possession.

Kamndaya, S., and M. Mkinga. 2008. "Tanzania: Wildlife Use Can't Be Left to Villagers' Control, Says Minister." *Citizen* (Dar es Salaam), March 7. http://allafrica.com /stories/200803070667.html.

Kikula, I. S. 1997. *Policy Implications on Environment: The Case of Villagisation in Tanzania*. Uppsala: Nordic Africa Institute.

Kipobota, C. 2010. *Community Mobilization against the Government Proposed Land Use Planning in Loliondo Division, Arusha Region Tanzania: Research and Opinion*. Report prepared by the Legal and Human Rights Center. Dar es Salaam: Legal and Human Rights Center.

KIPOC. 1992. *Korongoro Integrated People Oriented to Conservation (KIPOC) Principal Document no. 4: The Foundation Program.* Program profile and rationale. Loliondo.

Kjekshus, H. 1976. *The Villagization Panacea: A Review of Tanzania's Ujamaa Policy.* Oslo: Norsk utenrikspolitisk institutt.

———. 1977. "The Tanzanian Villagization Policy: Implementational Lessons and Ecological Dimensions." *Canadian Journal of African Studies* 11 (2): 269–82.

———. 1996. *Ecology Control & Economic Development in East African History: The Case of Tanganyika, 1850–1950.* London: James Curry.

Koponen, J. 1986. *People and Production in Late Colonial Tanzania.* Vol. 107 of *The Meek Shall Inherit the Earth.* Monographs of the Finnish Society for Development Studies 2. Uppsala: Scandinavian Institute of African Studies.

———. 1989. *Famine, Flies, People and Capitalism in Tanzanian History: Some Critical Historiographical Comments on Works by John Iliffe and Helge Kjekshus.* Helsinki: University of Helsinki, Institute of Development Studies.

Laltaika, E., and E. Sulle. 2009. *A Review of the Socio-economic Aspects of the Sukenya Farm.* Report prepared for PINGOS, UCRT, and PWC. Arusha: PINGOS.

Lane, C. 1996. *Pastures Lost: Barabaig Economy, Resource Tenure, and the Alienation of Their Land in Tanzania.* London: IIED.

Lane, C. R., and J. N. Pretty. 1991. *Displaced Pastoralists and Transferred Wheat Technology in Tanzania.* London: Sustainable Agriculture Programme of the International Institute for Environment and Development.

Leader-Williams, N., R. D. Baldus, and R. J. Smith. 2009. "The Influence of Corruption on the Conduct of Recreational Hunting." In *Recreational Hunting, Conservation, and Rural Livelihoods,* edited by B. Dickson, J. Hutton, and W. M. Adams, Science and Practice 4, 296. Oxford: Blackwell.

Leader-Williams, N., J. A. Kayera, and G. L. Overton, eds. 1996. *Tourist Hunting in Tanzania.* Occasional Paper of the IUCN Species Survival Commission no. 14. Gland, Switzerland: IUCN.

Lekan, T. 2011. "Serengeti Shall Not Die: Bernhard Grzimek, Wildlife Film, and the Making of a Tourist Landscape in East Africa." *German History* 29 (2): 224–64.

Lele, S., P. Wilshusen, D. Brockington, R. Seidler, and K. Bawa. 2010. "Beyond Exclusion: Alternative Approaches to Biodiversity Conservation in the Developing Tropics." *Current Opinion in Environmental Sustainability* 2 (1–2): 94–100.

Letara, J., J. MacGregor, and C. Hesse. 2006. *Estimating the Economic Significance of Pastoralism: The Example of the* Nyama Choma *Sector in Tanzania.* Edinburgh: International Institute for Environment and Development.

Leu, M. 2000. "Maasai Protest against Investor: Delegation Seeks Audience with the President." *Arusha Times,* April 8.

Li, T. M. 1996. "Images of Community: Discourse and Strategy in Property Relations." *Development and Change* 27 (3): 501–27.

———. 1999. *Transforming the Indonesian Uplands: Marginality, Power and Production.* Singapore: Harwood Academic; Institute of Southeast Asian Studies.

———. 2000. "Constituting Tribal Space: Indigenous Identity and Resource Politics in Indonesia." *Comparative Studies in Society and History* 42 (1): 149–79.

———. 2002. "Engaging Simplifications: Community-Based Resource Management, Market Processes and State Agendas in Upland Southeast Asia." *World Development* 30 (2): 265–83.

———. 2003. "Situating Resource Struggles: Concepts for Empirical Analysis." *Economic and Political Weekly* 38 (48): 5120–28.

———. 2010. "Indigeneity, Capitalism, and the Management of Dispossession." *Current Anthropology* 51 (3): 385–414.

Liverman, D. 2004. "Who Governs, at What Scale and at What Price? Geography, Environmental Governance, and the Commodification of Nature." *Annals of the Association of American Geographers* 94 (4): 734–38.

Loefler, I. 2004. "In Case We've Forgotten, There's Money in Wildlife." *East African,* Business, February 16. http://www.theeastafrican.co.ke/business/-/2560/242512/-/view/printVersion/-/bsdjvuz/-/index.html.

MacDonald, K. I., and C. Corson. 2012. "'TEEB Begins Now': A Virtual Moment in the Production of Natural Capital. *Development and Change* 43 (1): 159–84.

Madulu, N., et al. 2007. *Assessment and Evaluation of the Wildlife Management Areas in Tanzania.* Wildlife Division, MNRT.

Mamdani, M. 1996. *Citizen and Subject: Contemporary Africa and the Legacy of Late Colonialism.* Princeton, N.J.: Princeton University Press.

———. 2000. *Beyond Rights Talk and Culture Talk: Comparative Essays on the Politics of Rights and Culture.* New York: St. Martin's.

———. 2002. "Good Muslim, Bad Muslim: A Political Perspective on Culture and Terrorism." *American Anthropologist* 104 (3): 766–75.

———. 2011. "The Invention of the Indigene." *London Review of Books* 33 (2): 31–33.

Massey, D. B. 1991. "The Political Place of Locality Studies." *Environment and Planning A* 23 (2): 267–81.

———. 1994. *Space, Place, and Gender.* Minneapolis: University of Minnesota Press.

———. 1995. "Places and Their Pasts." *History Workshop Journal,* no. 39: 182–92.

———. 2009. "Concepts of Space and Power in Theory and in Political Practice." *Documents d'Anàlisi Geogràfica* 55 (55): 15–26.

Mbaria, J. 2002a. "Game 'Carnage' in Tanzania Alarms Kenya." *East African,* News, February 4. http://www.theeastafrican.co.ke/news/-/2558/239546/-/view/printVersion/-/t76oofz/-/index.html.

———. 2002b. "No Hunting without Ujamaa Consent." *East African,* News, December 1. http://www.theeastafrican.co.ke/news/-/2558/240212/-/view/printVersion/-/s1yq99z/-/index.html.

———. 2007. "Scramble for African Wildlife." *East African,* Magazine, March 5. http://www.theeastafrican.co.ke/magazine/-/434746/253422/-/view/printVersion/-/12r6eo7/-/index.html.

Mbaria, J., and R. Mgamba. 2003. "Loliondo Hunting: Kenya Urged to Take Dar to

ICJ." *East African*, News, December 8. http://www.theeastafrican.co.ke/news/-/2558
/241990/-/view/printVersion/-/icp2blz/-/index.html.

Mbattiany, O. 2009. "Tanzania: Loliondogate 2 Has Become a Police Project." *Pambazuka News*, September 17. http://www.pambazuka.org/en/category/advocacy
/58811/print.

Mbembe, A. 2001. *On the Postcolony*. Berkeley: University of California Press.

McAfee, K. 1999. "Selling Nature to Save It? Biodiversity and Green Developmentalism." *Environment and Planning D: Society and Space* 17 (2): 133–54.

McCarthy, J. 2005. "Scale, Sovereignty, and Strategy in Environmental Governance." *Antipode* 37 (4): 731–53.

———. 2006. "Neoliberalism and the Politics of Alternatives: Community Forestry in British Columbia and the United States." *Annals of the Association of American Geographers* 96 (1): 84–104.

———. 2012. "The Financial Crisis and Environmental Governance 'after' Neoliberalism." *Tijdschrift voor Economische en Sociale Geografie* 103 (2): 180–95.

Meitaya, D., and Y. Ndoinyo. 2002. "A Rejoinder to the Ministry's Press Release on Loliondo and OBC." *Arusha Times*, Opinion, August 17. http://www.arushatimes.co
.tz/2002/33/features_2.htm.

Meitaya, P. 2008. "Community Experiences with Tourism Development in Loliondo Tanzania: The Good, the Bad and the Ugly." Presentation to the Travelers' Philanthropy Conference 2008, December 3–5, Ngurdoto Lodge, Arusha. http://www
.travelersphilanthropy.org/resources/TPhil_conf_proceedings/proceedings
/partalala-meitaya-tp-2-presentation.pdf.

Ministry of Natural Resources and Tourism, United Republic of Tanzania. 2000. *The Wildlife Conservation (Tourist Hunting) Regulations*. Dar es Salaam: Government Printer.

———. 2002a. "Response and Explanations regarding the Article in the East African Newspaper Titled 'Game Carnage in Tanzania Alarms Kenya.'" *East African*, April 1.

———. 2002b. *The Wildlife Conservation (Wildlife Management Areas) Regulations*. Dar es Salaam: Government Printer.

———. 2007. *The Wildlife Conservation (Non-Consumptive Wildlife Utilization) Regulations*. Dar es Salaam: Government Printer.

———. 2010. *Tanzania Tourism Sector Survey: The 2008 International Visitors' Exit Survey Report*. Dar es Salaam: Government Printer.

———. 2011. *Tanzania Tourism Sector Survey: The 2009 International Visitors' Exit Survey Report*. Dar es Salaam: Government Printer.

Mitchell, D. 2000. *Cultural Geography: A Critical Introduction*. Oxford: Blackwell.

Mkumbukwa, A. R. 2008. "The Evolution of Wildlife Conservation Policies in Tanzania during the Colonial and Post-Independence Periods." *Development Southern Africa* 25 (5): 589–600.

Monbiot, G. 1994. *No Man's Land: An Investigative Journey through Kenya and Tanzania*. London: Macmillan.

Moore, D. S. 1993. "Contesting Terrain in Zimbabwe's Eastern Highlands: Political Ecology, Ethnography, and Peasant Resource Struggles." *Economic Geography* 69 (4): 380–401.

———. 1998a. "Clear Waters and Muddied Histories: Environmental History and the Politics of Community in Zimbabwe's Eastern Highlands." *Journal of Southern African Studies* 24 (2): 377–403.

———. 1998b. "Subaltern Struggles and the Politics of Place: Remapping Resistance in Zimbabwe's Eastern Highlands." *Cultural Anthropology* 13 (3): 344–81.

———. 1999. "The Crucible of Cultural Politics: Reworking 'Development' in Zimbabwe's Eastern Highlands." *American Ethnologist* 26 (3): 654–89.

Murphree, M. W., and S. C. Metcalfe. 1997. *Conservancy Policy and the CAMPFIRE Programme in Zimbabwe*. Mount Pleasant, Harare: Centre for Applied Social Sciences, University of Zimbabwe.

Mwalongo, Rose. 2010a. "3 Held in Loliondo over Women's Rally." *Guardian*, April 14. http://www.ippmedia.com/frontend/functions/print_article.php?l=15575.

———. 2010b. "NGO Staff Held in Loliondo Released." *Guardian*, April 15. http://www.ippmedia.com/frontend/functions/print_article.php?l=15616.

Namanyere, Y. Katembo. 2011. "Land Grabbing Is Recipe for Socioeconomic Disaster." *Citizen*, letter to the editor, August 22. http://www.thecitizen.co.tz/editorial-analysis/46-letters-to-the-editor/13996-land-grabbing-is-recipe-for-socioeconomic-disaster.html.

Nash, R. 1982. *Wilderness and the American Mind*. New Haven, Conn.: Yale University Press.

Ndagala, D. K. 1982. "Operation Imparnati: The Sedentarization of the Pastoral Maasai in Tanzania." *Nomadic Peoples* 10: 28–39.

Nelson, F. 2005. "Communities, Conservation and Conflicts in the Tanzanian Serengeti Preserving Rights to Gain Benefits." In *Natural Resources as Community Assets: Lessons from Two Continents*, edited by B. Child and M. W. Lyman, 121–45. Madison, Wis.: Sand County Foundation; Washington, D.C.: Aspen Institute.

———. 2007. *Emerging or Illusory? Community Wildlife Management in Tanzania*. London: IIED.

Nelson, F., and A. Agrawal. 2008. "Patronage or Participation? Community-Based Natural Resource Management Reform in Sub-Saharan Africa." *Development and Change* 39: 557–85.

Nelson, F., B. Gardner, J. Igoe, and A. Williams. 2009. "Community-Based Conservation and Maasai Livelihoods in Tanzania." In Homewood, Kristjanson, and Trench 2009, 299–334.

Nelson, F., and S. ole Makko. 2005. "Communities, Conservation, and Conflicts in the Tanzanian Serengeti." In *Natural Resources as Community Assets: Lessons from Two Continents*. Madison, Wis.: Sand County Foundation; Washington, D.C.: Aspen Institute.

Nelson, F., R. Nshala, and W. A. Rodgers. 2007. "The Evolution and Reform of Tanzanian Wildlife Management." *Conservation and Society* 5 (2): 232.

Neumann, R. P. 1992. "Political Ecology of Wildlife Conservation in the Mt. Meru Area of Northeast Tanzania." *Land Degradation & Development* 3 (2): 85–98.

———. 1995. "Local Challenges to Global Agendas: Conservation, Economic Liberalization and the Pastoralists' Rights Movement in Tanzania." *Antipode* 27 (4): 363–82.

———. 1996. "Dukes, Earls, and Ersatz Edens: Aristocratic Nature Preservationists in Colonial Africa." *Environment and Planning D* 14: 79–98.

———. 1997. "Primitive Ideas: Protected Area Buffer Zones and the Politics of Land in Africa." *Development and Change* 28: 559–82.

———. 1998. *Imposing Wilderness: Struggles over Livelihood and Nature Preservation in Africa*. Berkeley: University of California Press.

———. 2001. "Disciplining Peasants in Tanzania: From State Violence to Self-Surveillance in Wildlife Conservation." In *Violent Environments*, edited by M. Watts and N. Peluso, 305–27. Ithaca, N.Y.: Cornell University Press.

———. 2005. *Making Political Ecology*. Human Geography in the Making Series. New York: Oxford University Press

———. 2011. "Political Ecology III: Theorizing Landscape." *Progress in Human Geography* 35 (6): 843–50.

Ngoitiko, M. 2008. *The Pastoral Women's Council: Empowerment for Tanzania's Maasai*. London: International Institute for Environment and Development.

Ngoitiko, M., M. Sinandei, P. Meitaya, and F. Nelson. 2010. "Pastoral Activists: Negotiating Power Imbalances in the Tanzanian Serengeti." In *Community Rights, Conservation and Contested Land: The Politics of Natural Resource Governance in Africa*, edited by F. Nelson, 269–89. London: Earthscan.

Ngorongoro NGO Network. 2009. *Pastoralists Eviction in Loliondo: History, Process, and Impact*. Loliondo: NGONET.

Nkolimwa, Dominic. 2010. "Minister: Loliondo Stand-Off Resolved." *Guardian*, July 28. http://www.ippmedia.com/frontend/functions/print_article.php?l=19259.

Nkwame, Valentine Marc. 2008. "Wounded Maasai Moran Fights for Dear Life: Who Shot Him Is the Question!" *Arusha Times*, May 17. http://www.arushatimes.co.tz/2008/19/front_page_1.htm.

Norton-Griffiths, M., and C. Southey. 1995. "The Opportunity Costs of Biodiversity Conservation in Kenya." *Ecological Economics* 12 (2): 125–39.

Norwegian People's Aid. 2009. "Violence against Pastoralists Continues: Violations of Pastoralists' Rights in Tanzania Continues at an Incredible Pace. Now Local NGOs Are Calling for the Minister for Natural Resources and Tourism to Resign after She Claimed in Parliament That the Local People Had Burnt Their Own Homes." *Norwegian People's Aid*, August 21. http://otto.idium.no/nf.no/?module=Articles;action=Article.publicShow;ID=8401.

Nshala, R. 1999. *Granting Hunting Blocks in Tanzania: The Need for Reform*. Policy Brief no. 5. Dar es Salaam: Lawyers' Environmental Action Team (LEAT).

Nyerere, J. K. 1966. *Freedom and Unity: A Selection from Writings and Speeches 1952–1965*. Dar es Salaam: Oxford University Press.

———, ed. 1968a. *Freedom and Socialism: A Selection from Writings and Speeches, 1965–1967.* Dar es Salaam: Oxford University Press.

———. 1968b. "The Arusha Declaration: Socialism and Self-Reliance. In Nyerere 1968a, 231–50.

Ojalammi, S. 2006. "Contested Lands: Land Disputes in Semi-arid Parts of Northern Tanzania: Case Studies of the Loliondo and Sale Divisions in the Ngorongoro District." PhD diss., University of Helsinki.

O'Malley, M. E. 2000. "Cattle and Cultivation: Changing Land Use and Labor Patterns in Pastoral Maasai Livelihoods, Loliondo Division, Ngorongoro District, Tanzania." PhD diss., University of Michigan, Ann Arbor.

Ortello Business Corporation. 1992. "Loliondo Game Controlled Area: A Proposal for Wildlife Conservation, Management and Rural Development." In *Concept Paper of His Excellency Brigadier Mohamed Abdul Rahim al Ali for the Government of the United Republic of Tanzania.* Report.

Packer, C., H. Brink, B. M. Kissui, H. Maliti, H. Kushnir, and T. Caro. 2011. "Effects of Trophy Hunting on Lion and Leopard Populations in Tanzania." *Conservation Biology: The Journal of the Society for Conservation Biology* 25 (1): 142–53. doi:10.1111 /j.1523–1739.2010.01576.x

Parkipuny, M. S. ole. 1979. "Some Crucial Aspects of the Maasai Predicament." In *African Socialism in Practice: The Tanzanian Experience*, edited by A. Coulson, 136–57. Nottingham, England: Spokesman.

———. 1989a. "The Human Rights Situation of Indigenous Peoples in Africa." *Fourth World Journal* 4 (1): 1–4.

———. 1989b. "So That Serengeti Shall Never Die." In *Nature Management and Sustainable Development: Proceedings of the International Congress, Groningen, the Netherlands, 6–9 December 1988.* Amsterdam: IOS.

———. 1991. *Pastoralism, Conservation and Development in the Greater Serengeti Region.* IIED Issue Paper no. 26. In *Dryland Networks Programme Issues Paper.* London: IIED.

Parkipuny, M. S. ole, and D. J Berger. 1993. "Maasai Rangelands." In *Voices from Africa: Local Perspectives on Conservation*, edited by D. M. Lewis and N. Carter. Washington D.C: World Wildlife Fund.

Peck, J., and A. Tickell. 2002. "Neoliberalizing Space." *Antipode* 34 (3): 380–404.

Peluso, N. L. 1993. "Coercing Conservation: The Politics of State Resource Control." *Global Environmental Change* 3 (2): 199–217.

Peter, F. 2010. "Activists Up in Arms over Loliondo Report." *Guardian*, February 24. http://www.ippmedia.com/frontend/functions/print_article.php?l=13819.

Peterson, D., T. Peterson, and M. Peterson. 1997. *Dorobo Fund for Tanzania Newsletter.* Arusha.

———. 1998. "Philosophical Background of Dorobo Fund Priority: Holistic Community Resource Management." *Dorobo Fund for Tanzania Newsletter.*

Philemon, L. 2010. "Government Moves on Loliondo." *Guardian*, February 25. http:// www.ippmedia.com/frontend/functions/print_article.php?l=13857.

Polanyi, K. 1944. *The Great Transformation: The Political and Economic Origins of Our Times*. Boston: Beacon Press.

———. 1957. "The Economy as Instituted Process." In *Trade and Market in the Early Empires: Economies in History and Theory*, edited by C. Arensberg and H. Pearson, 243–70. New York: Free Press.

Postero, N. 2007. *Now We Are Citizens: Indigenous Politics in Postmulticultural Bolivia*. Stanford, Calif.: Stanford University Press.

Pratt, C., and R. Yeager. 1976. "The Critical Phase in Tanzania 1945–1968: Nyerere and the Emergence of a Socialist Strategy." *History: Reviews of New Books* 4 (8): 170–71.

Price Waterhouse. 1996. "The Trophy Hunting Industry: An African Perspective." In Leader-Williams, Kayera, and Overton 1996, 12–13.

Ranger, T. 1983. "The Invention of Tradition in Colonial Africa." In *The Invention of Tradition*, edited by E. Hobsbawm and T. Ranger. Cambridge: Cambridge University Press.

Renton, A. 2009. "Tourism Is a Curse to Us." *Guardian*, The Observer, September 6.

Rigby, P. 1983. "Time and Historical Consciousness: The Case of Ilparakuyo Maasai." *Comparative Studies in Society and History* 25 (03): 428–56.

———. 1992. *Cattle, Capitalism, and Class: Ilparakuyo Maasai Transformations*. Philadelphia: Temple University Press.

Robertson, M. M. 2006. "The Nature That Capital Can See: Science, State, and Market in the Commodification of Ecosystem Services." *Environment and Planning D* 24 (3): 367.

Rogers, Peter. 2002. "The Political Ecology of Pastoralism, Conservation, and Development in the Arusha Region of Northern Tanzania." PhD diss., University of Florida, Gainesville.

Sachedina, H. T. 2008. "Wildlife Is Our Oil: Conservation, Livelihoods and NGOs in the Tarangire Ecosystem, Tanzania." PhD diss., University of Oxford.

———. 2010. "Disconnected Nature: The Scaling Up of African Wildlife Foundation and Its Impacts on Biodiversity Conservation and Local Livelihoods." *Antipode* 42 (3): 603–23.

Said, E. 1978. *Orientalism*. London: Penguin.

Schneider, L. 2004. "Freedom and Unfreedom in Rural Development: Julius Nyerere, Ujamaa Vijijini, and Villagization." *Canadian Journal of African Studies* 38 (2): 344–92.

———. 2006a. "Colonial Legacies and Postcolonial Authoritarianism in Tanzania: Connects and Disconnects." *African Studies Review* 49 (1): 93–118.

———. 2006b. "The Maasai's New Clothes: A Developmentalist Modernity and Its Exclusions." *Africa Today* 53 (1): 101–29.

———. 2007. "High on Modernity? Explaining the Failings of Tanzanian Villagisation." *African Studies* 66 (1): 9–38.

Schroeder, R. A. 1999. *Shady Practices: Agroforestry and Gender Politics in the Gambia*. Berkeley: University of California Press.

———. 2008. "Environmental Justice and the Market: The Politics of Sharing Wildlife Revenues in Tanzania." *Society and Natural Resources* 21 (7): 583–96.

———. 2010. "Tanzanite as Conflict Gem: Certifying a Secure commodity Chain in Tanzania." *Geoforum* 41 (1): 56–65.

———. 2012. *Africa after Apartheid: South Africa, Race, and Nation in Tanzania.* Bloomington: Indiana University Press.

Schroeder, R. A., and R. P. Neumann. 2006. "Manifest Ecological Destinies: Local Rights and Global Environmental Agendas." *Antipode* 27 (4): 321–24.

Schutter, O. de. 2009. "Large-Scale Land Acquisitions and Leases: A Set of Core Principles and Measures to Address the Human Rights Challenge." http://www2.ohchr .org/english/issues/food/docs/BriefingNotelandgrab.pdf.

Scott, J. 1998. "Compulsory Villagization in Tanzania: Aesthetics and Miniaturization." In his *Seeing like a State: How Certain Schemes to Improve the Human Condition Have Failed,* 223–61. New Haven, Conn.: Yale University Press.

Seidman, R. B. 1975. "Law and Development: The Interface between Policy and Implementation." *Journal of Modern African Studies* 13 (4): 641–52.

Shetler, J. B. 2007. *Imagining Serengeti: A History of Landscape Memory in Tanzania from Earliest Times to the Present.* Athens: Ohio University Press.

Shivji, I. G. 1973. *Tourism and Socialist Development.* Dar es Salaam: Tanzania Publishing House.

———. 1993a. *Report of the Presidential Commission of Inquiry into Land Matters.* Vol. 1, *Land Policy and Land Tenure Structure.* Dar es Salaam: United Republic of Tanzania.

———. 1993b. *Report of the Presidential Commission of Inquiry into Land Matters.* Vol. 2, *Selected Land Disputes and Recommendations.* Dar es Salaam: United Republic of Tanzania.

———. 1998. *Not Yet Democracy: Reforming Land Tenure in Tanzania.* Dar es Salam: International Institute for Environment and Development (IIED)/HAKIARDHI.

———. 1999. *The Land Acts 1999: A Cause for Celebration or a Celebration of a Cause?* Oxford: Oxfam.

Shivji, I. G., and W. B. L. Kapinga. 1998. *Maasai Rights in Ngorongoro, Tanzania.* Dar es Salaam: IIED (International Institute for Environment and Development)/ HAKIARDHI.

Smith, D. 2014. "Tanzania Accused of Backtracking over Sale of Masai's Ancestral Land." *Guardian,* November 16, 2014

Smith, N. 1992. "Contours of a Spatialized Politics: Homeless Vehicles and the Production of Geographical Scale." *Social Text* 33: 54–81.

———. 2008. *Uneven Development: Nature, Capital, and the Production of Space.* Athens: University of Georgia Press.

Spear, T. T., and R. D. Waller. 1993. *Being Maasai: Ethnicity & Identity in East Africa.* London: James Curry.

SRCS. 1986. *Toward a Regional Conservation Strategy for the Serengeti, December 2–4*

1985, at Serengeti Wildlife Research Centre, Seronera, Tanzania. Policy document based on findings of the meeting.

Stiglitz, J. E. 2003. *Globalization and Its Discontents.* New York: W. W. Norton.

Sulle, E., E. Lekaita, and F. Nelson. 2011. *From Promise to Performance? Wildlife Management Areas in Northern Tanzania.* Dar es Salaam: TNRF, UCRT, Maliasili Initiatives.

Sundet, G. 1997. "The Politics of Land in Tanzania." PhD diss., University of Oxford.

———. 2005. *The 1999 Land Act and Village Land Act: A Technical Analysis of the Practical Implications of the Acts.* http://www.fao.org/fileadmin/templates/nr/images /resources/pdf_documents/kagera/tanzania/1999_land_act_and_village_land_act.rtf.

Swyngedouw, E. A. 1989. "The Heart of the Place: The Resurrection of Locality in an Age of Hyperspace." *Geografiska Annaler.* Series B, *Human Geography,* 71 (1): 31–42.

TAHOA. 1998. *A National and Global Perspective on the Tourist Hunting Industry in Tanzania: The Past, the Present, the Future, and Its Role in National Development.* Dar es Salaam: Tanzania.

TALA, FEMACT, NGONET, and PINGOS Forum. 2012. "The Tanzania Civil Society Organizations (CSOs) Position on Ongoing Avaaz Campaign on Stop Serengeti Sell Off." Press release.

Tanzania Natural Resource Forum. (2008). Meeting among the wildlife division, WMA authorized associations, village and district representatives, and the tourism industry on wildlife conservation regulations pertaining to wildlife use on village lands and in game controlled and open areas. Proceedings and observations, April 28–29, 2008. Impala Hotel, Arusha.

Thirgood, S., C. Mlingwa, E. Gereta, V. Runyoro, R. Malpas, K. Laurenson, and M. Borner. 2008. "Who Pays for Conservation? Current and Future Financing Scenarios for the Serengeti Ecosystem." In *Serengeti III: Human Impacts on Ecosystem Dynamics,* 443–470. Chicago: University of Chicago Press.

Thomson Safaris. 2009a. "The Enashiva Nature Refuge." August 21. *Thomson Safaris' Outlook.* Thomson Replies to Online Rumors. Get the Facts Here. Blog. http:// thomsonsafaris.wordpress.com/2009/08/21/ena_nat_ref/.

———. 2009b. "Our Open Letter to 'The Observer.'" September 6. *Thomson Safaris' Outlook.* Thomson Replies to Online rumors. Get the Facts Here. Blog. http:// thomsonsafaris.wordpress.com/2009/09/06/our-open-letter.

———. 2009c. "The Thomson Safaris Story." August 12. *Thomson Safaris' Outlook.* Thomson Replies to Online Rumors. Get the Facts Here. Blog. http://thomsonsafaris .wordpress.com/2009/08/12/ts_story/.

———. 2009d. "Thomson Safaris' Rebuttal to Alex Renton's Article in 'The Observer.'" September 21. *Thomson Safaris' Outlook.* Thomson Replies to Online Rumors. Get the Facts Here. Blog. http://thomsonsafaris.wordpress.com/2009/09/21/thomson -safari

———. 2010a. "Investigative Report Summary." February 23. *Thomson Safaris' Outlook.* Blog. http://thomsonsafaris.wordpress.com/2010/02/23/investigative.

———. 2010b. "Setting the Record Straight." April 20. *Thomson Safaris' Outlook.* Thom-

son Replies to Online Rumors. Get the Facts Here. Blog. http://thomsonsafaris
.wordpress.com/2010/04/20/setting-the-rec.

———. 2010c. "Sukenya: Freedom at Last." June 15. *Thomson Safaris' Outlook.* Thomson Replies to Online Rumors. Get the Facts Here. Blog. http://thomsonsafaris
.wordpress.com/2010/06/15/sukenya_freedom/.

———. 2010d. "Sukenya Leaders Support TCL." March 11. http://thomsonsafaris
.wordpress.com/2010/03/11/sukenya_leaders.

———. 2012. *Supporting Tanzanian Communities.* December 18 video. http://www
.thomsonsafaris.com/giving-back; https://www.youtube.com/watch?x-yt-cl
=85027636&x-yt-ts=1422503916&v=f-2Eyoanh9U.

Tomlinson, C. 2002. "Big-Game Hunting Threatening Parks: Africa; A Tanzania Company Is Accused of Altering Migratory Patterns of Animals in the Region to Benefit Business." *Los Angeles Times,* March 10. http://articles.latimes.com/2002/mar/10
/news/mn-32073.

Ubwania, Z. 2011. "Tanzania: Civil Society Organisations Call for Lasting Solution to Loliondo Land Crisis." *Citizen* (Dar es Salaam), May 15. http://allafrica.com/stories
/201105160271.html.

United Republic of Tanzania. 1999. *The Land Act, 1999.* Dar es Salaam: Government Printer.

Vandergeest, P., and N. L. Peluso. 1995. "Territorialization and State Power in Thailand." *Theory and Society* 24 (3): 385–426.

Waller, R. 1976. "The Maasai and the British, 1895–1905: The Origins of an Alliance." *Journal of African History* 17 (04): 529–53.

———. 1985. "Ecology, Migration, and Expansion in East Africa." *African Affairs* 84 (336): 347–70.

Warren, A. 1995. "Changing Understandings of African Pastoralism and the Nature of Environmental Paradigms." *Transactions of the Institute of British Geographers,* n.s., 20 (2): 193–203.

Watts, M. 1983. *Silent Violence: Food, Famine and Peasantry in Northern Nigeria.* Berkeley: University of California Press.

———. 1994. "Development II: The Privatization of Everything?" *Progress in Human Geography* 18 (3): 371.

———. 2001. "Petro-violence: Community, Extraction, and Political Ecology of a Mythic Commodity. In *Violent Environments,* edited by N. L. Peluso, and M. Watts, 189–212. Ithaca, N.Y.: Cornell University Press.

———. 2004. "Antinomies of Community: Some Thoughts on Geography, Resources and Empire." *Transactions of the Institute of British Geographers* 29 (2): 195–216.

West, P. 2006. *Conservation Is Our Government Now: The Politics of Ecology in Papua New Guinea.* Durham, N.C.: Duke University Press.

West, P., J. Igoe, and D. Brockington. 2006. "Parks and Peoples: The Social Impact of Protected Areas." *Annual Review of Anthropology* 35: 251–94.

Western, D. 2001. "Taking the Broad View of Conservation: A Response to Adams and Hulme." *Oryx* 35 (3): 201–3.

Western, D., and H. Gichohi. 1993. "Segregation Effects and Impoverishment of Savanna Parks: The Case for Ecosystem Viability Analysis." *African Journal of Ecology* 31 (4): 269.

Western, D., S. C. Strum, and R. M. Wright. 1994. *Natural Connections: Perspectives in Community-Based Conservation.* Washington, D.C.: Island Press.

Wildlife Division, Ministry of Natural Resources and Tourism, United Republic of Tanzania. 2003. *Reference Manual for Implementing Guidelines for the Designation and Management of Wildlife Management Areas (WMAs) in Tanzania.* Funded by GTZ and USAID through WWF Tanzania. Dar es Salaam: Wildlife Division

Wildlife Sector Review Task Force (WSRTF). 1995. *A Review of the Wildlife Sector in Tanzania.* Vol. 1, *Assessment of the Current Situation.* Dar es Salaam: Ministry of Tourism, Natural Resources and Environment.

Williamson, J. 1993. "Democracy and the Washington Consensus." *World Development* 21 (8): 1329–36.

Wily, L. A. 1998. "The Village, Villagers and the Village Land Bill." Paper prepared for the Land Management and Natural Resources Programme, Arusha Region, November.

Winichakul, T. 1997. *Siam Mapped: A History of the Geo-body of a Nation.* Honolulu: University of Hawaii Press.

Wolford, W. 2007. "Land Reform in the Time of Neoliberalism: A Many-Splendored Thing." *Antipode* 39 (3): 550.

World Bank Group/Multilateral Investment Guarantee Agency (MIGA). 2002. *Tourism in Tanzania: Investment for Growth and Diversification.* Washington, D.C.: MIGA and United Republic of Tanzania in cooperation with the Promote Africa Program.

Zoomers, A. 2010. "Globalisation and the Foreignisation of Space: Seven Processes Driving the Current Global Land Grab." *Journal of Peasant Studies* 37 (2): 429–47.

INDEX

African Wildlife Foundation (AWF): and community-based conservation, 70; and Korongoro Integrated People Oriented to Conservation, 67–68; and market-led conservation, 134; and the Serengeti Regional Conservation Strategy, 66, 70; and Tanzania National Parks Association, 70; and wildlife management areas, 55
al-Ali, Mohammed Abdulrahim, 1, 82, 89
authorized associations (AAS), 61–62
Avaaz, 1, 4, 26–27, 165; Maasai support of, 12

Barabaig, 30
Bearcroft, John, ix, x–xi, 103
buffer zones, 29–30, 57, 66–68, 70, 168

CAMPFIRE (Communal Areas Management Program for Indigenous Resources), 68, 71, 134
Canadian International Development Agency (CIDA), 30
Claridge, Lucy, 116
colonial rule: conservation efforts, 38–41; hunting regulations, 85
Commission on Land Reform, 160
common pool management, 42
community-based conservation (CBC): and African Wildlife Foundation, 70; conservation, economic value of, 161; and Dorobo Tours and Safaris, 138–40; and Frankfurt Zoological Society, 70; and high-end tourism, 140–42; and hunting, 57; and land rights, 147–48; and Maasai liberation, 147; and market value of nature, 133–35, 136–37; and pastoralism, 56–57, 101–2; results, 59; and tourism, 57; village authority, 122; village cooperation, 59; and the Wildlife Division, 57; and Wildlife Management Areas, 59. See also village-based joint-venture tourism
community-based natural resource management (CBNRM), 133–34
conservation: during colonial rule, 38–41; and dispossession, xviii–xix, 5, 10, 11–13, 17,

18–21, 20, 29–30, 73, 76–79, 82, 89, 91–92, 96, 98–99, 101–2, 122, 147 (see also Ngorongoro Conservation Area [NCA]; Serengeti National Park); and foreign investors, 12–13; fortress conservation, 37, 38–42, 96; hunting, 57–58; market-based approach, 70–73, 143; market value, 132–35, 136–37; and nation-state, 14–15; as nature versus urbanization, x–xi; and pastoralism, 155–56; safari tourism, 101; trophy hunting, 84–86, 89–90, 94–95; wildlife (see Ngorongoro Conservation Area [NCA]; Tanzania National Parks Association [TANAPA]; Wildlife Division [WD]); wildlife outside protected areas, 58. See also community-based conservation (CBC); ecotourism; tourism

dispossession: for conservation, xviii–xix, 5, 10, 11–13, 17, 18–21, 20, 29–30, 73, 76–79, 82, 89, 91–92, 96, 98–99, 101–2, 122, 147 (see also Ngorongoro Conservation Area (NCA); Serengeti National Park); effect on women, 106; fear of, 96
Dorobo Tours and Safaris, 126–50; agreement terms, 128, 137; community development initiatives, 14, 138; contracts with Maasai villages, 13–14; cultural encounters, 136; Dorobo Fund for Tanzania, xxi; and ecotourism, 138–40; expansion, 143–44; founders' ties to Maasai, 126, 127; founding of, 126–27; Maasai, relationship with, 130–31, 138–40; name, significance of, 126–27; and pastoralism, 127, 138; Tanzania Wildlife Corporation, relationship with, 136; as village-based joint-venture tourism, xix, 128, 131, 134, 136–37, 138, 143, 146; Wildlife Division, relationship with, 128–30, 136–37, 138–40. See also village-based joint-venture tourism

ecotourism: and conservation, 161–62; high-end tourism, 140–42; revenue, 138–40; state control over, 148–50; village-based joint-venture tourism, 146–48; villages, role of, 146

205